Planning the British Economy

PAUL HARE

Economics Department
University of Stirling

MACMILLAN

First published 1985

Published by
Higher and Further Education Division
MACMILLAN PUBLISHERS LTD
Houndmills, Basingstoke, Hampshire RG21 2XS
and London
Companies and representatives
throughout the world

Printed in Hong Kong

British Library Cataloguing in Publication Data
Hare, Paul
Planning the British economy.—(Radical economics)
1. Great Britain—Economic policy—1945–
I. Title   II. Series
330.941′ 0858   HC256.6
ISBN 0-333-36110-5
ISBN 0-333-36111-3 Pbk

To Sue, Kathryn and Cheryl

Contents

List of Tables and Figures

Tables

Figures

Preface

As an economist with a long-standing research interest in the planned economies of Eastern Europe, as well as China, it was probably inevitable that I would eventually turn my attention to the prospects for planning in my own country, Britain. At first sight, the prospects seemed rather dim and any story that one might tell about planning in Britain would therefore be quite brief. However, more careful reflection suggested that there was actually a great deal to say, and that some form of planning could make a significant positive contribution to improving Britain's economic performance.

Of course, there could be no question of importing wholesale the methods and institutional arrangements of economic planning from some other country. However, by investigating the strengths and weaknesses of planning systems in several countries, including some market-type economies where alternative forms of decentralised planning are employed principally to guide the allocation of investment resources, we can draw some useful conclusions about lessons for Britain. Similarly, Britain's own past experience of planning, as well as a range of theoretical arguments to do with economic information and the rate and pattern of investment, all have implications for the kind of planning system that would suit British conditions. These implications then require sufficient elaboration to show how the proposed form of decentralised economic planning would fit into the existing institutional structure, and what new institutions it would entail.

These issues are all discussed thoroughly in what follows, including a specific set of proposals for British planning and some comparisons with other recent proposals such as the

Alternative Economic Strategy. In setting out my argument, I felt that many points could be explained more clearly in the context of some concrete suggestions, but some aspects of my proposals should nevertheless be regarded as quite tentative and preliminary rather than as a blueprint for immediate action. Thus in some respects I see this book as a contribution to a debate about the future shape of economic policy in Britain, and therefore welcome other contributions, including further development of the ideas presented here.

In a work of this kind the author cannot make progress without the support and co-operation of numerous colleagues. My own greatest debts are to some of my academic colleagues who commented on one or more chapters and took part in discussions about various parts of my argument and proposals. I would particularly like to thank Athar Hussain, Saul Estrin, David Simpson, David Ulph and Neil Fraser. In addition, I am grateful to Labour Party and TUC officials for giving up their time to assist me, both by ensuring that I was fully informed about their respective organisations' official positions, and by commenting constructively on my own views; Henry Neuberger (Labour Party) was especially helpful in this regard. Wherever possible I have tried to take account of critical comments advanced by the above individuals, and a few others. However, none of the above can be held responsible for any of the views set out below; indeed in some cases I am all too aware that significant areas of disagreement remain between myself and some of the above commentators.

Unlike some research projects, this one did not require large resources. In order to hold meetings with various officials and academics, however, it was necessary to travel down to London quite frequently, and I am grateful to the Carnegie Trust for providing the necessary financial support. In addition, Ann Cowie and Catherine McIntosh managed to transform my handwriting into an impressively neat and clear typescript in a remarkably short time; I can hardly thank them enough for their efforts and for their patience in accommodating my frequent amendments and revisions.

Finally, I would like to thank my wife and daughters for their contribution to this book: my wife for tolerating far too many unsociable weekends while I was busy writing; and my daughters for keeping out of my way when required and for providing pleasant and often entertaining company when I needed to relax. I hope that in 1985 I shall have more time for the family than I had in 1984.

Economics Department   Paul Hare
University of Stirling
Scotland
January 1985

1
Introduction

The suggestion that the British economy could usefully introduce some form of national economic planning arouses a wide range of responses, from implacable hostility, through indifference, all the way to fervent support. These enormous differences in response can, for the most part, be explained in terms of three major factors, namely:

(1) Ideological attitudes and theoretical standpoints concerning the relative merits of resource allocation via markets or planning;
(2) The accepted explanation of Britain's present economic predicament, and hence the role that planning may or may not play in its amelioration;
(3) The interpretation of past British and other countries' experience of planning and lessons that may be drawn from it.

It is helpful to separate these factors because, although they are frequently found in particular combinations in practice, they are clearly conceptually distinct and our eventual conclusions about planning should be more firmly based if this is recognised from the outset.

The first part of this chapter is devoted to a short sketch of some aspects of the first factor, the question of ideology and theory in relation to planning and markets. This will help to clear the ground for some of the subsequent analysis. Some of the explanations advanced for Britain's relative economic decline (the second factor) are reviewed in Chapter 4, while British and other countries' experience of economic planning are investigated thoroughly in Chapters 2 and 3 respectively. Section 1.2 of the present chapter deals with some topics which are relevant to planning – such as manpower planning and its relationship to the education system – which are not covered in any detail elsewhere in the book. The reader should not thereby assume that these topics are unimportant or peripheral; it is simply that we lack the space to examine all aspects of planning to the same depth, and so some selection has been necessary. Finally, Section 1.3 provides some statistical material on Gross Domestic Product (GDP), investment and related items which is referred to again in later chapters.

Chapters 4 and 5 are the book's principal theoretical chapters. While the former covers indicative planning and other relatively technical aspects of planning, the latter pays more attention to political and social aspects. For if planning is to have a broad appeal, it is insufficient merely to seek improvements in the technical functioning of the economy as it is presently constituted. This is not to minimise the very real difficulties of bringing about such technical improvements, but rather to insist that planning should be accompanied by measures to ensure democratic accountability of investment, production, trade and other significant economic decisions. One facet of this is a proposal to associate planning with widespread workplace democracy; another is the development of planning councils linked to the various planning agencies recommended below. Both of these are discussed in Chapter 5.

Some of the important institutional issues connected with economic planning are covered in Chapters 6 and 7. Chapter 6 begins relatively cautiously by taking the existing institutional framework as its starting point. It considers the problems of controlling the nationalised industries in the existing management framework, and the question whether it would be advisable or expedient to extend the scope of state control as part of the process of introducing an economic planning system. Similar questions of control also arise later in the chapter in connection with the financial institutions and policy towards international transactions. A fairly recent institutional innovation, the Development Agencies, and the even newer Enterprise boards established by a few local authorities are also outlined in Chapter 6.

Proposals for new planning, and planning-related institutions form the subject of Chapter 7. The first two sections are concerned with national level and lower level institutions respectively. In both these areas there are several concrete proposals in the existing literature, and these are compared critically with my own proposals. The third section of Chapter 7 reviews the whole field of wage and price control in a planned economy, beginning by emphasising the important role that markets, and market forces, should continue to play in such an economy: it then considers price and wage control in turn. In the course of the analysis it will be necessary to review alternative theories of the inflationary process in general, and wage determination in particular, as well as the role of profits in the economy. The latter is especially important because, for some supporters of planning, profits tend to be regarded as somehow 'unsocialist' and hence, presumably, undesirable. In this section I argue that it would be more appropriate to take precisely the opposite view.

Finally, Chapter 8 concludes the book by summarising briefly our principal findings and proposals. It also outlines the main elements of what has come to be called the Alternative Economic Strategy (AES), a radical approach to economic policy in Britain, and one which will already have been referred to in passing in several of the earlier chapters. In Chapter 8, my objective in introducing the AES is to show that, at least in so far as it concerns economic planning, it cannot be regarded as a convincing alternative to my own proposals. Since I can hardly claim that my present views should be regarded as the last word on economic planning, I hope that this element of controversy in Chapter 8 will stimulate an informed and constructive debate on possible forms of economic planning in a developed, predominantly market-type economy such as Britain. The last part of Chapter 8 widens the discussion to include other developed, market economies. We note that much of the analysis presented here, though not of course all the institutional detail, should apply to other countries equally well. Hence the book may be regarded as a study of planning in advanced countries, taking Britain as a special case to investigate in detail.

1.1 Planning and Markets

With the inception of its first five year plan in 1928, the Soviet Union became the first country in the world to adopt a system of national economic planning. Interestingly, the Western world was just entering the Great Depression of the 1930s, from which it did not fully recover until the Second World War, as the Soviet 'experiment' was getting under way. Prior to the 1917 Revolution which brought a communist government to power in Russia, Marxists and other less radical socialists had rather little to say about planning and, indeed, were often critical of utopian attempts to spell out in detail how a new, post-capitalist society might function. There was, however, some measure of agreement about the features which the new society should not contain.

These included the exploitation of labour which was held to characterise production relations, production for the market and the law of value, private ownership of the means of production, and the forms of private income resulting from ownership (profits, rents, etc.). Thus it was argued that a socialist society would be characterised by public (or state) ownership of at least the principal means of production, with property income then being transformed into a new category of 'income for society'. In addition instead of output being produced *for the market* in accordance with the dictates of the law of value (whereby investment in various branches is allocated in line with the relative profitabilities of different productive activities), it would be produced directly *for use*, guided by an all-embracing plan for the economy.

So in the early writings which made reference to a post-capitalist, or socialist society, it was apparent that capitalist forms of production for private profit were to be superseded by some kind of planning system. Beyond such generalities, however, it is impossible to find any detailed accounts of the resulting system. Perhaps in consequence, it was widely believed just after the October Revolution that planning would prove to be quite a simple matter. Lenin, for instance, suggested in some of his writings that planning would entail little more than basic numeracy and some accounting skills, which ordinary workers should certainly be able to manage. In the chaotic aftermath of the Revolution, with Civil War and the most appalling economic collapse and dislocation, this rather simplistic view never received a completely fair test. Nevertheless, subsequent experience did indicate that centralised state planning of the Soviet kind could not be undertaken successfully with the simple skills envisaged by Lenin. Indeed, as we know, it was only at the end of the 1920s that the statistical systems, administrative procedures and techniques of economic analysis were sufficiently well developed to enable the centralised planning system to function effectively. Even with the plethora of controls that had been developed by then, moreover, it did not prove possible to leave behind every last trace of the capitalist economic system. For instance, despite some consumption rationing and centralised labour allocation, the bulk of consumer goods and labour were allocated through markets, with individuals responding to relative prices and relative wage rates, respectively. But in the most important sphere of production, little remained of production for profit aside from very small scale production and repair businesses run by individual artisans. With its manifold imperfections, on which we enlarge in Chapter 3, this new, extremely centralised planning system soon demonstrated that it was viable, in the sense that it was capable of mobilising the Soviet economy's resources and directing them into a massive investment programme which stimulated an impressively rapid rate of economic growth. In the 1930s and subsequently, therefore, the Soviet Union has provided us with an unequivocal empirical demonstration of the viability of centralised planning.

During the 1930s, however, few Western economists were aware of this Soviet experience, and much of what was known – for instance the brutal collectivisation of agriculture, and the purges – generated considerable and understandable political antipathy, despite the Soviets' undoubted economic achievements. Only a few economists, such as Maurice Dobb, retained sufficient sympathy for the Soviet planning experiments to be impressed by them.

This conjuncture of rapid Soviet economic progress with the Great Depression in Europe and North America was accompanied by a curious, and by now famous economic debate. Ironically, the debate concerned the feasibility of economic planning and it was conducted exclusively in theoretical terms. Mises and Hayek among others sought to argue that economic planning was not feasible, while Lange and Taylor outlined a possible planning mechanism which demonstrated that it was (see Hayek, 1935; Lange, 1936; Taylor, 1936). Although considerable work has since been done on planning mechanisms (centralised or decentralised non-market allocation procedures), for example by Hurwicz, Arrow, Weitzman (see Hurwicz, 1977; and Cave and Hare, 1981; also Weitzman, 1970), the terms of debate have actually changed. It is no longer about feasibility, since by now it is clear to all that some form of economic planning is possible. Instead, the debate now concerns issues to do with efficiency on the one hand, and economic freedom on the other, sometimes buttressed by appeals to the social benefits of decentralised, market-type resource allocation as contrasted with the 'dead hand of planning'. Needless to say, it is one of the principal aims of this book to show that this latter epithet is by no means always justified.

Let us now review the debate rather more fully. Mises and Hayek began their analyses by visualising a Walrasian model of the economy, a system of interacting markets. In this system, economic information is highly dispersed among the individual economic agents, such as firms and households, and prices are the only type of information transmitted throughout the economy and available to all. Hence an individual agent takes its decisions in the light of its own local information, together with the prevailing prices. Naturally, for any arbitrary set of prices the resulting supplies and demands may not be in balance, or equilibrium, in all markets. However, if prices rise in response to excess demand and fall when there is excess supply then the whole system will eventually arrive at an equilibrium position. (Note: it is now understood that this line of argument is not generally valid since equilibrium in this model may not be stable; for more discussion of this general equilibrium model, see Chapter 4.)

Leaving aside numerous technical deficiencies of the above argument, what it demonstrates is that price information alone is sufficient to co-ordinate economic activity in the presence of highly dispersed information on technology, budget constraints and preferences. The next step in the argument is to point out that this complex co-ordination problem is what the planners have to solve in a planned economy, but without the aid of the free market adjustment process just discussed. In effect, the planners have to solve an enormous system of equations of the form, supply equals demand, for all goods and services in the economy and it was assumed that they would have to determine some centralised procedure for doing so. At this point, Mises and Hayek could offer two reasons for the impossibility of planning; one was concerned with computation, the other with information.

Certainly in the 1930s, and even today it must be conceded, finding an accurate estimate of a set of equilibrium prices, essentially by solving directly the corresponding set of supply–demand balances presents insuperable computational difficulties. The equations involved are both numerous and complex, so that even the fastest modern computers can only solve highly aggregated systems of supply–demand balances within a reasonable time; anything larger and hence more detailed is clearly beyond present computing capacities and *a fortiori* quite impossible at the time of the debate we are discussing.

The second reason concerned information. Here it was argued that before the above computations could even commence, it would be necessary to assemble huge volumes of information from individual firms and households in order to evaluate the required supply and demand relationships. However, the cost of doing this, in terms of man-hours and other resources, would be so great as to be prohibitive. By the time the information had been collected, the underlying economic situation would have changed in some important respects and the whole process would inevitably take far too long. Indeed it would take so long that the information finally assembled might only bear an extremely tenuous relation to the real constraints and preferences of individual agents. As a modern instance of this problem, it is worth mentioning the common experience that the compilation of even a moderately aggregated input–output table (say 50–100 sectors) can take three to five years.

The argument therefore demonstrates beyond doubt the impossibility of planning, according to Mises and Hayek. Or does it? In fact, a closer inspection of the argument reveals that it only demonstrates the impossibility of perfectly centralised planning. This observation suggests two directions in which an alternative argument might be constructed. The first direction involves retaining the idea of centralisation, but no longer insisting on perfection. After all, the market mechanism itself is far from perfect in its practical operation so it is perhaps not surprising that the search for an alternative in terms of perfect planning proved so fruitless. The Soviet economy that we commented on earlier in this section provides us with a viable instance of centralised planning, and so belongs to this category of centralised planning with imperfections. The second direction looks for a decentralised planning mechanism which 'mimics' the outcomes of the familiar market-type adjustment process sketched above.

Lange and Taylor both solved this problem in the 1930s and developed the first price-type planning procedure. They independently envisaged an economy in which the central planners might determine some or all of the economy's investment (cf. our discussion in Chapter 4), and also fixed all prices – for inputs, outputs, producer's goods and consumer goods. This, of course, is a huge undertaking in itself, but considerably less so than what the

Figure 1.1   *Price-type planning procedure*

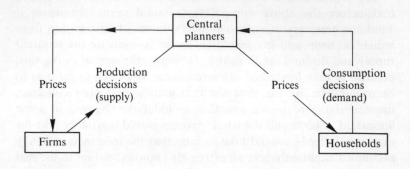

Note Arrows show the direction of information flows; notice that, very unrealistically, the procedure does not require any horizontal information flows at all (cf. Cave and Hare (1981), Section 3.3, and Hare (1981b)).

centralised model entailed. The functioning of the procedure is illustrated in Figure 1.1 above.

The planners set prices, observe the resulting demands and supplies chosen by households and firms and adjust prices in the light of any apparent imbalances: thus prices would rise in the case of excess demand, and fall with excess supply. After a series of such adjustments, the process should (under suitable conditions which I shall not dwell on here) converge to a set of equilibrium prices and the resulting plan can then be implemented simply by confirming the final prices. Thus economic co-ordination is achieved without any need for the planners to collect information about preferences, technology and so on as in the centralised model of planning; moreover, the calculations required to adjust the prices, though numerous, are basically quite elementary and would not have presented any great difficulties even with 1930s technology.

This theoretical argument, together with Soviet and later on other countries' experience, made clear that economic planning was feasible. More recent discussion, therefore, has tended to focus on economic comparisons which are rather less easy to evaluate unambiguously, namely the relative efficiency of alternative economic systems, and their respective contributions to economic and other aspects of freedom.

It is fashionable at present to argue for the superiority of free market allocation on both the above counts (see, for instance, Minford *et al.*, 1980; Friedman and Friedman, 1980), a standpoint which is also commonly associated with a monetarist approach in macroeconomics. The policy implications require the minimum possible government intervention in the economy in areas such as industrial policy (cf. Redwood, 1984; Burton, 1983) and embody a touching faith in the efficacy of unimpeded market processes (cf. Kirzner, 1973). Needless to say, planning of any kind can hardly expect to receive serious attention alongside such views. Yet the theoretical and empirical evidence to support this extreme, pro-market position is extremely weak, to say the least.

Even the basic notion of an unimpeded market process is fraught with ambiguities, since everywhere one finds that governments have enacted laws and regulations governing contract, transfers of property, the recognised forms of company, the formation and closure of companies, and so on. In addition, it is commonplace to find quite complex tax structures in place, even in the most market-oriented economies. Hence it is virtually impossible to point to significant instances of market processes in which there is no public intervention or regulation: as a result, despite the claims of ardent pro-marketeers we actually know rather little about how free market processes might work. And it seems to me that the interesting question is not so much about how to reduce all aspects of government intervention in the economy, but rather about how to determine the appropriate boundary between public and private spheres of influence, without any preconceptions as to where the boundary should lie.

Another pointer in the same direction is the simple observation that transactions effected within firms are typically not market transactions. Without going into a detailed exegesis on the theory of the firm (on which see, for instance, Loasby (1976)), it is clear that firms develop and grow whenever transactions and contractual arrangements concerned with some production process are expected to be conducted more efficiently by a single organisation than by a whole series of separate market links. This is partly a matter of judgement, and so partly influenced by the legal and other arrangements mentioned in the preceding paragraph. Nevertheless, the firm is another area in which the interesting question to ask concerns a boundary issue, in this case the proper boundary between market and non-market transactions.

With these examples in mind, it is certainly not obvious *a priori* that non-market allocation or public intervention (the two are not the same, though they are often confused) should be excluded from other spheres of economic life, especially not on such flimsy grounds as the assertion that 'markets are best'. Furthermore, as is explained at greater length in Chapter 4, even the more formal general equilibrium theory provides no support for the view that resource allocation through markets is always desirable, let alone 'best'. For in general this theory offers no explanation of resource allocation within firms and many of the markets needed for deriving conventional efficiency results (especially futures markets and markets for contingent goods) simply do not exist. Hence it is possible to argue, as we do, that a form of decentralised economic planning could be developed which has a strong chance of improving on the resource allocation generated by the unaided market.

As far as efficiency and freedom are concerned, the strong claims made about the virtues of markets are at least questionable. True, with sufficiently strong assumptions, it can be claimed that markets are efficient, but we have already remarked above that these assumptions will rarely hold. Equally, individuals may have freedom to choose their jobs and consumption patterns, and to set up new businesses (and to go bankrupt), but this is always subject to legal and other constraints which govern what is socially acceptable. Economic freedom is never absolute, and nor should it be since all societies need to concern themselves with working conditions and practices, the environmental impact of economic activity and the health and safety aspects of both production and consumption. Such externalities are not accommodated in the standard market model and call for some form of intervention to correct them. In sum, it is apparent that there are a great many reasons for not simply accepting the results of resource allocation achieved entirely through a system of free markets.

However, this book is largely about the specific instance of Britain, so it may be useful to conclude this section by making the discussion rather more conrete. Britain has a highly developed economy which is usually classified as 'mixed', in the sense that both public and private sectors have an important rôle to play. The bulk of productive activity is in private hands, but certain industries are nationalised (e.g. coal, steel, the railways, etc.; see Hare (1984); in both these cases, the resulting output is typically sold through markets). However, another important part of the public sector consists of the supply of a range of services, such as health and education, provision of which is normally free, or almost free. Finally, the public sector also acts as an enormous financial intermediary, which collects tax revenue and reallocates much of it back to households in the form of pensions, social security benefits, and so on.

These features of the British economy are assumed to continue into the period when the planning system proposed later on is fully operational. This key assumption is maintained throughout the book. Consequently, the recommended planning system has to allow for the fact that Britain is and will remain a mixed, substantially market-type economy. Thus while it may often be justified to intervene to influence the outcomes of market processes, I would not expect it to be necessary to supersede the market altogether in many cases. I take this view right from the start, partly because I see no advantage for Britain in moving over to a highly centralised, non-market, Soviet approach to economic planning; and partly because forms of planning which take advantage of market forces, as exemplified by Japan and France (see Chapter 3), seem both more attractive and more relevant to British circumstances. In addition, in putting forward proposals for planning it seems to me essential to consider carefully what might be politically acceptable and feasible under present conditions. This, too, leads me to favour an approach to planning which makes use of the market mechanism wherever possible, while intervening actively to influence the economy's investment activity and hence the future shape of the British economy.

1.2 Education and Manpower Planning

The last section ended with a reference to investment, and this is where the emphasis lies in much of the subsequent argument in later chapters. But although it may be easy to accept that, however it is done, planning is essentially about long term economic decision-making and the information required to take such decisions, it is less clear that we are right to confine attention to investment. My own justification for so limiting the scope of this investigation is quite simple. I take the view that raising living standards and developing the economy can only come about as a consequence of a whole range of economic changes, for virtually all of which some investment is the major precondition. Hence if, through a combination of economic planning and more conventional macroeconomic policy measures, we can improve the volume and composition of investment in Britain then a major contribution will have been made to ameliorating our economic performance.

Nevertheless, I freely concede that investment is not the sole precondition for successful development, and in this section I discuss two other factors from the many which might be regarded as just as crucial. These factors receive little or no attention later on, not because I personally regard them as insignificant, which I do not, but merely because of the tight space constraints under which this book was written. The two factors are education and manpower planning.

Now it is possible to regard education simply as a consumption good (or more precisely, a service), but in an economic context it has the additional function of imparting knowledge and skills to the future labour force. One aspect of this is the dissemination of elementary numeracy and literacy and the spread of the broad values and social conventions according to which British society functions. The education system seeks to provide everyone with this basic level of education, essential for everyday life in a developed society, but beyond that it rapidly becomes more specialised. The specialisation can either take the form of pursuing particular academic subjects (e.g. mathematics) to a high level, with little or no immediate regard for the resulting job opportunities, or a more vocational programme might be pursued in which a course of study is directed at a specific job or type of job. Such programmes typically draw on a range of academic disciplines and try to achieve some degree of integration. Vocational training of this kind can either be undertaken by individuals wishing to enter a particular profession (e.g. social work training, computer programming and systems analysis), or it can be arranged by firms wishing to improve the qualifications of those they have already taken on (e.g. day-release schemes, management training, etc.). In the former case individuals undertaking training, as well as those running the relevant courses, have to make their own judgements about the likely availability of jobs, while in the latter a definite job is already assigned before the training starts. It is most common for these various forms of further training to take place immediately or very soon after the period of compulsory, full-time education, but increasingly it is becoming necessary for people to contemplate periods of retraining in mid-career as economic and social change becomes rather more rapid.

All this education and training gives rise to both costs and benefits. The costs are of two kinds: first, the direct resource costs of the education and training activities themselves in terms of staff, buildings, teaching materials and so on; and secondly, the opportunity cost incurred by those being taught, in terms of the wages they might otherwise have earned (or leisure they might have enjoyed). The arrangements for funding particular courses obviously affect the relationship between the corresponding private and social costs involved and in the British case this relationship exhibits an astonishingly wide range of variation. Thus students on some courses (e.g. university undergraduates) receive both a maintenance grant and in most cases full payment of fees from public funds, so that the net private cost of undertaking such a course must be very low; while in other instances (e.g. most language schools or computing courses) participants normally have to pay full fees and support themselves during the course, so the private cost is essentially equal to the social costs. It is not clear to the present author whether any economic rationale could be offered for our diverse practice in this sphere. Certainly, thinking of education as a form of investment, the widely different financial arrangements associated with different types of education and training seem remarkably similar in principle to the distortions we discuss later (see Chapter 4 in particular) in the tax treatment of different forms of personal saving and investment.

Aside from intangible, though possibly quite important benefits of education through its effect on subsequent consumption norms and patterns, its most significant benefit is the higher incomes and better working conditions to which it affords access. To a large extent, these are private benefits received by the individuals concerned, though higher income tax payments help to offset the public cost of any educational subsidy that may have been received. Often, specified qualifications and courses are required even to enter a particular field of work (e.g. nursing, teaching). In these cases, even though the final incomes received may not be higher than in alternative occupations, the benefit to those undertaking the relevant courses is simply that they can get closer to their preferred type of work. Naturally, satisfying preferences in this way does not yield any additional revenue to the government, so the benefits are wholly private.

From a social point of view, the benefits take the form of a better allocation of the labour force to particular jobs, and higher marginal products (and hence the higher incomes discussed above). The former is a benefit because it is most likely that assigning people to jobs that match their skills and preferences as closely as possible will result in a well-motivated work-force, with most people doing their jobs well. The latter is much more contentious since the marginal productivity theory of wages is open to attack and many wage rates and relativities appear to depend at least as much on established conventions and expectations as on any objective measure of productivity. However, this is not the place for a full discussion of theories of income distribution. All we need for present purposes is the postulate that, at least for groups of workers, there is a strong positive association between their income and a suitable measure of productivity. Then we are correct to claim that education and training confer both private and social benefit, as stated.

Given all this it is pertinent to ask whether government intervention, presumably channelled through the Department of Education, should be used to improve the volume and composition of the education and training provided in Britain. A related issue, which brings us to the second of the two factors mentioned at the start of this section, namely manpower planning, concerns whether the Department of Employment, together with the Manpower Services Commission could between them provide sufficiently well founded medium and long term projections of future manpower needs to be helpful in educational planning.

Inevitably, some co-ordination of education and manpower needs already takes place, in areas such as teacher training and medicine. However, these are both professions which regularly experience an excess supply of aspiring and qualified young entrants, so it is not difficult for educational institutions to allocate a specified quota of places (except, in the case of teachers, for a few important specialisms such as mathematics). Also, both are in the public sector, and can therefore use public expenditure forecasts to determine the scale of employment envisaged in future years. In the opposite situation, when there is a shortage of specialised personnel experienced by some private sector industry, it is less obvious what the appropriate response should be. Training courses can be multiplied, but may not attract recruits of sufficient quality. Or wage rates for the personnel in short supply may start to drift upwards, creating windfall gains for those already in post, but raising the private returns to new entrants, hence attracting more and better applicants.

However, this market-type adjustment is subject to several shortcomings. First, it can only work at all if the changed wage relativities are accepted by other groups of workers, rather than becoming a pretext for obtaining corresponding wage increases for them. The chances of success are probably greatest for relatively new occupations such as computing or for workers in completely new industries such as North Sea oil. Secondly, the dissemination of information about relative wage rates and job characteristics, especially through to educational institutions, is extremely slow and erratic; consequently, even if the market mechanism works it can be expected to act quite slowly. Lastly, choice of occupation is, for many people, a very long term decision, which means that any sudden change in market signals will only be taken seriously if it is expected to persist. Hence this is another reason for market forces to act slowly to reallocate the labour force: it applies with particular force to those occupations which require a substantial period of initial training (investment in human capital).

This is the context in which educational and manpower planning would take place. However, if investment planning together with other policies succeeded in raising the growth rate and maintaining the economy rather closer to full employment than it has been in recent years then we should soon begin to experience serious shortages of particular labour skills. This is because the skill mix of the unemployed population probably corresponds quite poorly to that required for the new jobs created by economic expansion. There are actually two problems here. One is that in Britain a relatively small proportion of the work-force has anything above a fairly basic and general level of training in specific skills, as compared with the principal competitor countries. In these countries, more people progress to the higher levels of the education system and more people undergo a period of formal technical or vocational training. In Britain, by contrast, more training takes place informally, in spare time or on-the-job. The result is a work-force less well qualified than other countries' and, since much British training is geared to the requirements of specific firms and tasks, probably less flexible and adaptable than elsewhere.

Aside from this issue of the overall proportion of skilled workers in the working population, the other problematic aspect of the skill mix is the composition of the skilled population itself. Partly because of the rapid pace of technological and economic change experienced recently, the demand for traditional skills such as those required by the metal-working industries has declined sharply, while that for various kinds of electronic engineer, systems analysts and so on has expanded from nothing to a high level. Some of these changes have either been unexpected, or were expected to be temporary, or of modest proportion, and the 'education and training industry' has not adapted quickly enough. Moreover, firms in some of the traditional industries have responded to falling demand for their products by cutting back recruitment, especially in grades requiring extensive training (e.g. apprentices, management). Given Britain's emphasis on on-the-job training, the consequence has been to reduce the overall amount of training on offer, since the newer industries have tended to recruit people with suitable paper qualifications and, as already noted, educational institutions cannot yet meet all the demand for such courses. The only factor offsetting this trend is the range of training and work experience programmes organised by the Manpower Services Commission, especially for younger people.

In relation to the economic planning discussed in subsequent chapters, based on a return to full employment and growth, some important questions arise concerning the development of the labour force and its training and education. These include the following:

(1)   How (and how well) can we predict the demand for unskilled and the numerous types of skilled workers required by the economy?

(2)   If there are shortages and surpluses of different skill categories, how readily can one type of worker be substituted for another, with or without some additional training to facilitate the substitution?

(3)   How can the education system help to improve the match between the demand and supply of the various types of skilled worker?

(4) How far can other factors, such as changes in relative wages and working conditions, bring about the same result?

(5) How should education and training programmes be funded and to what extent should subsidies and other supports be designed to achieve a broad equality of treatment between different programmes?

and so on.

These questions, of course, require thorough investigation and detailed answers, not unlike the responses that we shall be offering to questions about investment in the remainder of this book. However, it seems to me that it would scarcely be possible to give adequate answers to the above questions, without writing another book. While there is evidently scope for such a book, since the whole area of manpower planning and related issues has been relatively neglected since the period of wartime planning, the above discussion was simply intended to draw attention to a few of the interesting issues.

1.3 Statistical Material

To provide some factual background to the analysis of later chapters, this section presents some tables on various aspects of investment in the UK, together with some international comparisons.

Table 1.1 shows gross and net investment in relation to the economy's total output. The gross investment ratio reached a post-war peak around 1970, and has gradually declined since then. While the net investment ratio also reached its peak at about the same time, it has fallen dramatically since then, to little more than a third of its 1970 value. Given this, it is hardly surprising that the economy has performed so poorly, especially in the last decade or so. As far as growth rates are concerned, it can easily be calculated from Table 1.1 that over the whole period 1950–82, GDP grew at the rate of 2.3 per cent p.a. Breaking the period into sub-periods, GDP grew at 2.8 per cent. p.a. during 1950–70, slowing down to 1.3 per cent p.a. during 1970–82. Gross investment grew at 4.6 per cent p.a. from 1950–70, while it has since stagnated and then fallen.

Table 1.1   *Output and investment in the UK*

Year	GDP* £10^9	Net domestic product† £10^9	Gross investment‡ £10^9	Net investment§ £10^9	GI/ GDP (%)	NInv/ NDP (%)
1950	96	86	15.8	7.3	16.5	8.5
1955	111	99	20.4	10.3	18.4	10.4
1960	125	112	24.9	12.4	19.9	11.1
1965	146	131	32.7	17.4	22.4	13.3
1970	166	147	39.1	20.1	23.6	13.7
1971	170	150	39.6	19.9	23.3	13.3
1972	172	152	39.5	18.9	23.0	12.4
1973	186	164	41.8	20.5	22.5	12.5
1974	184	162	40.6	18.8	22.1	11.6
1975	183	160	40.3	17.3	22.0	10.8
1976	190	166	40.9	17.0	21.5	10.2
1977	192	167	39.9	15.0	20.8	9.0
1978	198	172	41.2	15.1	20.8	8.8
1979	201	174	41.6	14.7	20.7	8.4
1980	196	168	39.3	11.6	20.1	6.9
1981	194	166	35.6	7.2	18.4	4.3
1982	198	169	37.6	8.5	19.0	5.0

*   GDP at factor cost in 1980 prices.
†   GDP at factor cost, less capital consumption, at 1980 prices.
‡   Gross domestic fixed capital formation at 1980 prices.
§   Net domestic fixed capital formation at 1980 prices.
Sources: *National Income and Expenditure, 1971*, Tables 1.8.
         National Income and Expenditure, 1983, Tables 2.1, 11.4.
         National Income and Expenditure, 1977, Tables 1.1, 2.1.

Table 1.2   *Gross & net capital formation and GDP by sector*

(a)   *Personal sector*

Year	GDP*	NDP*	Gross I*	Net I*	GI/GDP (%)	NI/NDP (%)
1972	11.1	9.9	2.50	1.26	22.5	12.7
1973	13.3	11.7	2.27	0.71	17.0	6.1
1974	15.0	13.2	2.04	0.23	13.6	1.7
1975	17.8	15.6	3.15	0.90	17.7	5.8
1976	20.9	18.3	3.55	0.94	17.0	5.1
1977	23.4	20.4	4.37	1.34	18.7	6.6
1978	26.9	23.3	5.09	1.46	18.9	6.3
1979	31.5	27.0	6.37	1.90	20.2	7.0
1980	36.5	31.1	7.21	1.80	19.8	5.8
1981	40.0	33.9	7.61	1.48	19.0	4.4
1982	43.9	37.4	9.96	3.46	22.7	9.3

(b) *Industrial and commercial companies*

Year	GDP*	NDP*	Gross I*	Net I*	GI/GDP (%)	NI/NDP (%)
1972	29.1	26.6	3.84	1.34	13.2	5.0
1973	33.7	30.8	4.86	1.93	14.4	6.3
1974	37.3	33.6	5.93	2.26	15.9	6.7
1975	45.9	41.2	6.88	2.17	15.0	5.3
1976	53.2	47.4	8.07	2.26	15.2	4.8
1977	64.8	57.7	9.79	2.70	15.1	4.7
1978	75.8	67.4	12.0	3.62	15.9	5.4
1979	87.7	77.7	13.9	3.89	15.8	5.0
1980	99.8	87.9	14.8	2.87	14.8	3.3
1981	106.9	93.6	14.5	1.19	13.6	1.3
1982	114.6	100.4	14.7	0.55	12.8	0.55

(c) *Public corporations*

Year	GDP*	NDP*	Gross I*	Net I*	GI/GDP (%)	NI/NDP (%)
1972	5.6	4.1	1.77	0.30	31.6	7.3
1973	6.4	4.7	2.07	0.40	32.6	8.5
1974	8.0	5.8	2.86	0.68	35.8	11.7
1975	10.6	7.8	3.92	1.08	37.1	13.8
1976	13.0	9.6	4.70	1.30	36.1	13.5
1977	14.5	10.5	4.78	0.77	32.9	7.3
1978	16.5	12.0	4.94	0.40	30.0	3.3
1979	18.0	12.8	5.62	0.42	31.2	3.3
1980	21.2	15.0	6.65	0.41	31.4	2.7
1981	23.7	16.8	6.90	0.02	29.2	0.1
1982	26.1	18.8	7.22	−0.04	27.7	−0.2

* At current prices, £10^9.
Source: *National Income and Expenditure, 1983*, Tables 1.10, 10.3 and 11.6.

Table 1.2 decomposes Table 1.1 into sectors (omitting financial institutions and government). It shows that net investment by industrial and commercial companies, as well as by the public corporations has fallen virtually to zero, whereas that by the personal sector (presumably housing and small businesses, in the main) has held up reasonably well in recent years. Table 1.3 is concerned with a similar exercise, but this time it concentrates on net investment and in an industrial breakdown. It is quite remarkable to observe that, as a consequence of the present depressed economic conditions, net investment in manufacturing, construction and transport has fallen below zero; i.e. in effect, disinvestment is taking place in these industrial groups.

Table 1.3 *Net fixed capital formation by industry group*

Industry	1972	1973	1974	1975	1976	1977	1978	1979	1980	1981	1982
Agriculture, forestry and fishing	496	591	345	166	147	125	185	16	-124	-281	100
Extraction of mineral oil and natural gas	280	473	1104	2245	2842	2181	1612	769	454	548	605
All other energy and water supply	121	-348	-294	-28	-125	-432	-268	-183	4	54	20
Manufacturing (revised definition)	1347	1570	1882	1237	786	895	1168	1275	175	-1407	-1830
Construction	118	327	290	218	107	72	84	128	-77	-236	-183
Distribution, hotels and catering; repairs	1	1921	1738	1078	934	1365	1521	1870	1433	1140	1407
Transport	679	683	405	215	-11	224	268	149	-57	-588	-638
Communication	899	1205	855	524	435	173	127	161	269	136	23
Banking, finance, insurance, business services and leasing	1992	2509	2608	2065	2314	2385	2884	3507	3833	4032	4404
Other services	5548	6165	5006	4337	4287	3335	2848	2840	2582	2296	2792
Dwellings	6030	5340	4568	5124	5253	4499	4612	4086	3127	1540	2028
Total	18950	20498	18808	17349	17034	14973	15152	14665	11620	7179	8500

Source: *National Income and Expenditure, 1983, Table 11.4*

Figures show gross domestic fixed capital formation less capital consumption. All figures are in £m at 1980 prices.

Table 1.4 *Capital–output ratios* by industry group*

Industry group	1972	1977	1982
Agriculture, forestry and fishing	4.82	5.53	4.38
Energy and water supply	9.41	7.77	5.98
Manufacturing.	2.94	3.16	3.98
Construction	0.64	0.90	1.06
Distribution, etc.	1.58	2.03	2.51
Transport	7.82	7.53	7.30
Communication	4.61	5.40	5.13
Banking etc. (including leasing)	2.18	2.62	3.13
Other services	3.43	3.71	4.08
Dwellings	25.1	25.2	25.7
GDP (factor cost)	4.65	5.08	5.57
GDP less dwellings	3.40	3.76	4.18

* Defined as gross capital stock at 1980 replacement cost ÷ GDP at 1980 prices.

Source: *National Income and Expenditure, 1983,* Tables 1.9, 2.3 and 11.8.

Table 1.4 turns from measures of the volume and composition of investment, to one measure of its productivity, namely capital–output ratios. These ratios should be treated with some caution, but they show how much capital stock is required to generate a unit of GDP in each industry group. Hence a high ratio indicates that in a particular branch a relatively large amount of investment has typically been required to raise output by one unit, and conversely for a low ratio. Ratios can fluctuate somewhat from year to year depending on the state of demand and hence capacity utilisation, changes in relative prices, and the timing of major investment programmes. In the UK, capital–output ratios in most industries have tended to be higher than those of our principal competitors; consequently, a given volume of investment sustained over a period is likely to generate less additional output in Britain than elsewhere. This is one of the problems we shall be discussing later on.

The final Table 1.5 compares investment ratios in the UK and several other countries. As is apparent from the table, the UK's investment ratio has been at or close to the lowest among the countries shown there. This combined with the UK's relatively high capital output ratios noted above goes a long way towards explaining the rather low growth rates. It also justifies our concentration on the investment process and investment planning in much of the remainder

Table 1.5   *Investment ratios:* international comparisons*

Country	1970	1980
Austria	26.2	25.2
Belgium	22.6	21.3
Canada	21.0	22.8
France	25.8	21.7
West Germany	26.4	22.8
Italy	21.2	19.8
Japan	35.0	32.0
UK	18.5	17.4
USA	16.5	18.5

* Defined as gross domestic fixed capital formation ÷ GDP; original data in current prices.

Sources: *UN Monthly Bulletin of Statistics,* Feb. 1973, Table 62, and Feb. 1984, Special Table F.

The final Table 1.5 compares investment ratios in the UK and several other countries. As is apparent from the table, the UK's investment ratio has been at or close to the lowest among the countries shown there. This combined with the UK's relatively high capital output ratios noted above goes a long way towards explaining the rather low growth rates. It also justifies our concentration on the investment process and investment planning in much of the remainder of this book.

2
British Experience

2.1 Wartime Planning

In the early stages of the Second World War, economic activity in Britain came increasingly under government control, in order to ensure that the goods and services required for the war effort were produced as and when required. Administratively, this involved the establishment of three new ministries, the Ministry of Aircraft Production (MAP), the Ministry of Supply and the Ministry of Production. In addition, the Central Statistical Office (CSO) was set up to improve the flow of economic information to and between the departments concerned with planning. Two committees co-ordinated the planning function of government departments. The first was known as the Steering Committee, attended by Permanent Secretaries of the economic departments, while the second was the Lord President's Committee, attended by the corresponding Ministers.

Since Britain is a country where the great bulk of resource allocation is effected through the market mechanism, it is useful to consider why this mechanism was at least partly suspended during the war, with substantial agreement from political, business and trade union circles. It is not enough merely to point to the enormous wartime need for aircraft, weapons and other military equipment, since at least in theory, such a demand might have been met through the placing of orders in the normal, commercial way. However, the nature of aircraft production and the production of certain other military items (e.g. ships, heavy guns, military vehicles, etc.), with their substantial economies of scale, was conducive to central intervention, at least in order to agree on standard designs to ensure long production runs. Also, under wartime conditions of a severe labour shortage, it was widely feared that reliance on market allocation would inevitably lead to severe inflation. Such an inflationary process would start with wages, as a result of efforts to attract additional labour into defence-related areas of production; this would soon put further pressure on consumer goods markets and force up prices and money wages there too.

Indeed, even with some labour direction, introduced early in the war and gradually strengthened, serious inflationary pressure was to be expected. For on the supply side of the economy, the concentration of investment on the expansion of defence-related production, with severe restrictions on much civilian production in order to release resources for the war effort, meant that consumer goods production could hardly be relied on to expand. Many items, especially consumer durables, virtually disappeared from the shops for the duration of the war while others were in short supply and/ or subject to some form of official rationing. At the same time, employment was sharply increased, generating incomes, and hence additional purchasing power, with no corresponding supply of goods and services to meet the ensuing demand. Hence some measures to reduce inflationary pressure in consumer goods markets were essential. These measures included higher taxes, some forced savings, and the rationing already mentioned. Taken as a whole, even this was insufficient to equate demands and supplies at the prevailing prices. As a result, there was a limited amount of inflation during the war, as well as a considerable accumulation of cash balances by the population, which could only be spent after the war. Of course, there was also some evasion of the controls and some 'black' economic activity, but in general the degree of compliance was impressively high, and probably only feasible in the special circumstances of the war.

Now it is just about possible to imagine that the war's huge transfers of resources into military production could have been achieved through the operation of market signals. However, experience of the First World War strongly suggested that, aside from general inflation, this would have been accompanied by unacceptable shifts in income distribution: away from wages and towards profits, and favouring profits on military goods in particular. Hence it would be easy to condemn certain groups for so-called war-profiteering. Such economic rationality, which actually requires high profits on war production, would probably undermine popular political support for the war and so be socially divisive at a very critical time. In order to maintain civilian morale and support, it was essential to protect real wages to the extent possible, and this could only be done through a plethora of increasingly complex and interlinked controls. The market was not merely suspended, but temporarily superseded during the war and for a time afterwards.

It would be inaccurate to suppose that all the controls grew up at once. What actually happened was closer to the experience of Eastern Europe, where it is commonly found that the introduction of some controls or targets, especially where the resources concerned are in short supply, leads to shortages elsewhere and hence the need for even more centralised allocation to ensure that scarce goods and services are provided preferentially to high priority users. In the British case, the most severe shortages were initially of foreign exchange and manpower. But attempts to allocate these to individual firms soon translated these general shortages into shortages of specific goods and services, which in turn required their own allocation arrangements. Hence at least for major users, commodities such as coal and steel came to be allocated centrally, while essential consumer goods (by definition, therefore, having numerous small users and no major ones) came to be rationed.

As explained very clearly in Mitchell (1966, ch. III), the main technique used in wartime planning was referred to as budgeting; not surprisingly, it bears a striking resemblance to the material balance methods used in post-war Eastern Europe and the Soviet Union. Each budget was worked out for a given, relatively homogeneous commodity group, the principal ones involved being steel, coal, timber and parts of non-ferrous metals and chemicals. They were calculated in physical terms, which in wartime conditions was quite adequate: the emphasis was always on raising production related to military objectives and given this, there was no need for standards of value – prices – that would have facilitated economy-wide comparisons of costs and benefits. Moreover, most prices were in any case regulated administratively and profits above a rather modest level were taxed away. As for the scope of centralised allocation, many commodities were never centrally allocated at all, though over much of the economy, certain key inputs were centrally controlled. Also in each central budget, there was no attempt to account for the uses and/or sources of every last unit of the commodity group concerned. Hence the interconnections that were

Figure 2.1   *A typical budget*

Sources		Uses	
Sources		*Uses*	
Imports	Domestic sources	Exports	Domestic uses
	Main suppliers (listed individually)		Main users – branches related to military
	Other suppliers (taken together)		needs (listed individually)
			Other users

recognised by the planners were relatively few, and there was never anything like a complete model of the economy (such as an input-output model; such techniques had not then been developed very far and the few available computers could not have managed the attendant calculations) implicit in the planning procedure that gradually emerged through trial and error.

A typical budget is shown in Figure 2.1. In principle, sources and uses should balance; if not, it is the task of the administrators concerned to make adjustments in one or more entries to achieve balance. Even then, however, the assumptions made in one balance may well not accord with those made for another, so successive iterations of information exchange and balancing should be conducted in order to achieve a feasible plan overall. Frequently, there was not enough time to do a thorough job of plan balancing and again, just as in Eastern Europe, some errors and imbalances remained when the finally approved allocation was announced. Plans were implemented by issuing either licences to users permitting them to make specified purchases or by instructions to producers or dealers to supply specified amounts to approved users.

Devons (1950) provides what is perhaps the most perceptive account of wartime planning, explaining in considerable detail the assignment of targets to the factories involved in aircraft production and the supply of major components. The allocation of manpower, viewed as the principal factor constraining output in the short run, was also analysed, along with the trade-offs that had to be taken into account. Interestingly, and agreeing with the above account of planning in general, there was never any attempt to assign all the required inputs through centralised procedures, and the main producing firms engaged in extensive sub-contracting. This was possible because the sphere of planning only covered a relatively narrow range of economic activity. Even though most production was subject to government controls both during and for some period after the war, there was enough flexibility in the unplanned parts of the economy (and this included most small firms even in those branches otherwise subject to planning) to supply those inputs needed for aircraft production that were not centrally planned.

It is crucial to emphasise here the reasons for the success of this wartime planning. First, it was geared to very specific objectives, namely the production of aircraft needed for the war effort; and the planning system in general was based on the highest priority for military production. Yet even with such a clear objective – essentially, the maximisation of military production – Devons remarks that it still presented considerable problems to firms seeking to formulate, and then implement, an economic plan, in consultation with higher authorities. The practical difficulty of interpreting an overall objective in the context of an individual firm and its production possibilities is immense: it is extremely unclear what exactly it requires the firm to do. This, combined with persistent shortages of many materials and products, generates all the planning distortions so familiar from Soviet-type planning. Even allowing for the distortions, however, the specificity of wartime economic objectives did allow the centralised form of planning to be highly effective.

Secondly, as already remarked, its scope was also quite limited, focusing on a small number of key firms, the allocation of very few inputs, with much of the emphasis on manpower allocation. Thus in no sense could wartime planning be described as comprehensive, and for the most part it was left to normal commercial practices operating through the market to fill in any gaps in the central plan.

Thirdly, its aims and methods were widely supported not only by the firms involved, including their work-forces in so far as their views can now be ascertained, but also by the population in general. Where these conditions are not all fulfilled, one cannot expect a centralised form of planning to function so effectively.

Immediately after the war, the newly elected Labour government quickly abolished the Ministry of Production and the Ministry of Aircraft Production, but continued most of the powers under which wartime plans were implemented. As Mitchell (1966, p.61) explains,

The Government extended the powers to control prices and supplies for five years; imports and foreign exchange were still subject to strict control; the power to control borrowing was retained; and the power to control building by licence. But conscription of labour (except for the armed Forces) was immediately ended, and direction of labour also ended, except for a few Essential Works Orders.

But the retention of planning powers is not the same as the continuation of planning. And indeed, although some centralised allocation continued, notably of foreign exchange and materials still in short supply, it was no longer done in the framework of an effective overall plan. Nevertheless, the 1947 *Economic Survey* did open with a section on planning, although it emphasised the importance of freedom for the individual, especially in choosing his or her place of work, and the need to conduct planning in a way which minimised its infringement on individual liberties. The Survey went on to note that planning required both an organisation possessed of adequate knowledge about national resources and needs, and a set of economic 'budgets' to relate needs to resources.

The budgets for manpower, and national income and expenditure assumed greatest importance in 1947, supplemented with analysis of the foreign exchange position and prospects, investment, and particular scarce resources such as fuel and power. A serious attempt was made to allocate resources in a balanced way but in practice this aim was frustrated by a number of factors which, for brevity, are merely listed here:

Confusion between targets, forecasts and desires as between different items within any given economic balance;
Misjudgements about trade prospects – exports expanded more slowly and imports became more expensive than expected; balance of payments crises;
The impact of certain persistent resource shortages in limiting the achievement of key output targets, e.g. housing, coal;
In the light of the previous paragraph, the reluctance of government to intervene more forcefully than it actually did in many spheres: self-imposed restraint.

Although these very real difficulties called into question even the possibility of continuing to plan along wartime lines under conditions of peace (and the planning mechanism was already falling into disuse by 1950), it should be pointed out that they are not wholly avoidable in any system of planning. Given the inevitable constraints on the government's freedom of manoeuvre, dictated by political considerations among others, and the general acceptance of, and preference for, a substantially market-oriented economy, all but the third factor must simply be tolerated. Shortage conditions, however, were eliminated by the early 1950s in Britain and have not recurred, so this is an aspect of the wartime and early post-war scene that we shall not need to consider again later.

Despite the above shortcomings of planning, the post-war demobilisation was effected remarkably smoothly. It was widely expected (and feared) in official circles that a rapid transfer of personnel from the forces and defence-related production into civilian activity would be accompanied by rising unemployment. In the event, the transfer was more rapid than initially envisaged and yet the early post-war years were characterised by a severe labour shortage. Some branches, such as those concerned with manufacturing consumer goods, expanded more sharply than the government expected, while others suffered from a mixture of labour and material shortages, e.g. housebuilding. I presume that what must have happened was as follows: many manufacturers perceived that wartime demand for consumer goods had been suppressed by a variety of non-market means; they saw that cash balances were available to buy virtually anything that could be produced, as soon as the wartime restrictions were relaxed. By producing the goods they generated employment.

Having noted the decline of the wartime approach to planning, it is important to appreciate why it was not replaced with some other approach. One reason had to do with fears of inflation. The government and TUC did enter into discussion about ways of controlling money wages, but the TUC stuck firmly to its insistence on 'free collective bargaining', refusing to entertain any form of government control. In the circumstances, a firm commitment to full employment embodied in an officially accepted plan might have been accompanied by quite unacceptable inflationary pressure from the side of wages.

However, as Budd (1978, pp.75, 76) points out, this can hardly be the full story, since even in the absence of a plan, something close to full employment was maintained and money wage increases were surprisingly modest. By 1951 it appeared that full employment and sustained improvements in living standards could be achieved without planning, using the new, Keynesian methods of demand management to regulate what was still an essentially capitalist economy. It was this apparent success that undermined any arguments about new forms of planning; and it was Britain's subsequent economic failure that stimulated the revival of planning in the early 1960s.

As far as institutions were concerned, the decline of planning was associated with the re-emergence of the Treasury as the pre-eminent government department concerned with economic policy (Worswick and Ady, 1962, ch.XV). This affected both the range of economic issues that were regarded as the concern of government – the policy agenda – as well as the set of instruments likely to be employed. According to Pollard (1982, ch.4), the basic attitude of the UK authorities both just after the war, and subsequently, came to be characterised increasingly by a contempt for production, that is, real output and economic activity, as compared to financial and macroeconomic indicators such as the balance of payments, inflation and the public sector borrowing requirement (PSBR). Moreover, there was a feeling that the economy possessed some 'underlying growth rate' that governments themselves could at best only influence marginally: hence economic policy should concentrate on demand management. Yet such an absurd conclusion surely neglects the fact that many government policies have been very harmful to production, frequently for short run reasons.

It should not be supposed that no one defended planning after the war. Franks (1947), for instance, made out an impressively forceful case for planning in a series of lectures. He justified planning on four grounds:

(1)   Considerations of military security;
(2)   Fear of unemployment;
(3)   The need to encourage industries to take risks, plan ahead, invest;
(4)   The general world economic situation and the changed position of the UK.

He went on to argue that the traditional economics of the free market was no longer helpful in analysing the UK, and the government should increasingly assume the role of 'general manager' of the economy. The government was to take few decisions itself, but should communicate clear objectives and information on resource constraints to other agencies. Interestingly, Franks recognised that good planning would entail taking some risks and making mistakes; a cautious, 'safety first' approach would be entirely foolish. Planning could succeed in the post-war world because closer relations between government and industry had already been established during the war, and the statistical and economic services required to service and inform the planning apparatus had also been developed. Nevertheless Franks' approach attracted little support and was soon left far behind by the onward march of Keynesian demand management.

2.2 The National Plan

A decade later, at the start of the 1960s, planning was no longer regarded as an irrelevant diversion from the mainstream of economic policy. Several factors had combined to bring about an atmosphere more favourable to economic planning. These included the realisation that Britain's economic growth, although faster than it had normally been before the Second World War, was seriously lagging behind our principal competitors, some of whom, such as France, were already using a form of economic planning; an increasing dissatisfaction with stop-go methods of economic management; and the fact that the post-war social reforms and extensive nationalisation had greatly enlarged the public sector and hence called for some attempt at co-ordinated forecasting and regulation.

Comprehensive public sector forecasting began in the late 1950s, initially as a technical matter carried on within the Treasury. However, in making its forecasts the Treasury had to liaise with the principal spending departments, liaison which soon grew into an interdepartmental committee. The Plowden Committee set up to review the planning of government spending recommended that public expenditure should be forecast five years ahead, a process which began in 1963 with the publication of forecasts extending up to 1967/8. This process contributed greatly to improvements in official statistics on public sector activities, and also encouraged some attempts to ensure that the forecasts for different departments were based on consistent assumptions about the economy's likely development.

Table 2.1 *Stop-go policies up to the early 1960s*

	Indicators of the economic situation			Policy
	Balance of payments	Unemployment	Rate of inflation	
1.	Surplus or balance	Low	Low	No change
2.	Deficit*	Low	Low	Contraction
3.	Surplus or balance*	High	Low	Expansion
4.	Deficit	High	Low	Expansion plus devaluation†
5.	Surplus or balance	Low	High	Incomes policy‡
6.	Deficit*	Low	High	Contraction
7.	Surplus or balance	High	High	Expansion plus incomes policy‡
8.	Deficit	High	High	Expansion plus devaluation† plus incomes policy‡

* A typical post-war cycle consisted of alternation between states 3 and 2, or 3 and 6.

† The £ sterling had been fixed in relation to the dollar in 1949; there was no serious consideration of devaluation by the government, but the option was analysed in the theoretical literature.

‡ An official incomes policy, a 'pay pause' had first been implemented in 1961 but worries about inflationary tendencies had already generated some discussion.

Considerable pressure was also building up among industrialists for the government to do something positive to moderate investment fluctuations. Frequent shifts of economic policy were held to generate uncertainty for investors, and hence depress the volume of investment even at the best of times; while the shifts themselves increased the amplitude of fluctuations. Yet for the most part, both then and subsequently, the changes in policy were justified by the immediate (short run) needs of the economy. According to what became the conventional wisdom, certain frequently published indicators of the economic situation were used as guides to the required changes in policy, as shown in summary form in Table 2.1. Expansionary and contractionary policies in relation to aggregate demand were implemented by a mixture of monetary policy (mainly the structure of interest rates, influenced by the then Bank Rate) and fiscal policy (taxation and government expenditure). Whatever the precise policy mix chosen on a particular occasion, the major impact fell on a limited number of consumer goods sectors, notably those with the highest income elasticity of demand and/or most susceptible to variations in the cost and availability of consumer credit, and on investment, particularly construction. This was the environment in which the revival of interest in planning took place: thus there was a reasonably clear view about the supposed defects of the existing policies (though not at that time supported by an overwhelming volume of evidence), and considerably less clarity about how planning was supposed to overcome them.

Nevertheless, Mr Selwyn Lloyd, who was Chancellor of the Exchequer in the Conservative Government of the time, introduced the notion of planning to the House of Commons during a debate on a balance of payments crisis in July 1961 (Mitchell, 1966, p.125). As subsequently elaborated, it turned out that he envisaged setting up a new body to examine the country's long term economic prospects and make recommendations about how to improve Britain's performance, both in general, and in particular branches. Virtually for the first time, growth was thereby elevated to a leading position in the ranks of the economic objectives to be pursued by British governments. However, in the light of our remarks towards the end of Section 2.1, it was uncertain (and remains so) whether this represented a fundamental shift in views about the *power* of the government to influence the growth rate, or merely the need *to be seen to act* on an issue that was assuming political prominence.

After some negotiation about the terms of reference between the interested parties, the new planning body was formally announced later in 1961 and held its first meeting in March 1962. The National Economic Development Council (NEDC), as it was named, comprised six nominees from the Trades Union Congress (TUC), six from the principal employers' organisations, two nationalised industry chairmen, three government Ministers (Chancellor of the Exchequer, Minister of Labour, President of the Board of Trade), two independent academic experts, and the Director-General of the National Economic Development Office (NEDO); the Office having been established to service NEDC by preparing background papers, and other reports. The Chancellor served as the NEDC's chairman. As an independent body, rather than part of the government machinery, the NEDC could justly claim that it was no mere mouthpiece for official views. On the other hand, that same independence also meant that it was easy for the government to ignore any unpalatable conclusions that might be reached by the new body.

Within a remarkably short period, NEDC began work on its first plan, for the period 1961–6. This envisaged that GDP would grow at 4 per cent p.a. over the period, which was well above the recent British performance, but very much in line with the growth rates being discussed at a number of OECD meetings around that time. Within the overall total, private and public consumption were both expected to grow somewhat more slowly than GDP, at 3.5 per cent p.a., while investment and exports were to grow by 5.3 per cent and 5.0 per cent p.a. respectively. Thus the share of investment in GDP would slowly rise and, since imports were only supposed to increase by 4.0 per cent p.a., the balance of payments should also improve.

This plan was based on 17 special industrial enquiries (4 in the public sector, 13 in the rest) plus a variety of patchy and often highly aggregated data on the remainder of the economy. The industries investigated were asked to report on the consequences for them of overall growth at 4 per cent p.a., identifying any particular problems likely to impede expansion, and suggesting possible remedies. It turned out, perhaps not surprisingly given the questions that were asked, that few significant problems were identified. Some general resource shortages might have been expected, and some mismatch between the patterns of demand and output, but none of this could be investigated adequately without a fully developed input-output type of model to assist. Despite this weakness, the data-base for the plan was an improvement on anything done before and some important steps had been taken towards the organisation of systematic data collection for planning purposes.

Mitchell (1966, p.133) suggests that the planned increase in exports was not firmly based on a model of export demand. Instead, it was merely a balancing item in the plan, indicating what exports would have to be to enable the other elements of the plan to work. Since the required growth rate was far higher than that achieved during the 1950s, this meant that the plan embodied a considerable degree of optimism from the time of its inception.

Given the paucity of difficulties and real constraints identified in the plan, one can only wonder why British economic growth had not previously been much more rapid. Conversely, it could be expected that the plan should be easy to implement. However, this was not to be. Political uncertainties undermined the government's own commitment to the plan while long-term weaknesses of the British economy, not explicitly identified in the plan, prevented any dramatic improvement in performance. As emphasised by Budd (1978, p.102), in a critical comment, 'the plan did not impose any constraints on short run policies'. It outlined a possible future without making clear what steps were required to ensure that we arrived there. Nevertheless, this tentative resumption of planning laid the foundations which were to be built on by the Labour Government that came to power in 1964. Let us therefore turn to the well-known National Plan.

When the Conservatives resurrected the idea of planning in the early 1960s, the Labour Party was caught by surprise, with no well-developed policy of its own in that area. However, it soon recovered and attacked the Conservatives for not doing enough to make planning an effective component of economic management. Following the 1964 election, Labour proceeded to make its intentions and hopes clear to all. The first step was to reorganise the machinery of government. Responsibilities were shuffled between departments to form the Ministry of Technology (Min. Tech.), and the Department of Economic Affairs (DEA); the latter was given regional policy and prices and incomes policy, as well as taking charge of economic planning.

Labour believed that neither a (small) section within the already powerful Treasury, nor an independent and rather weak body such as the NEDC would be influential enough to impose planning on other government departments or the private sector. Hence the DEA was formed to act as a counterweight to the Treasury on economic matters. The division of responsibilities between the two departments was not just that between long term (DEA) and short term (Treasury) policy, but was based more on functional lines. The Treasury retained its traditional responsibilities for monetary matters and the exchange rate, as well as the control of public expenditure, while the new DEA took on the co-ordination of industry and the mobilisation of real resources. At the same time, Min. Tech. sponsored a number of key industries, such as computers, machine tools and manufacturing machinery, vehicles and mechanical engineering, electrical and process plant, etc. (Broadway, 1969, ch.2). Evidently, however planning developed it could be foreseen that problems of co-ordination between all those bodies were likely to arise.

The DEA inherited many of the NEDO personnel and for a short period it appeared that the Conservatives' NEDC/NEDO apparatus was being superseded. However, within two months it was realised that the regular, close contact between government, trade union leaders and senior businessmen could continue to play a fruitful rôle. Accordingly, the system was reconstituted with only minor changes; for instance, the NEDC chairman was now to be the minister in charge of the DEA. It was intended that NEDC would contribute to the planning process by commenting on draft plans at various stages, and by making suggestions about policies that would assist the development of particular industries. To facilitate the latter, the formation of industry economic development councils (EDCs, or little Neddies, as they came to be called) which had commenced rather half-heartedly under the Conservatives, was undertaken with renewed vigour; by summer 1965, 11 EDCs were already functioning, and more were in preparation.

Aside from these direct and indirect government-industry links, a regional dimension to planning was also seen as important. This was partly because regional problems, especially high local unemployment, were a politically sensitive issue in many constituencies, and partly to improve information flows to the national level departments concerned with economic matters, notably the DEA. Planning was unlikely to be effective unless the impact of plan-related decisions on particular regions could be allowed for in the calculations. Moreover, once a regional structure was in being, it would only be a small further step for the regions themselves to formulate their own plans within the framework of the national-level plan for the whole economy. Unfortunately, this process had barely been started when the whole idea of national planning fell out of favour again, as we shall see below. The regional apparatus comprised a series of Regional Planning Councils with memberships appointed from local experts and interest groups (local authorities, business, trade unions, etc.), and Regional Planning Boards staffed by officials from various government departments. The Boards were largely intended as information channels for the government, though they also provided reports and advice to the

Councils to assist the latters' deliberations on regional implications of national plans, and in connection with their work on regional plans.

Planning could only succeed if Britain's recurrent tendency to generate inflationary pressure, especially when the pressure of demand took the economy close to full employment, could somehow be moderated. It was argued that this required earnings to rise more or less in step with productivity, though in fact the National Plan published in 1965 envisaged that consumption should rise more slowly than GNP, to release additional resources for investment and exports. This appears to require that personal incomes (mainly earnings from employment) should rise more slowly, and profits more rapidly than GNP as a whole. Leaving aside this discrepancy, the DEA entered into discussions with management and trade union bodies to establish an agreed framework in which the so-called prices and incomes policy could be conducted.

A 'Statement of Intent' was signed by government, TUC and employers' representatives which envisaged that prices and incomes policy should serve two principal purposes:

(1) To keep under review the general movement of prices and of money incomes of all kinds;
(2) To examine particular cases in order to advise whether or not the behaviour of prices and of wages, salaries or other money incomes is in the national interest as defined by the Government after consultation with management and unions (quoted in Mitchell, 1966, p.159).

Item (1) was assigned to the existing NEDC/NEDO machinery already discussed, but (2) became the responsiblity of a new body set up in April 1965, the National Board for Prices and Incomes (NBPI). An accompanying White Paper set out the principles of price and income formation which were to guide the new Board, with price increases permitted only when unavoidable cost increases were experienced, and wage increases subject to a 3–3.5 per cent wage norm, together with a list of recognised exceptional circumstances when higher wage increases were allowed. Initially, the policy relied on the consent and co-operation of trade unionists and management, but when this appeared to be inadequate after a few months, it was soon given a statutory basis. The Government, through the DEA, had the power to refer proposed price and wage increases to the NBPI but in practice there were few powers to enforce whatever increases were approved. Moreover, even when embodied in legislation, the policy still had to rely on co-operation from the other 'social partners'. Unfortunately, with the increased economic difficulties of the mid-to late 1960s, this co-operation gradually turned to antagonism, especially from the trade union side. By 1969, prices and incomes policy was virtually dead for the time being.

As for the National Plan itself, this was produced remarkably quickly by Labour's new DEA, in consultation with a wide range of interested parties from government, the trade unions and industry. The plan sought to elaborate the implications for the economy as a whole, as well as for individual branches, of a 25 per cent growth in GNP over the six-year period 1964–70. The implied 3.8 per cent p.a. rate of growth, although slightly below the previous NEDC plan discussed above, was still well above what the economy had been achieving. If sustained, it would evidently have brought the UK's performance much closer to that of our main competitors.

Industries were asked to consider the implications of such a rate of growth for required investment, manpower, imports and other inputs, as well as for marketing, including the expected split between domestic and overseas sales. The plan combined the various industry answers with information about government spending and estimates of private consumption to yield an outcome that, at least formally, was reasonably well balanced at the macroeconomic level. The resulting plan was somewhat more detailed and comprehensive than the NEDC plan had been, but the extremely tight timetable for drawing up the plan still left little time for proper balancing after completion of the industry surveys. As a result, the plan failed to point out and/or resolve potential bottlenecks or surpluses and so once again made the mistake of suggesting that plan fulfilment would not present any exceptional difficulties.

Yet despite this, the plan did envisage some quite significant changes in the structure of the economy over the plan period. For instance, along with the overall GNP growth rate of 3.8 per cent p.a., investment in manufacturing and construction was to rise by 7.5 per cent p.a., most other components of investment were to grow by 4.0 per cent p.a. or more, while the growth of private consumption was to be limited to a relatively modest 3.2 per cent. The latter would presumably depend on some success with the prices and incomes policy discussed above, but the required growth in investment could only come about in the wake of a resurgence of investor confidence. Part of the plan's aim, of course, was to improve the informational basis for investment decision-making in order to improve the quality of these decisions and maintain investment at a high level; thus if all firms believed in the overall growth targets, then their individual investment decisions, based on attempting to maximise profits, should be compatible with that belief. If this theory was correct, then the plan ought to have been a self-fulfilling prophecy.

Perhaps partly for this reason, the plan had few real teeth, and only included a rather unimpressive 'check list of action required' to make the plan work. Since nothing was done directly to ensure that this action really happened, the status of the plan targets was in doubt from the outset. Moreover, it was never clear how the growth projections for particular branches should be translated into the concrete investments required to put the plan into practice. Individual firms received little or no guidance as to what was expected of them, and the plan itself provided neither compulsion nor incentives (e.g. based on taxes and subsidies, as in France). Consequently, the notion of a self-fulfilling prophecy made no sense in practice.

Even the formal, macroeconomic balance in the plan could not be given a great deal of weight, for two reasons. First, the plan seemed to imply that the economy would be faced with a serious labour shortage by the end of the decade, but failed to explain how it might be resolved. Secondly, the balance of payments projections only came out all right because exports were assumed to grow about twice as fast as they had been doing previously. Given the government's then determination to maintain what already appeared to many to be an overvalued exchange rate for the pound, and a tendency for production costs in Britain to drift upwards slightly faster than elsewhere, this was not very plausible, without some support from other policies. This view was soon to be confirmed by events, since it was a foreign exchange crisis in July 1966 that led to domestic deflation and the abandonment of the plan; and just over a year later, a further crisis led to the inevitable devaluation.

Thus the plan was sacrificed to the exigencies of short term macroeconomic policy, though even if it had not been it contained so little provision for implementation that it is hard to believe it could have had much impact on the economy. With its unclear objectives, and being produced at a time when planning was briefly 'in fashion', it is tempting to conclude that the National Plan was largely a political exercise, without much serious intent. Budd (1978, p.118) regarded the plan as a combination of ambitious forecasts and feeble policies which were nothing like enough to resolve the real problems. The National Plan hardly began the task of changing the real constraints facing the economy, and its rapid failure following a period of quite unjustified optimism left planning in Britain discredited for many years.

While all this was happening, another experiment in public intervention was gathering momentum. This was the Industrial Reorganisation Corporation, better know as the IRC (for a detailed study of the IRC, see Hague and Wilkinson, 1983). The development of NEDC and then the EDCs for many individual industries was one of the factors lying behind the creation of the IRC, since it stimulated official thinking about the need for, and possibility of selective intervention. Another factor was the 1960s merger boom. Market forces were generating a great deal of industrial reorganisation and restructuring, but there was a widespread view that much of the activity was purely defensive, e.g. forming a larger unit to reduce the likelihood of a successful takeover bid. In this situation, an agency such as the IRC might be able to promote mergers that would be more clearly in the national interest, establishing new firms able to compete more effectively in world markets, or innovate more rapidly. The latter was an important issue for Min. Tech., the ministry having been set up in the first place because of the Labour government's view that new technology and faster innovation were essential for a sustained improvement in Britain's economic performance.

Proposals for an agency of the IRC type were already being developed in Min. Tech. in mid-1965, and some ideas had been discussed with industrialists. The principal difficulties arose in two areas: first, to assemble sufficient support, both political and economic, for the IRC to get off the ground; and second, to determine the remit of the IRC in such a way as to foster industrialists' confidence in the new body while also satisfying most of its government supporters. Support came from a number of quarters, notably the DEA (which eventually sponsored the IRC legislation, though without taking over completely from Min. Tech.),

Harold Wilson's (the then prime minister) economic adviser Dr T. Balogh, and various other government departments.

The question of the IRC's remit proved a more contentious issue, and the ensuing debate was virtually a rehearsal for the same thing a decade later, when the National Enterprise Board (NEB) was being considered (see next section). According to the most modest views, the IRC should simply be a merger broker, using a judicious mixture of persuasion and financial incentives to bring about the mergers it believed to be especially desirable. Balogh, among others, saw the IRC as something grander than this. He was impressed by the enormously successful trusts which dominated parts of US and German industry and wanted the IRC to act as a catalyst in the formation of similar bodies in Britain, able to use the most advanced technology, and benefit from economies of scale. The more radical Labour Party theorists wanted to take this notion even further, by establishing the IRC as a state holding company, with the power to set up new enterprises in areas where the government wished to see faster development, with or without private sector participation.

In the event, it was the more cautious conception of the IRC which gained approval, as indicated in the IRC Act of 1966, Section 2(1):

> The Corporation may, for the purpose of promoting industrial efficiency and profitability and assisting the economy of the United Kingdom or any part of the United Kingdom
>
> (a) promote or assist the reorganisation or development of any industry; or
>
> (b) if requested by the Secretary of State, establish or develop, or promote or assist the establishment or development of any industrial enterprise.

To fulfil these broad and imprecisely defined responsibilities, the Corporation was given an overall financial limit of £150m. In all other respects, the Corporation had a free hand to decide on the sectors and/or firms which required its attention, and the form which its intervention should assume. It was given no guidance as to the criteria it should employ, nor about priorities, so inevitably its early months were largely occupied with such general considerations, rather than with specific interventions.

Let us now consider what the Corporation actually did in its regrettably brief life – it was abolished by the Conservative government in 1971. In reviewing the IRC's activities and achievements, it is important to bear in mind that it was not some new government department, nor a wholly private concern, but a publicly funded agency that was nevertheless expected to act independently of government. It was always a small organisation, and many of its board members were prominent industrialists, a point which undoubtedly helped to reassure the private firms with which the IRC came to deal; the same point was taken up in a more critical vein by parts of the Labour left, who saw it as indicating a sell-out of the IRC concept to placate private sector interests.

The IRC was involved in over fifty mergers, including some very large ones such as those involving GEC, AEI and EE, as well as the merger of British Motor Holdings and Leyland Motors to form British Leyland. According to Hague and Wilkinson (1983, p.235) this amounted to less than 2 per cent of the mergers consummated in the period 1967–70. So how did the IRC decide where to act? In general, it was interested in proposals likely to improve the balance of payments; it also studied NEDC and DEA reports on various industries and produced its own review of the economy, describing each sector in terms of a few key indicators. Initially, however, it was quite literally waiting for 'customers'.

Aside from its merger business, the IRC also supported a number of schemes that came under Section 2(1)(b) of the Act. In principle, these required an initiative from the DEA (Secretary of State), but in most cases the IRC or the firm concerned took the first move: the IRC would then ask the Secretary of State to request it to intervene. This line of development was a form of 'selective investment', and like any prudent investor the IRC was often at pains to ensure that the management concerned was sufficiently strong to overcome the foreseeable difficulties. It did this either through the influence of its representatives on the boards of companies where supported investment was occurring, or more directly by insisting on changes in senior management as a condition of support. As can be seen, the IRC tended to become much more involved in management than private sector financial institutions normally did (or do). It was beginning to behave in some respects like a development or investment bank of the kind that is well established in some other countries. Moreover, for the government it provided a mechanism whereby industrial support could be offered and negotiated 'at arms' length', hence support could be rapid and flexible. Like the other activities of the IRC, this mechanism clearly had considerable potential for development; it could have served as a powerful lubricant of government–industry relations at what is othewise a rather delicate interface.

It is not easy to evaluate the success of the IRC. Many of its schemes had barely come to fruition when its life was abruptly terminated by an incoming government initially hostile to such interventionism and in any case, success could only be judged over a much longer period. Moreover, some of the supported mergers and other interventions might eventually have happened anyway, either independently or through some other mechanism, so the precise role of the IRC is difficult to disentangle from other factors. Nevertheless, the institution rapidly assembled a highly competent and effective team and managed to gain the respect of much of the business community, who saw the IRC filling a real gap in Britain's economic management structure. Consequently, its demise was widely regretted.

Several books have been written which, among other things, review the period from the mid-1960s discussed in this section. Two in particular stand out from the rest, and provide some useful observations with which to close this section: the first is by a politician, Dell (1973), and the second by an industrialist, Knight (1974). Dell is concerned about the growth of mechanisms for intervening in industry since the end of wartime controls in the early 1950s. Thus there was the Restrictive Trade Practices Act in 1956, the Monopolies and Mergers Act in 1965, and in the latter year also, the NBPI that was discussed above. These provisions can cause great uncertainty for firms, as they are unsure whether their actions will be referred to the appropriate body, and if so, whether any subsequent recommendations would be accepted by the government.

Another area of concern is the arrangements and criteria for industry policy, especially when the government is funding invest-ment projects. Many decisions in this sphere have been taken by committees, or other groupings of officials, leaving the location of responsibility rather unclear. For this reason, Dell favours a system, either within the government machine, or operating through some form of paragovernmental agency like the IRC, which ensures that intervention in general is in the public interest and defensible as such, while any specific intervention should be the responsibility of an identifiable individual. Problems of risk and judgement would still remain, but Dell appears to want intervention to be conducted in such a way that objectives are clear and responsibility limited.

For government agencies these are understandable aims, but Knight (1974) makes clear that they should certainly not be the sole considerations. His book relates to his experience in Courtaulds, both in developing a company strategy (cf. the discussion in Section 2.4, below) and in relating to various government agencies. On the former, he summarises the stages whereby Courtaulds became a vertically integrated fibres-textiles group, with a management style based on profit centres. Rather than establishing a formalised and possibly rigid divisionalisation of the company, it became the practice to expand the area of responsibility of the more successful managers. Within the management structure there was an emphasis on good, rapid information flows for control purposes.

On the latter, the relations with government agencies, much attention is devoted to ICI's takeover bid for Courtaulds, subsequently referred to the Monopolies Commission and blocked. The company believed that the Commission, by adhering to the conventional, static model of monopoly, completely misunderstood its competitive market position, and hence drew inappropriate conclusions. Aside from this particular reference, Courtaulds was also affected to some extent by Restrictive Practices legislation, and by references to the NBPI in the late 1960s. Moreover, the government frequently sought information from the company about a whole range of issues to do with developments in the textiles industry. All this contact with government consumed enormous amounts of time and effort which might have been better employed in running the business.

In this sense, government intevention can impose an extremely high cost on a company, so that in addition to Dell's criteria it is important to add the further condition that the expected economic benefits of intervention should exceed these costs by a substantial margin. Interestingly, two areas of intervention attracted relatively favourable comment from Knight: these were regional policy and investment incentives (on the latter, note that these comments pre-date the introduction of selective incentives in the 1970s; see the next section). With these policy areas, government objectives were reasonably clear, the policies themselves were quite simple so that little management input was needed to establish whether or not any given project qualified for support. Also the policies merely sought to reinforce the kinds of incentive already generated by normal market forces, so that they were never seen as a threat to the accepted ways of doing business. Perhaps it was because of these important advantages that Knight is able to claim that these policies were so effective. In any case, both Dell and Knight have drawn attention to issues that were relatively neglected in all the discussion surrounding the National Plan, issues that we shall return to later in this volume.

2.3 The Labour Government, 1974–9

The government that came to power in the wake of the first oil crisis of late 1973, the miners' strike and the three-day week imposed by the previous Conservative administration found itself in a most unenviable situation. Its views and aspirations about the proper conduct of economic policy in order to realise the Labour Party's socialist ideals had to contend with severe, and in some respects even worsening, short term economic difficulties. However, rather than discussing the whole range of social and economic policies put forward by the 1974–9 Labour government, I shall restrict attention to those aspects of policy with a bearing on economic planning. These are: the industrial strategy (planning agreements and the National Enterprise Board), policies on prices and incomes (the social contract), and the debate about industrial democracy.

In political terms, this set of policies was seen as an internally consistent package, designed to secure support from the Labour Party's key constituencies. Thus the social contract, with its price controls and assurances about public expenditure, was intended to secure trade union co-operation over wages. And by involving workers, particularly trade unionists in discussions about restructuring and other forms of industrial adjustment, it was hoped that the development of effective industrial democracy throughout the economy would facilitate economic change. Finally, the industrial strategy itself signalled the government's commitment to more and better investment, and hence an improved growth performance. Among other things, this would make the level of employment more secure and hence make economic restructuring more acceptable socially.

Unfortunately, as we note below, the effects of short run policy considerations and priorities constrained the government's ability to progress towards its longer term objectives. When the government allowed its radical ambitions to be checked, some observers concluded that it was merely accepting the realities of operating within a predominantly market (capitalist) economy under very unfavourable conditions, while those on the left of the political spectrum were highly critical, presumably believing that the 'realities' should somehow have been superseded.

In the 1970s, there was no serious attempt to repeat the exercise of formulating an overall national plan of the kind discussed in the last section. Instead, the selective approach to industrial policy, as exemplified in the 1960s by the IRC, dominated the picture. Of course, industrial policy and planning are not quite the same; but to the extent that the former includes policy concerning the volume and structure of investment, and other elements of policy affecting the longer term development of the economy, then it falls within the scope of planning as far as the present book is concerned. In fact, the Labour government often presented its industrial strategy as a flexible, company-by-company approach to planning.

A theoretical basis for such selective intervention was provided by Stuart Holland (1972, 1975). He argued that the increasing concentration of the economy, accompanied by the increasingly strong position of multinational corporations within it, had already produced a qualitative change in the British economy's nature and functioning. To mark this change, Holland developed the concept of the 'mesoeconomy'. In traditional economic analysis, the elements of the analysis are individual firms, frequently assumed to operate in competitive, or almost competitive markets, and in policy discussion these are juxtaposed directly to central government and its agencies: there are no intermediate levels in the traditional theory. According to Holland, the new, large firms were powerful enough to dominate many of their markets; and, moreover, their international inter-connections allowed them to evade many of the intended effects of domestic economic policies. Thus although not constituted as sovereign states, these firms were increasingly able to undermine the authority normally supposed to reside in the nation state and hence called for the introduction of new instruments of regulation to redress the upset balance of power between government and firms. It was the large, powerful firms which Holland referred to as the mesoeconomy, indicating something intermediate between government and the more familiar, competitive firms. In their somewhat emasculated form, planning agreements and the National Enterprise Board were the Labour government's response to Holland's call for new policy instruments.

Before examining these policies in detail, it is appropriate to insert here some critical remarks about Holland's theoretical stance. First, while the rise of the multinationals is an important and interesting fact about the post-war world, it is not at all clear why this fact should imply anything special for the British economy as compared to other countries. In particular, I do not believe that a convincing case has been made out for the proposition that Britain's relatively poor economic performance has much, if any connection with the role and power of multinational corporations.

Secondly, multinational corporations may or may not succeed in undermining to some degree the authority traditionally enjoyed by government but it surely does not follow automatically that any new instruments of policy are required. It is true that the size and power of the multinationals has grown more or less in default of any effective, countervailing controls, either national or supranational. Nevertheless, a case for new policy instruments cannot be based on the mere existence of multinationals, but should rest on some assessment of the costs and benefits of their prevailing modes of operation. It seems to me that the alleged harmful impact of multinationals has often been greatly exaggerated to the comparative neglect of benefits such as technology transfer and the ability to engage in effective marketing in a wide range of countries. Aside from this general point, the practical problems of effectively controlling multinational companies are illustrated by the example of Chrysler, referred to later in this section: clearly there is still much to learn.

Thirdly, there is no point (except, perhaps, in propaganda terms) in introducing new policies towards industry without a presumption that they will have some real effects, and that these effects are likely to represent an improvement on what would have happened anyway. The question of real effects is largely a question of power, and the willingness of governments to exercise it to impose their wishes on large corporations; it raises a number of issues which all post-war British governments have found both delicate and intractable. For a Labour government, especially that of the mid-1970s, the issues are especially difficult since the development of any, remotely forceful industrial policy is seen by some as a challenge to the very existence of the market capitalist type of economy. For those on the Labour left, such a challenge has sometimes been quite deliberate and overt; but in view of the real constraints and power relations affecting British economic policy, the degree of panic that afflicted some of the country's leading industrialists in the 1970s was quite absurd. In practice, the challenge proved to be vacuous (further critical discussion of Holland's views can be found in Tomlinson, 1982).

In the operation of industrial policy, governments have a range of policy options open to them. These include:

(1)   Taxes and subsidies applicable to all economic units within a specified category, e.g. all business firms, or all firms above a certain size (*general taxes and subsidies*);

(2)   Measures as in (1), but applicable only to certain sectors and/ or regions (*specific taxes and subsidies*);

(3)   Measures as in (2), restricted to selected firms (this is really what is meant by *selective intervention*);

(4)   *Prohibitions and restrictions* on certain types of economic activity (e.g. regulation of industrial location through the issue of industrial development certificates, referred to as IDC control);

(5)   *Instructions* that certain activities (such as particular investment projects) must be carried out by specified firms within a given time period;

(6)   *Compulsory transfers* of all or part of the ownership of specified firms, either within the private sector (compulsory merger or reorganisation) or from private to public sector (partial or complete nationalisation).

General taxes and subsidies evidently fall within the scope of conventional fiscal policy, while specific ones either represent regional policy, or a broadly defined, substantially non-discriminatory form of industrial policy. Thus both of these categories largely accept the basic assumptions of a market economy, and merely change some of the parameters which affect the market signals that firms observe. Consequently, all governments have felt able to apply policies of this sort, without attracting critical attention. Selective intervention goes much further because it does discriminate between firms and hence arouses fierce opposition from firms losing out.

Prohibitions and restrictions encompass an extensive range of policies which restrict what private firms (and often public sector organisations such as the nationalised industries, as well) are permitted to do, or where they may locate. The argument for such policies, even in a thoroughgoing market economy, is that market signals left to themselves can stimulate firms to make choices which, although privately profitable, are highly undesirable from a social point of view. Pollution, and industrial location, are the two principal examples of external diseconomies where this issue arises; since there is widespread agreement on the need for public controls in these areas, they too have formed part of the policy armoury since the war. However, the intensity of such controls has varied over time and it remains a matter for debate. For it is important to appreciate that although, taken individually, a case could probably be made for each control that is employed, their overall effect is inevitably to impede economic growth and development. Hence there is likely to be a trade-off between the rate of development as conventionally measured and the quality of our environment, and it is not easy to determine the most appropriate policy mix in this context.

To compensate for the negative effects of the above controls, it might be expected that policies involving instructions to firms could be used to enforce development in regions/branches deemed desirable by the relevant governmental authority. But this is a field into which governments have hesitated to tread, because it would bring them into serious conflict with private sector interests. Moreover, it is possible in principle to channel market forces along the desired lines without generating such conflict. For example, a government agency or department could draw up a technical specification of a project and then invite firms to tender for the right to undertake it. If the project is one where the subsequent management and control resides with the public sector, such as a project to build a new motorway, then the tendering process is just the conventional one. On the other hand, if it is envisaged that the project will be run, and the output it generates marketed, by a private sector firm, then an invitation to tender is really asking the private sector to assess what subsidy is required to make the project commercially viable. The nature and amount of the subsidy must depend on whether the tendering firms believe that the project involves a product with a reasonable market, provided costs can be kept down or, more fundamentally, whether they doubt the very existence of a potential market. In the latter case, private sector caution could prevent the project from proceeding at all, and even in the former case, limited competition from alternative suppliers could result in unduly high subsidies being paid. Thus policies of this kind are likely to prove either contentious, if the government simply issues instructions, or expensive, if it seeks to utilise the market mechanism wherever possible.

Partly for this reason, industrial policies that include compulsory transfers are sometimes proposed. For a reorganisation within the private sector, continued public support could be the 'carrot' that induced the rationalisation to be carried out, while the 'stick' of outright nationalisation could be held in reserve to counter any breakdown of co-operaton. In addition, the public sector could act in an entrepreneurial role by setting up new enterprises in areas of activity regarded as belonging to potential future leading sectors, especially if the existing organisational structure of the private sector appears to be inhibiting such development.

Here it is important to remark that market signals need to be generated, received and processed appropriately before they can be acted on. Thus a given set of organisations (e.g. the existing private sector) may simply fail to perceive, or be unable to act on certain market signals indicating the potential profitability of new developments. For instance, a new technological process may make it profitable to produce a whole range of new products. But if the designers of the process are unfamiliar with the markets in which the new products would be sold and the potential producers of these products are unaware of the significance (or even the existence) of the new process, then development may be extremely slow. It is in this sense that market signals must be received and processed by appropriate agents before any response is likely. Moreover, this difficulty is quite separate from the further problems that arise from any inadequacy of the market signals themselves. Consequently, there need be no contradiction for a state body to fulfil an entrepreneurial function as suggested above, even in a predominantly market-type economy.

Finally, it may also be argued that compulsory transfers may be justified if the state wishes to improve its control over the private sector: ownership and management of one or more major enterprises in many leading sectors both yields information about production conditions, allowing taxation and other forms of intervention to be more efficiently conducted, and gives the government greater influence over the volume and structure of investment than it might otherwise have.

In the light of the above discussion of Holland's theoretical position and alternative elements of industrial policy, let us now consider the Labour government's industrial strategy of the 1970s. The strategy, as already noted, involved a combination of planning agreements and the NEB, supplemented by proposals to bring a number of industries wholly or partly into the public sector. The prime candidates for such nationalisation included shipbuilding, aircraft production and road haulage; and plans were afoot to establish the British National Oil Corporation (BNOC), giving the public sector a stake in North Sea Oil developments.

As originally set out in the Labour Party programme prior to the 1974 election, planning agreements were seen as the instrument whereby a future Labour government would gain a decisive say in the affairs of the leading 100 or so major companies. By influencing the companies' development strategies, the system of planning agreements was to achieve certain broadly specified objectives to do with employment (e.g. in particular regions), investment and exports. It would do so by supplying the government with regular (and hopefully, reliable) information on investment, prices, product development, marketing, exports and import requirements, with government financial support in the form of selective aid being contingent on each company's co-operation with government aims (Coates, 1980, p.100). Thus in terms of the previous taxonomy of industrial policy, planning agreements can be regarded as a mixture of selective intervention and instruction with financial inducements largely eliminating the need for direct compulsion. Nevertheless, firms would be compelled to enter into planning agreements with the Department of Industry, trade unionists would be involved in the negotiations at all stages and, as just noted, financial aid would be contingent on agreement.

By the time planning agreements reached the statute book, through the 1975 Industry Act, all of these conditions had been abandoned, mainly due to pressure from industrialists opposing the new forms of intervention. Thus agreements were to be voluntary, and for the most part the discussions leading up to an agreement would be between management and the Department of Industry, with little or no participation by the relevant trade unions. Moreover, the contingency condition for financial support had also disappeared, and nothing more was heard about the need to establish planning agreements with up to 100 leading companies, except from disgruntled left-wingers who still harboured the illusion that that was the agreed policy. Finally, the change from Tony Benn to Eric Varley as minister at the Department of Industry signalled a shift in approach from a radical to a more moderate and cautious industrial policy.

On paper, the policy that emerged was not totally out of line with the Labour government's initial intentions, but it had been watered down significantly and it was not pursued with any noticeable vigour. In terms of concrete effects, only two planning agreements were ever signed. One involved a nationalised industry, the NCB, but it was never clear what difference such an agreement could make to an industry already in the public sector. The other involved the then ailing Chrysler Corporation, the Department of Industry offering substantial financial help in order to keep Chrysler's UK plants in operation. The attempt to make the assistance conditional on a planning agreement soon backfired, however. For in the face of continuing financial difficulties, Chrysler's US management negotiated the sale of its UK operations to the French company, Peugeot: the Industry Department was virtually presented with a *fait accompli* and, to avoid further job losses it could do little but accept the deal, effectively writing off much of Chrysler UK's debts at the same time. The planning agreement was powerless to prevent Chrysler from exploring alternative dispositions of its assets, and did nothing to improve communication between the corporation and the government. This unfortunate and embarrassing episode no doubt discouraged officials from continuing negotiations with other companies with much enthusiasm. It points to a real area of difficulty in relating to multinational companies which must be allowed for when judging how and whether to control them.

With only two signed agreements and neither very effective, this experience in the 1970s cannot really be regarded as an adequate test of a planning agreements approach to industrial policy. However, it was sufficient to reveal some of the problems of the approach. To some extent these arose from its voluntary character, but more importantly, it was never clear what the formal, legal status of any agreement was supposed to be. Hence there was always room for doubt about what was being agreed, with whom and for what purpose. In negotiations with industrialists almost universally hostile to planning agreements, it was easy for this uncertainty to be exploited. Hence if a similar approach was to be tried again, it would be essential to reduce the area of uncertainty and ambiguity in the policy. Some ideas along these lines are discussed in Chapter 7.

The National Enterprise Board (NEB) suffered a rather similar fate to the planning agreements system, in the sense that its final form was much less radical than the initial proposals. Nevertheless, the NEB did get off the ground and achieved a measure of success; it even survived for some time the transition to a Conservative government in 1979. By taking over some existing firms, and by setting up some new ones on its own initiative, it was expected that the NEB would:

> influence major companies in every manufacturing sector through competitive stimuli by giving a lead on investment, would reorganise the industrial structure in each major sector in line with longer term public need rather than short term market considerations, reduce private monopoly power by inserting public enterprise competition, and create a more evenly balanced regional location of industry. (Speech by Eric Heffer, 1974; quoted in Coates, 1980, p.90.)

Leaving aside any question of the feasibility of realising these very ambitious and diverse aims merely by forming a single new institution, it was apparent as soon as the 1975 Industry Act emerged from the legislative process that the NEB would be able to do no more than scratch the surface of Britain's deep-seated industrial problems. Its initial allocation of £1000m for its first four years, of which the last £300m could only be released on parliamentary approval, was simply insufficient to transform the direction and structure of investment in the country. In additon, much of the money was committed in advance to continue subventions to British Leyland, Rolls-Royce 1971 and a few other 'lame ducks' that were transferred from Department of Industry to NEB supervision. Without Department of Industry approval, the NEB could acquire no more than 30 per cent of the shares of any company, nor could it invest more than £10m. Thus if the NEB was to function as an independent institution, as the government appeared to envisage, it to confine most of its attention to small and medium sized companies. Although remote from the Labour Party's original intentions for the NEB, this is largely what happened in practice.

The Board was instrumental in initiating some valuable developments in areas of modern technology where the private sector appeared to be laggard, such as bio-technology, micro-electronics, opto-electronics, etc. With occasional notable exceptions (e.g. Inmos), most of these developments were on quite a small scale. Rather than dominating various branches of British industry, therefore, it would be more accurate to describe its role as catalytic.

The Board's first chairman, Sir Don Ryder (later Lord Ryder) took the view that commercial criteria should inform NEB decisions. He favoured the kind of wide-ranging intervention for which the NEB was established, but was unwilling to underwrite loss-making enterprises even to meet social aims such as employment protection. In this he was strongly supported by the already more moderate Industry Department, with the result that the NEB's first guidelines made clear that normal commercial returns were to be expected on the Board's activities as a whole (except where some selective assistance for persistent loss makers was channelled through the NEB). Individual firms should only receive NEB support if there was judged to be a reasonable prospect of achieving or restoring profitability in the longer term. None of this would preclude the NEB from taking risks which existing private sector institutions seemed unwilling to countenance, or indeed from forming a totally different judgement about the prospects for some venture as compared to the private sector. The NEB could therefore act (and did) as a state funded venture capitalist, but its ability to pursue wider social or economic objectives was severely constrained. Thus it turned out to be a larger and more ambitious version of the IRC discussed in the previous section. Such a rôle made it more acceptable to industry, and probably more effective as a result, but it inevitably attracted considerable criticism both from those who would have preferred social objectives such as employment protection to carry greater weight, as well as from those who thought the NEB should have been establishing a novel kind of state socialist sector, rather than assist an essentially capitalist economy to function better. The NEB is discussed further in Section 6.3.

Given the scale of retreat from early radicalism to subsequent modest reforms, both in regard to planning agreements and the

NEB, the following conclusion by Coates (1980, p.98) seems quite fair:

> From 1975 the Government settled into a straightforward tripartite industrial strategy of the kind governments have pursued in Britain ever since the war. True, this Government used greater amounts of public money, and the NEB remained an important interventionist agency, . . . But the criteria by which it acted did not differ significantly from those dominant in private financial agencies. The scale and manner of its operation were insufficient to put the Government visibly 'in charge' of private investment, as the Labour Left appear to have hoped.

The only aspect of industrial policy in which retreat was less evident concerned the programme of nationalisation. The mid-1970s saw the formation of British Aerospace, British Shipbuilders and the British National Oil Corporation (BNOC).

Creating these new public enterprises, either by taking over and combining existing private enterprises, or, as in BNOC's case, *ab initio*, was certainly in line with Labour Party promises before the 1974 election. For each company, the arguments favouring nationalisation were somewhat different. Thus aerospace was seen as a sector possessing major strategic significance as well as offering tremendously large export opportunities. Given the economies of scale that characterise the sector, as well as the costly and risky nature of new product development it was argued that successful development could best be assured within the framework of a single, state-run company, rather than by a number of loosely related but substantially independent private firms. Since a considerable proportion of British Aerospace business is conducted with the Ministry of Defence and with other nationalised industries (e.g. British Airways), this argument has some force since the new arrangement could, in principle, help to improve the co-ordination of both investment and current transactions within the public sector. However, the Thatcher government evidently decided that these benefits are quite compatible with a large private shareholding in British Aerospace, since a major flotation of shares took place in 1982.

In complete contrast to British Aerospace, British Shipbuilders was formed as a response to persistent decline in the industry since the 1950s. Presumably, therefore, the new company was seen as a convenient vehicle for rationalisation, a process which is still, albeit painfully, going on. In this respect it is not greatly different from the situation at British Leyland, referred to above, though the two companies did not follow quite the same route into the public sector. Nevertheless, in one guise or another, state sponsored rationalisation of industry has gathered pace in the last decade or so, and all the signs are that it is set to continue for much longer. Adapting our older and once prosperous industries to suit present-day domestic and world market conditions is an arduous and time-consuming task. Nationalisation is merely one of a range of possible instruments that may be applied to facilitate such adaptation.

Finally, BNOC was viewed as a means of giving the British government (and hence, indirectly, the British people) a significant stake in the North Sea Oil developments. It was justified partly on the grounds that a public stake, both in production and trading aspects of the oil business, would make it easier to cream off some of the profits into the public revenue; and partly by claiming that government needed to be well informed about the oil industry in order to design tax schemes efficiently. Of course, the latter argument could be applied to any industry, and it is not altogether clear why it was held to apply with particular force to the oil industry. In its original form, BNOC encompassed both production and trading activities. However, its production activities have been privatised since 1982, with the formation of the new company, Britoil, in which the government only retained a minority shareholding.

From these diverse instances of nationalisation that took place under the 1974 Labour Government, it is not easy to discern a coherent theme, nor anything that has more than tangential relevance to economic planning. Indeed, it seems more likely that the amount of the government's time and energy expended on the passage of nationalisation Acts through parliament would have diverted attention from more important matters, such as how to improve and develop the planning process. However, this issue is touched on again in Chapter 6, below.

Overall, then, it has to be concluded that Labour's industrial policy in the mid-1970s turned out to be a disappointment. One reason for this, as already emphasised, was the ideological confusion, as a result of which parts of the policy rested on the continuance of a well-functioning, market-type economy, while others tacitly assumed its obsolescence and supersession by something quite different. Given the assumptions and outlook of the present book, therefore, one of the principal tasks for the later chapters is to elucidate the forms of planning and industrial policy compatible with a predominantly market-type economy.

Another reason for the disappointment was the breakdown of other elements of the policy package, notably the social contract and industrial democracy. When it came to power in 1974, the Labour government found itself committed to honour wage agreements negotiated under the previous administration, including the general policy of indexing wages to the cost of living, as soon as the latter exceeded a specified base by more than 7 per cent. The timing of this policy could scarcely have been more unfortunate, since it coincided with the first oil crisis which not only raised industrial costs and the cost of living but also provoked an abrupt end to the rapid economic expansion which had characterised the world in the early 1970s. Consequently, while adjustment to the new economic conditions required a fall in the real wage, the prevailing incomes policy allowed it to remain constant or even drift upwards. It was not surprising, as a result of all this, that the mid-1970s experienced a rapid acceleration in the rate of inflation in Britain, reaching almost 30 per cent p.a. before dropping back to more moderate levels.

The experience of the early 1970s, combined with vociferous opposition from the trade unions, made a formal incomes policy a political impossibility for the Labour government; indeed the Conservatives' Pay Board was abolished almost as soon as it came to power. Nevertheless, many in the Labour leadership were well aware that their hopes for faster economic growth could not be realised without some agreement on wages and other components of income, an agreement that would include at least the government and trade unions, but preferably the employers as well (the CBI). What emerged, eventually, was the *social contract*, an understanding between the government and the trade unions whereby, in return for wage restraint (guided by norms to be determined each year) the government undertook to:

> improve the social wage,
> restrict dividend payments by firms,
> control prices.

By the social wage is meant the various contributions to consumption provided by the public sector. Broadly interpreted, this includes publicly provided services such as health care, education, refuse collection, and so on; as well as transfer payments made through the social security system, like pensions, supplementary benefit and child benefit. The argument was that if workers could see these elements of their real living standards steadily improving, then they would be less inclined to seek unreasonable nominal wage increases and so sustain the inflationary process.

Similarly, restrictions on dividends were intended to reassure workers that their own restraint would not merely result in higher incomes for those already better off than themselves. However, with moderately competitive markets such controls alone could not be very effective, except in helping to propagate the view that government policy was in some sense 'fair'. In practice, of course, the restrictions would be accompanied by a more rapidly rising share price than would otherwise have occurred, and hence income in the form of capital gains (taxed at a lower rate than dividends) would accrue to shareholders. For this reason, it is not clear that shareholders' income can be controlled effectively, except by measures which directly limit profits.

This line of argument provides one justification for price controls, since they can stipulate the amount of profits which firms are permitted to include in their prices. Another justification is that they may encourage managers to resist demands for very large wage increases if the controls prevent wage rises in excess of the agreed wage norm from being passed forwards into prices. But if the workers do then succeed in securing substantial wage increases, then the net effect could simply be a squeeze on profits and hence a decline in the ability and willingness of firms to undertake capital investment. The latter consideration gradually resulted in the acceptance of exceptions to the Price Code inherited from the Conservative government. After initially strengthening the Code, the Labour government soon faced irresistible pressure from firms to allow price increases that would enable them to fund investment from retained earnings. Extended even to firms paying wage increases in excess of the prevailing norm, this exception considerably weakened the effectiveness of price control, albeit for the best of reasons, since no one wanted to see real investment decline any further.

Thus increasingly, both price and dividend control took on a cosmetic appearance, with very limited real effect. As a means of controlling wage increases, another instrument was available to the government, namely the allocation of public sector contracts. The government did in fact announce that it would not give contracts to firms which granted wage increases above the norm. However, such a policy is subject to serious practical limitations. In the first place, if all firms in a particular branch of industry have made an above-norm award (e.g. because of a national agreement with the relevant trade union), then the public sector has to deal with at least one of them and the wage award provides no basis for discrimination. Secondly, in the case of large, multinational firms, the government may simply be unwilling to discriminate either in relation to its own contracts or in regard to investment subsidies, for fear of driving the firms concerned to locate their new investment elsewhere in the EEC. Hence contract allocation is also rather less powerful an instrument than one might imagine.

From all the above, it follows that the unions themselves, and their willingness to enter into agreements with the government constituted the only really effective means of wage regulation in the mid-1970s; and it worked surprisingly well, especially in view of the limited extent to which the government delivered on its own promises. As the rate of inflation approached 30 per cent in 1975, it was apparent that many union leaders, including those on the left, were becoming increasingly aware of the futility of leap-frogging wage awards and of the dangers of uncontrolled hyperinflation. Thus even though an official incomes policy of the traditional sort remained politically unacceptable, there was widespread support for a more informal policy such as the social contract.

The wage norm for each year's pay round was to be settled through discussions between the government and the TUC, in the light of current trends in the rate of inflation and other economic indicators, such as progress with the government's side of the social contract. However what actually happened was a good deal more complex than this statement suggests. To understand this, it is worth presenting a brief account of the main events. These are summarised in Table 2.2 below, and then commented on.

What the table shows is a policy on incomes regulation which initially commanded widespread support, the support slowly but surely being eroded. The early months of 1979 have been referred to as the 'winter of discontent'; they were characterised by extensive industrial action to obtain above-norm wage increases, and the resulting strikes undoubtedly helped to alienate many members of the public from the Labour government, creating the conditions for a Conservative victory in the June 1979 election.

Table 2.2   *Incomes policy, 1975–9*

Pay round	Official policy	TUC backing	Outcome
1975/6 (Stage 1)	Freeze on high incomes + £6/ week flat rate increase.	Yes	Earnings up 13.9 per cent over the year of Stage 1. Inflation still around 14 per cent.
1976/7 (Stage 2)	4.5 per cent norm.	Yes	Earnings up 8.8 per cent. Inflation still at 17.1 per cent in May 1977.
1977/8 (Stage 3)	Public sector pay rises limited to 10 per cent; 12 month rule between settlement; no catch up awards.	No, but opposition not sustained at all effectively. TUC sought an 'orderly return to free collective bargaining'.	Earnings up 14.2 per cent, inflation down to 7.8 per cent (+ cuts in personal taxes).
1978/9 (Stage 4)	5 per cent norm; no special cases.	No; strong grass roots opposition.	Settlements mainly in the range 10–15 per cent.

But for present purposes, it is important to understand why union and popular support for Labour's incomes policy declined so catastrophically in the late 1970s, after such a promising start. From the trade unions' standpoint, the main difficulty was that they were being asked to co-operate with a set of policies which was not providing the benefits that union leaders and their members had been led to expect. Short term economic pressures (and the short term appeared to get longer and longer) forced the government to restrain, and in some cases actually to cut back public spending, so that any hopes of raising the social wage rapidly dwindled. Moreover, largely for balance of payments reasons, the general stance of government policy became increasingly deflationary with the result that unemployment rose to more than 6 per cent of the labour force.

Thus trade union support for the later stages of Labour's approach to incomes policy would also have been construed as support for these highly unpalatable results of government decisions: not even the most docile and quiescent unions could stomach that.

Yet the government itself was increasingly convinced that some form of incomes policy was essential in the longer term, as a means of containing inflationary pressure in the economy. In practice, the sheer size of the public sector apparently dictated the need for income regulation in that sphere, though there was room for much debate about the most suitable methods; and the prevalence of comparability arguments between public and private sectors seemed to imply that pay policy should be applied more widely. Unfortunately, government and TUC moved further apart, while the TUC leaders found it more and more difficult to control their own members. In the circumstances, it was not surprising that the incoming Conservative government in 1979 dropped all attempts to secure TUC co-operation. Instead, it supported its pay guidelines for the public sector with increasingly stringent cash limits on the various components of public expenditure and was prepared to allow rising unemployment to serve as the principal regulator of wages. It appeared that twenty years of experience with various forms of incomes policy had failed to advance either the theory or the practice of the policy to any noticeable extent.

Industrial democracy suffered a fate similar to that of incomes policy outlined above. It began as a firmly espoused manifesto commitment which, as Coates (1980, p.132) explains, covered two main areas. The first of these concerned the strengthening of workers' rights and protections, a field where the Labour government did register significant progress. In legislative terms, the progress comprised the passage of two important Acts: the Employment Protection Act, and the Trade Unions and Labour Relations Act, the latter of which repealed the previous Conservative government's Industrial Relations Act and reinforced trade union rights.

The second area related to the sharing of managerial functions, giving workers, and notably their trade union representatives, positions on company boards. In addition, it involved stipulations about information disclosure, designed to improve the information available to workers about company policy, the financial position of the company, and so on, in order to provide a sounder basis for collective bargaining. Both the Trade Unions and Labour Relations

Act, and the 1975 Industry Act contained provisions on information disclosure, but in practice they turned out to be weak and cumbersome to operate, so hardly effective at all.

However, the question of sharing managerial functions gave rise to the greatest controversy over the period 1974–9, since there were deep divisions about it within the trade union movement as well as within the government itself and opposition from private sector employers to anything that smacked of power-sharing was extremely strong.

The Donovan Commission which reported in 1968 (Donovan, 1968) focused its principal recommendations on employment and trade union protection, and was extremely cautious about worker representation in management bodies; this was despite the fact that the TUC at that time supported the idea of worker directors, though only on a voluntary basis. Subsequently, the TUC developed a more positive approach to industrial democracy, incorporating the West German, two-tier management structure. The upper tier, the supervisory board, would contain equal numbers of shareholders' and workers' representatives, while the lower, executive board would contain full-time managers and be concerned with the day-to-day running of the business. The incoming Labour government promised an Industrial Democracy Act along these lines, but divisions within the Cabinet delayed action and eventually led to the establishment of a Committee of Inquiry to hear new evidence.

The ensuing Bullock Report (Bullock, 1977) put forward the so-called $(2X + Y)$ formula whereby companies with over 2000 employees should have a single board made up of equal numbers of worker directors (nominated by the relevant trade union branches) and shareholder nominees (these two groups are the $2X$), supplemented with a number of independent directors (Y). A minority report was more cautious than this, merely supporting the development of participatory machinery within firms rather than institutional changes sufficient to give the workers real control.

In any case, publication of the report sparked off a major campaign by the CBI, vigorously opposing the more radical Bullock proposals and arguing for a voluntary, step-by-step approach to industrial democracy. Such opposition might have been overcome had it not been for evident difficulties in other areas. For within the public sector, the government was already seeking to introduce some form of worker representation and also made suggestions about this in relation to its planned nationalisation of the aircraft and shipbuilding industries. The Post Office and the British Steel Corporation began experiments involving the appointment of worker directors, but in general the public sector unions turned out to be at best ambivalent about industrial democracy. Moreover, the situation was no better in the private sector, either. The TUC's reaction to the Bullock proposals was thus initially muted and cautious, but it soon revealed serious divisions. Unions on the left argued that Bullock simply failed to go far enough, and so would not give the workers enough power; in particular the recommendations were clearly designed to prevent worker directors from achieving a majority on any company board. On the other hand, the more right wing unions feared that worker involvement in management would conflict with, and perhaps introduce new difficulties and constraints into, traditional collective bargaining practices.

Given this mixture of opposition and division the government probably had little option but to delay its response to Bullock. Eventually, a White Paper appeared which marked a decisive retreat from Bullock: it favoured gradual, voluntary progess towards greater industrial democracy, with only limited statutory backing. Further consultations with management and trade unions were envisaged before an Industrial Democracy Bill could be presented to Parliament, but in the event, the General Election brought an already sluggish process to an abrupt halt.

The picture we have presented shows a government coming into office with a reasonably coherent, though perhaps over-ambitious programme, in which all the elements discussed above – the industrial strategy, the social contract and industrial democracy – were expected to be mutually supportive. In the event, problems of inflation and the balance of payments proved to be so persistent and pressing that the government was soon obliged to renege on some of its early promises by starting to cut public spending. At the same time, its weak and vulnerable position in Parliament, brought into sharp focus towards the end of the Parliament by Labour's need to enter into an alliance with the Liberal Party, led to weakness and vacillation in the implementation of policy. This factor explains why Labour had to retreat when its policies met with strong opposition, for instance over the measures to put the industrial policy into effect, and again over industrial democracy.

Despite its impressive claims, the Labour Party had no mandate to change the face of British society, and knew it.

2.4 Planning at the Level of the Firm

Much of the discussion in this chapter has concerned planning from the standpoint of government agencies, and has tended to regard planning as a branch of macroeconomics, dealing with investment, growth and related issues. However, more recent thinking about planning, such as that referred to in the previous section has also viewed it in more microeconomic terms, selecting particular branches of the economy or even some individual firms for special attention. Presumably, an important reason for planning at national level is to induce changes in the economic behaviour of firms. In that case, it is of interest to consider how externally produced plans interact with firms' internal processes. Of course, this interaction will depend on how firms conduct their own corporate planning, an observation which raises the problems mentioned in the following quote:

> Government could take a lead in improving the quality of corporate planning in the U.K. So far its approach has been largely through the planning agreements initiative. One of the biggest difficulties this faces is the practical one. Many organisations either do not have corporate plans and therefore have nothing which they can agree with government, or they produce plans in which top management has little confidence. To have a planning agreement, one presumably needs a plan. (Taylor and Hussey, 1982, p.64.)

The implication here is that the Labour government was a little premature in proposing a system of planning agreements when it assumed power in 1974. While many firms opposed the system 'in principle', it appears that there were also many that lacked a suitable internal planning mechanism with which a planning agreement could be linked. A similar sort of difficulty might also arise with the more conventional approach to indicative planning (reviewed critically in the next chapter). This would entail a central planning agency estimating and publishing a series of indicators about the likely development path of the economy. These indicators (or the relevant subset) would then form part of the information available to profit maximising firms to guide their decisions on current production and investment. But if there is no individual, organisation or department within the firm with the responsibility to receive and assimilate the plan indicators, drawing out their implication for the firm's activities, then the indicative plan will be ineffective. Hence, as is only to be expected, the impact of virtually any form of decentralised planning in a market-type economy will be conditioned by the response of individual firms, and this in turn largely depends on their internal planning procedures.

Now in the last two decades, many, perhaps most of Britain's larger firms have adopted some form of corporate planning, though the extent to which it is integrated with the other activities of a firm varies considerably. An extensive literature has grown up, particularly on theoretical approaches to corporate planning, much of which is usefully summarised in Taylor and Hussey (1982). These authors stress the need to consider several distinct perspectives on planning, regarding planning, for instance, as a central control system, a framework for innovation, a social learning process, a political process or as a conflict of values (ibid, p.43). In principle, a firm should not merely choose one or other of these approaches and disregard the rest; instead it should seek to combine them into a coherent whole adapted to its own peculiar circumstances and integrated into the management structure.

In most cases, however, the practice is not as neat and tidy as the above outline suggests that it should be. Thus in some firms planning is quite peripheral, perhaps only undertaken at all because it seems to be in vogue. Alternatively, it might be undertaken as an annual exercise, to review certain areas of the firm's functioning such as investment, innovation, market structure, and so on. In firms of this kind, planning could be helpful in structuring a process of exploration of current or prospective problems, and it may throw light on possible solutions. Such reviews may be requested by individual departments within a firm, or by top management for the benefit of a range of departments. Whatever procedure is used, it is apparent that conflict is likely as soon as proposed solutions approach implementation. For on the one hand, a departmental approach can easily run into trouble if it is not well co-ordinated with what other departments are proposing to do, while on the other hand an approach initiated by top management can also arouse opposition if there is insufficient consultation with the various interest groups within the firm. Thus the planning review may reveal problems and opportunities, but implementation is not easy.

Some authors sidestep these highly practical issues connected with organisational structure, incentives and information flows by putting forward a model of planning which simply ignores them. The literature of operations research frequently suffers from this defect, as does some of the theoretical literature on corporate planning. More seriously, Bray (1982), whose own experience should have left him with a better understanding of planning, argues that both national and enterprise level planning can be regarded as exercises in constrained optimisation. (This is a mathematical problem expressed in the form of an objective, such as profits in this case, to be maximised, subject to a number of constraints, here related to production and market conditions.) Thus he apparently believes that a series of national and enterprise level planning models could be set up and linked together through an appropriate, computerised information system to establish a co-ordinated, economy-wide planning system; and that it would be desirable to construct such a system in order to improve British economic management.

Personally, I find it hard to believe that Bray's approach will be remotely feasible for many years, for there is rather more involved in implementing his system than the purely technical problem of linking a number of computerised models. Even the technical side of his approach is difficult enough, however. But leaving aside the feasibility question, I am quite convinced that his collection of interlinked models would be a recipe for an astonishingly rigid economy, in which hardly anything could be done without checking its interactions with other sectors. In a rapidly changing world, in which our understanding even of the economy's present situation, let alone its possible future states, is necessarily extremely imperfect, it is surely absurd (or arrogant?) to pretend that any models we might construct could be adequate for the comprehensive analysis Bray has in mind. And since the models are therefore certain to be imperfect, as a result of the abstraction, selection, and simplification that they embody (see Loasby, 1976), it would be unwise to allow them to constrain choices about the future development paths which the economy might follow. Of course, this is not meant to imply that there are no real constraints, such as resource constraints, which must be respected along any development path. It is more in the nature of a comment on the necessarily poor representation of these constraints in a planning model.

Probably the most serious defects in the proposal to develop an economy-wide system of linked models for planning purposes are as follows: first, the approach assumes that we could specifiy a clear, economy-wide objective function to serve as the system's maximand; secondly, the approach makes very poor use of lower level information, including alternative 'theories' about the most appropriate developments in particular markets and technologies. Since the question of an objective function is discussed critically elsewhere in this volume, there is no need to dwell on it here. However, the second point is much more important for present purposes, since it concerns what happens at the level of individual firms.

This is the level at which corporate planning takes place. The information available to and sought by any individual firm is processed and assimilated, possibly using formalised mathematical models if that is found to be helpful, but certainly using the firm's 'theory of the business'. This is the firm's view of its business, its fundamental conception about the nature of its products, markets, technologies and so on, and their probable directions and modes of development. Some such conception, whether merely implicit in the thinking of one or more senior managers, or explicitly elaborated in a planning document, is essential to enable a firm to organise and indeed comprehend the mass of information presented to it by what is normally a very turbulent external environment. Much of what is involved in formulating a corporate plan concerns this filtering of environmental information in the light of the current 'theory of the business'.

In this context, the problem with economy-wide modelling is that it is very likely, for reasons to do with its own internal coherence, to impose a kind of artificial uniformity on the model-building methodologies adopted by different branches and firms. In some cases the results might be perfectly compatible with the firms' own approaches to analysing their respective businesses, but in many others they would not be. Thus many firms would be developing models, or providing information for external modellers, which were hardly relevant to their own ways of thinking about economic change. Alternatively, they might even find themselves being obliged to change their approach to suit the external models. Both of these possibilities choose to neglect each firm's own conception of its business and hence deprive agents, mainly firms but to some extent higher level planners as well, of an invaluable tool for organising information; moreover, only a relatively weak and unsophisticated replacement is offered, in the form of a uniform and standardised methodology for planning models.

Given the pervasiveness of environmental uncertainty to which firms must adapt (and which they themselves help to create through their earlier decisions), it may be argued that these remarks about planning models are beside the point; and that modelling is impossible and planning futile. Needless to say, this is not a view to which I subscribe, but it is nevertheless quite a widely held view and does therefore merit some comment. The essential point is that although the way we plan must take account of uncertainty, whether we are concerned with national level or enterprise level planning, it is not sensible merely to abandon planning altogether. Let us now examine what uncertainty implies for the form and structure of a planning system, focusing on the level of individual firms and their inter-relations with the wider economy.

On the former, Beck (1982), in connection with a discussion of developments in planning practice at Shell UK, emphasised a number of unsatisfactory features of conventional point forecasts under conditions of uncertainty. He points out, for instance, that they have frequently turned out to be wrong or misleading, an observation which has sometimes discredited the planning process of which they formed a part. The planning literature is full of articles on how to improve forecasts, though for effective planning they may not even be needed at all. 'Thus the fundamental role of the planner is to promote conceptual understanding, rather than provide numerical quantification . . .' (Beck, 1982, p.17). From this standpoint (which is in line with our comments on 'theories of the business', above) the planner's job is to pinpoint the key factors – which may well be social or political at least as much as economic – likely to affect the viability of developments in various areas of the business. Thus if the exchange rate is crucial for some investment projects, the planner should not seek to construct a point forecast of the rate. Instead, he should indicate that for certain types of project there is a critical region for the exchange rate; for rates above this region, these projects would not be profitable, while for rates below it they certainly would be. Naturally, it is impossible to follow this procedure for a large number of separate factors, but Shell has found it useful to group factors together in order to generate a small number (often as few as two) of scenarios. Each scenario should be internally consistent; in use, it needs to be considered along with at least one alternative, and should be regarded as a framework to guide decisions. Hence unlike the situation when conventional forecasts are used, decision-making responsibility is not taken over by the planners. Thus Beck's view, with which I substantially concur, is that an uncertain environment requires planning, but that it should be based on a scenario approach rather than conventional forecasting.

Scenarios are not without their own problems, of course. In particular they can give rise to some problems of management control, for it can be difficult to judge whether a certain decision was either appropriate at the time or was executed properly in relation to a given scenario. Also, it is not a simple matter to ensure that the different parts of an organisation co-ordinate their decisions properly with respect to a scenario. Both these points are more straightforward to resolve where decisions are based on more conventional forecasts.

On the interrelations of corporate planning and the economy as a whole, Beck's approach has some interesting implications. First, it emphasises the importance for successful economy-wide planning of knowledge about the internal workings of firms, especially the way in which their own internal planning functions. At the same time, it suggests that the practice could well be quite different in different firms, not least because different economic and social variables will be used to differentiate between alternative scenarios as we move from, say, electronics through to construction. Discussions over some forms of planning agreement, as began in the mid-1970s under the Labour government (see previous section), could have provided a means for government departments, especially the Industry Department, to learn more about these practices and hence design better policies; unfortunately, this opportunity to learn was virtually thrown away, as the government's whole approach towards industry became more cautious and circumspect.

Secondly, since the government and its agencies face much the same uncertainty about future developments in the economy as do individual firms, albeit reflected in indicators that are usually at a higher level of aggregation, some of the observations made above about planning by firms might also apply to higher levels, such as the avoidance of point forecasts and the preparation of scenarios.

Thirdly, following on from this, let us recall Beck's notion that planning should provide a framework for decisions. Given my view of planning, this should be narrowed down to decisions about investment and growth. Thus corporate plans guide (but do not predetermine) such decisions for individual firms. At high levels, too, plans should be a guide to decisions and choices. For governments, the relevant decisions are about policies: concerning the level and structure of public sector investment, affecting the level of aggregate demand, affecting business profitability, and so on. Hence a governmental plan should focus on a small number of policy packages (perhaps as few as two) and should set out in as much detail as is possible, or seems appropriate, the circumstances under which one or other would be chosen. Of course, the actual policy choice would normally be something intermediate between the extremes, but this approach would nevertheless provide firms with a much firmer basis for their own calculations than a simple forecast. In this context, it is worth noting that a major weakness of the National Plan was precisely that it failed to provide a guide to decisions. Lying somewhere in the region between forecast and hope, it nowhere specified who had to take what decisions in order to bring it to fruition and did not discuss the circumstances in which such decisions would have been economically justified.

2.5 Lessons from the Past

Since many of the lessons from Britain's past experiece with planning will be drawn out in later chapters, there is no need for a detailed account at this point. However, it is worth drawing attention to a few issues and conclusions which should be borne in mind throughout what follows. For convenience, these are presented as a numbered list of points.

(1) Except under the very special circumstances of wartime, the administrative direction of production and distribution does not offer a feasible approach to planning in Britain.

(2) For any form of planning, a sound, comprehensive data-basis is essential. Even though much of the planning described in

this chapter was not a resounding success, these endeavours have served the very valuable purpose of stimulating the collection of much better statistical data about many branches of the economy.

(3) In the market-type economy which I assume will continue in Britain for many years, it is important to consider very carefully how a planning system should mesh into the existing system of market signals. How do we judge whether markets are functioning well or badly, and when is it desirable for planners to act in concert with, or contrary to the prevailing market signals?

(4) Ironically, the role of the government in relation to an established planning system raises one of the most awkward problems. For it is highly unlikely that a plan could elicit a satisfactory response from the private sector without a very firm and sustained assurance that the government is also committed. Such a commitment involves questions of public expenditure, especially to do with investment, as well as the conduct of conventional macroeconomic policy as it affects the level of demand experienced by the private sector. As we saw in Sections 2.3 and 2.4, it has proved very difficult for governments to stick to their early promises, and the result has been an understandable loss of confidence in the whole planning process.

(5) Although not subscribing to the view that planning is merely a matter of defining objectives and specifying the relevant constraints, it remains the case that these aspects of planning are extremely important. A plan that does little more than describe some desirable future state, without identifying concrete objectives for the agents involved in fulfilling the plan, or elucidating the constraints they must contend with in doing so, is scarcely worth the paper it is written on. Equally, however, it would be a very serious error to see planning only in these limited terms.

(6) With the modest exception of the tripartite NEDO machinery, Britain has virtually no experience of a planning process in which the trade unions or other workers' representatives play a major role. This is the case both at national level, and at the level of individual firms, though for the latter there has been a good deal of development of consultative and

participatory machinery in the last decade or so. Despite calls for greater worker involvement, the Labour governments of the 1960s and 1970s proved most reluctant to override employers' objections to such a development. The unions themselves were also divided on this issue of workers' democracy.

3
Planning in Other Countries

Several countries or regions of the world operate their economies using, among other policy tools, some form of economic planning. It is only reasonable, therefore, to expect that some or all of these countries should be able to offer some lessons to do with the organisation, operation and effectiveness of systems of economic planning. While seeking to elicit such lessons, it would be wrong to suppose that Britain might ever simply wish to copy another country's procedures wholesale. There are many reasons why this would be neither desirable, nor in most cases even feasible, as I hope should become clearer in what follows. Nevertheless, it can be valuable to study experience elsewhere so that we might at least avoid unnecessary errors or misconceptions. Experience elsewhere also indicates the types of planning that are possible, illustrates the institutional frameworks required by the different types and reveals the range of instruments and objectives associated with each system.

In this chapter, I begin in Section 3.1 by discussing some aspects of Eastern European planning experience, regarding this as the most important case of economy-wide production planning. I pay particular attention to the debates about economic reform, and the slow shift away from the extreme centralisation of economic management that characterised the 1950s. Like Eastern Europe, France also experimented with economic planning soon after the Second World War, but the French approach was extremely decentralised and market-oriented. In terms of the more theoretical literature surveyed in the next chapter, it was regarded for a time as a kind of indicative planning, but in Section 3.2 of this chapter we merely outline its main concrete features. Japan is not generally thought of as a planned economy, but in fact the Ministry of International Trade and Industry (MITI) fulfils many of the functions of a central planning bureau in a guided market economy. For this reason, and because Japan's industrialisation since 1945 has been so successful, it merits some discussion in this chapter: accordingly, Section 3.3 is devoted to Japan, seen as an example of industry level planning geared to specific and restricted objectives. This is an interesting case to study, since sectoral planning is becoming increasingly popular in developed industrial economies, as indicated by the recent Alvey plan for the development of information technology in Britain (Alvey, 1982), the Telematic and Informatics Plan in France and the similar plan recently announced by the West German government. Finally, Section 3.4 draws out some lessons for Britain from these three very different types of planning experience.

3.1　Eastern Europe: Debates on Economic Reform

The traditional model

In the late 1940s, the whole of Eastern Europe adopted the Soviet-type model of a planned economy, with only minor variations between the individual countries. This model is based on a highly centralised and hierarchical economic administration, with state or co-operative ownership of virtually all means of production and a state monopoly over international transactions, mainly exports and imports of goods and services (see Cave and Hare, 1981).

Within this framework, plan formulation is initiated from the highest level planning organ, which we shall refer to for convenience as the Central Planning Bureau (CPB). The initial plan proposal is a set of aggregated targets setting out the main features of expected development in the coming plan period. For instance, the targets might include national income as a whole, the output of major branches of the economy (industry, construction, agriculture, etc.), private and public consumption, exports and imports, and so on. Once ratified or amended by the Council of Ministers, the targets are broken down by the ministries and other intermediate levels of the system into a set of draft production plans, one for each producing unit in the economy. The enterprises receiving these plans then have a chance to comment on them and propose changes; either reductions if they think the plan is too ambitious, or an alternative output mix, or alternative inputs if its structure is inappropriate for a particular enterprise, or increases if the original plan is too easy. Whatever happens at this stage of plan bargaining, the revised proposals are passed up the hierarchy so that economy-wide materials balances can be checked by the ministries and the CPB. These balances are important in a centralised economy where the bulk of resource allocation is determined by instructions rather than by market signals. They are worked out in order to ensure that supply and demand for the most important commodities and commodity groups, after allowing for exports and imports as well as all domestic transactions, are balanced. Almost invariably, many of the revised plan proposals will require further revision in order to satisfy the material balances. Eventually, a final version of the plan is approved by the CPB and Council of Ministers and, when decomposed again to enterprise level, this becomes the operational plan for each producing unit.

The process of plan formulation outlined above applies most fully to annual plans. Medium term (usually five-year) plans and long term (15–20-year) plans are largely constructed by the top levels of the system. They are never disaggregated in the same way as current plans and, as one would expect from their longer time perspective, they are mainly concerned with some of the key growth rates in the economy, and the allocation of labour and investment resources between branches. In addition, in the more open economies they have to pay a great deal of attention to the opportunities arising through trade with both East and West. In principle, the medium term plans should establish some of the guidelines needed to initiate the annual planning process. To some extent this happens in practice, though when the economic situation changes in such a way as to invalidate some of the central assumptions of the five-year plan, one would no longer expect annual plans to be at all closely tied to the five-year plan targets. Thus over a given five-year period, most of the economic adjustment that might be required, takes place via the annual plans, rather than through the five-year plan itself.

Having arrived at an annual plan, let us now consider what institutions and policy instruments are available to ensure its implementation, while remaining within the now traditional Soviet type model. The institutions involved include the Ministry of Finance and the banking system, the Statistical Office, the various branch ministries, the Materials Supply Bureau, the ministries dealing with foreign and domestic trade, and in most cases the Party and Trade Union hierarchies. Bureaux concerned with price and wage regulation are also likely to play a part in plan implementation, though the way in which this happens varies a lot from country to country. Policy instruments include instructions issued by the institutions just mentioned, as well as credit rules, tax and subsidy policy as it affects both domestic and international transactions, and rules to do with incomes, especially bonuses related to some aspect of economic performance.

An important further power possessed by the state authorities in Eastern Europe is the ability to make organisational changes: either affecting the whole economy or some of its larger branches, or more modestly, involving only one or a few enterprises. The central authorities can start up new enterprises, order mergers, or in extreme cases close down enterprises that are performing badly: it is important to note that unlike in a pure market economy or a mixed economy, no other agents have that power.

With such an extensive range of powers, one might imagine that plan fulfilment within this type of economic system would be quite straightforward and more or less automatic. Unfortunately, life is never that simple. Although it had some powerful advantages in the early stages of planning, the traditional system we have been sketching turned out eventually to have some very severe weaknesses, affecting both plan formulation and plan fulfilment. These provided much of the impetus behind the debates about economic reform from the late 1950s right up to the present day, and are discussed in the following sub-section.

The advantages of the system stemmed from its essentially simple but rather rigid structure. In the 1950s in particular, it was able to mobilise resources very rapidly, generating remarkably high growth rates of total output, at least until all the surplus labour available in agriculture had been absorbed into other sectors of each economy. Much of the growth so generated was quite labour intensive; and where it was not, it was nearly always based on the replication in each branch of standard designs of plant and/or equipment. Such a pattern of growth was initially feasible, though even then probably not the most efficient that could be imagined. Moreover, rather like the British wartime planning outlined in Chapter 2, it was at its most effective when the state's objectives were simple, as in the

1950s when the rapid development of heavy industry was everywhere the paramount goal. Finally, it should be emphasised that the above advantages of the centralised system had more to do with the centralised control over economic resources than with the detailed production planning that also characterised the system.

Limitations of the model

As the conditions for success in the 1950s gradually changed – resources were more fully utilised and economic objectives became more complex – the Soviet-type model became less adequate as a basis for economic management. Not only that, but even when working reasonably well in its own terms, this model was not in effect for long before it began to attract fundamental criticism. Most of the model's deficiencies that were identified early on had to do with problems of *information* and *incentives*, issues which have since been analysed at length in the theoretical literature on planning (Johansen, 1978; Kornai, 1980b). More recently, questions relating to technological *innovation* and the need for *institutional change* have come to the fore (Berliner, 1976 and Wiles, 1977). From the standpoint of the present book, a further issue also merits our attention, namely the problem of determining and making operational the plan *objectives* (see Johansen, 1978; Kornai, 1980a).

Many people still harbour the illusion that central planners are able to assemble all the information needed to formulate a comprehensive production plan in one place, the CPB, and process this information into a perfectly balanced plan which lower level agents can then implement. To some extent, this illusion was built into the Soviet-type model of a planned economy, and its practical impossibility explains some of the microeconomic inefficiencies of economies operating according to this model.

The sheer volume of information that would be needed to formulate a 'perfect plan' is far beyond the capacity of any organisation to assemble and process, even with the most modern data processing equipment to assist. Centrally planned economies circumvent this difficulty by aggregating economic information into broad commodity groups as it is passed up the planning hierarchy. As a result, material balances are not usually concerned with individual commodities, but rather with balancing the supply and demand of aggregates of commodities. However, a plan that is balanced in this way is unlikely to be perfectly balanced once it is decomposed to enterprise level for implementation. Consequently, such a plan is bound to embody innumerable errors of detail, involving shortages of some goods and surpluses of others. So at the implementation stage of planning, these problems will quickly emerge; they can be resolved either by informal and probably unofficial, transactions between enterprises, or by amendments to the plan, approved by higher bodies. (On theoretical aspects of this problem, see Hare, 1981a and b.)

But often, enterprises simply have to live with the situation as it turns out, since there might not be time for a properly balanced plan adjustment to be worked out. Anticipating this, as they soon learn to do, enterprises tend to request more material, labour and capital inputs than they really need, or try to propose fairly easy output targets, so that in the event of supply difficulties they will still be able to fulfil their plans. From the enterprise's point of view, this kind of behaviour is only natural, though from a social point of view it is likely to be very inefficient.

Another effect of the same informational problem is to make enterprises reluctant to change what they are doing, since regular supply and marketing arrangements provide some security against micro-level plan imbalances. If nothing is changing, however, there is hardly any need for planning, a curious paradox of extreme centralisation. Yet in an economy that is striving to grow rapidly, much has to change; so the central planners have to overcome a resistance to change which is largely generated by the functioning of the planning system itself. At the same time, the sheer complexity of detailed production planning forces the system to simplify the task of planning by restricting the range of goods to be produced, slowing down the rate of introduction of new technologies, favouring large units of production, and so on. On the demand side, there is a relative lack of attention to the requirements of users of products and the system tends to be slow to cater for demand for new products.

These shortcomings are likely to be especially damaging in relation to foreign trade, since successful exporting to the West requires the enterprises concerned to adapt flexibly to changing market demands. Yet in the traditional system, virtually all foreign trading transactions had to pass through the foreign trade ministry; and to a large extent, foreign trade was treated as a residual after domestic demands and supplies had been accounted for. The combination of poor organisational support and relatively low priority has impeded the development of East-West trade and probably helped to slow down the growth of productive efficiency in the more trade-dependent Eastern economies.

Satisfactory enterprise-level incentives for workers, and more particularly for managers, have proved remarkably hard to devise in the centrally planned economies of Eastern Europe. Ideological purists may feel that the whole question of monetary incentives should not arise at all in what is supposedly a socialist economy, and that some form of moral incentive – such as the desire to participate in and contribute towards the building of socialism – should provide workers and managers with adequate motivation. In practice, although this kind of motive can have some effect, it has never turned out to be enough, even when the emphasis on ideological matters is very strong.

Enterprise-level incentives were initially based on gross output targets, subsequently on indicators more closely related to profitability. While the latter is clearly preferable from an economic standpoint, in that it obliges enterprises to have some concern for their costs, all the targets that have been employed share a common defect, namely their short-run character. Thus in virtually all cases, managerial bonuses and worker incentive payments were tied to some aspect of fulfilling the annual plan. Although probably stimulating greater effort than the complete absence of bonuses, the short-run basis for bonuses has had two distorting effects, both of which tended to reinforce the problems identified above in relation to plan information.

The first was the effect on product mix and input choices. Taking the profitability indicator as an example, the bonus system encouraged enterprises to concentrate on making their most profitable products. That sounds perfectly reasonable until one realises that:

(1) Enterprises were not usually involved in marketing their output. The relevant ministry or the materials supply organs normally undertook to purchase whatever was produced, whether or not there was any demand for the goods concerned.

(2) Other enterprises would be reliant on particular supplies of inputs, so a distortion in one enterprise's product mix could hinder plan fulfilment elsewhere in the economy, especially in view of the lack of adequate slack in the system.

Given the need for aggregation to economise on information flows, these defects were hard to avoid. The central authorities were often nervous about delegating marketing responsibility to enterprise-level or about encouraging direct enterprise links to avoid product-mix distortions, fearing that this would undermine central control over the economy, imperfect though that inevitably was.

The second distortion was the stultifying effect on product and process innovation by enterprises. The emphasis on current product and plan fulfilment meant that enterprises were not too keen to change their production methods or introduce new products if this involved any interruption of their current operations. In the early phase of central planning, where the main aim was to achieve growth by mobilising additional resources, this shortcoming was less serious than it became later on.

An important aspect of the economic growth process is the institutional change that normally accompanies it, such as the formation, merger and dissolution of enterprises, the rearrangement of responsibilities among higher level economic agencies and so forth. Such changes, as noted above, are largely subject to central decision in the Soviet-type model which makes for a good deal of inflexibility at times. Moreover, rather than encouraging the development of a diversity of organisational forms, the centralised model tends to favour uniformity and simplicity, failing to recognise that different branches of the economy may be best served by very different types of economic organisation.

The final deficiency of the Soviet-type model is a rather surprising one, concerning the determination of plan objectives. According to the ideology of the model, the plan is intended to serve social needs and these needs are, in some unspecified way, objectively given to the central planners. Given these presuppositions, there clearly cannot be any problem to do with the plan objectives. Unfortunately, in practice, the assumptions are highly unlikely to be valid. For one thing, the whole concept of social need is highly elusive and it is far from clear why the perceptions of needs by a group of central planners should ever command universal acceptance. For another, the concept of the central planners as a homogeneous, united group is nowhere borne out in reality. Instead, the plan emerges from a complex process of interaction between rival central agencies with diverse objectives and resources. Such a view of the centralised model makes it substantially less attractive in social welfare terms than its own ideology asserts.

Reform proposals

Some or all of these problems are recognised and actively debated throughout Eastern Europe. The ensuing debates have generated a wide range of reform proposals and a rather more limited extent of actual change. Generally speaking, the proposals have either sought to retain the centralised model but introduce some changes to improve its functioning; or have envisaged some degree of decentralisation of economic management.

Measures in the first category include the formation of associations, reduction or change in the compulsory plan indicators, improvements in planning techniques and computerisation. Many of the planned economies began to combine enterprises into larger units from the mid-1960s, e.g. East Germany, Poland, USSR (from 1973), with the generic name of associations (for a useful discussion of these developments, see Bauer and Szamuely, 1978). Simultaneously, these new bodies, which in some cases had already existed in the guise of sub-departments within the branch ministries, were expected to strengthen central control and increase the autonomy of lower level units. The former would be achieved by reducing the number of separate economic units to whom plan instructions needed to be sent (or addressed, to use the standard terminology), and correspondingly raising their degree of aggregation. This reduces the centre's information processing load and so offers the possibility of achieving better control over the reduced number of plan targets that the central agencies still determine.

In this system, the associations themselves have considerable influence over resource allocation between their member enterprises, whether this concerns the details of materials allocation, choice of product mix and technology, or marketing. By locating this kind of decision rather lower down the planning hierarchy, it is more likely that the necessary information will be available to the decision-makers, and that they will be able to respond more quickly to changed circumstances than the traditional hierarchy could. Thus the additional autonomy for lower levels could improve the quality of planning and make it more flexible: such at least was the hope for this type of reform.

In the early days of the centralised model, the most important plan target for each enterprise was its gross output target. This reflected the growth/output orientation of the central planners and their associated neglect of costs and profitability. From an economic point of view, of course, gross output could hardly be a less appropriate target since, to the extent that enterprises possessed some scope for independent choice – and they always have some, even in the most centralised model – it stimulated high cost, high price production irrespective of the pattern of demand and relative costs. To mitigate these distortions, other targets were assigned and soon proliferated into a complex, and frequently imperfectly co-ordinated array of plan targets for each enterprise. Because of the practical difficulties of operating this system, and its sheer complexity, it is not surprising that reformers wanted to tackle the plan indicator problem. Two things were required to make progress: agreement on a suitable new indicator of enterprise performance, and revisions to the price system.

As far as indicators were concerned, the idea that some measure of enterprise profitability was most satisfactory soon became widely accepted. Such a measure is comprehensive, in that it encompasses all elements of costs and revenues; and at enterprise level it is clearly correct to regard wages as a cost and labour as a productive input that should be economised. Decisions about wage/profit shares are more properly dealt with at the macroeconomic level. Apart from a profitability indicator, several countries also impose sales targets on their enterprises as a legacy of the gross-output tradition but in some cases profit has now become the most important enterprise-level plan target.

Profits are measured in terms of the prevailing prices, so the spread of profits targets necessarily drew attention to the price system, and the principles of price formation. If prices bear little or no relation to costs, then profits targets themselves are bound to stimulate undesirable decisions about product and input mix, especially if there remains some tendency to reproduce shortage conditions in the economy, a sellers' market. Hence a price reform has often accompanied a shift to profits targets, though this is not the place for a detailed analysis of pricing in planned economies (see Hare, 1976; Bornstein, 1976). Essentially, however, profits targets and better pricing should eliminate many of the traditional distortions, and should make enterprise behaviour more concordant with central plan objectives. The one remaining shortcoming of this approach is its short-run bias. Operational plans are still based on a single year and enterprise performance is evaluated, correspondingly, for the same period. Thus there is a general tendency to inhibit activities and decisions with longer term consequences, such as most forms of innovation, unless specific instructions are issued by the central authorities. This is a serious defect and one which the centrally planned economies are far from resolving.

Another area in which the centralised model is open to some improvement is that of planning techniques and computerisation (on the latter, see Cave, 1980). The method of material balances was first developed in the Soviet Union in the 1920s, and only involves very simple calculations and the exchange of information between officials in various levels and departments of the planning hierarchy. It is fundamentally an administrative method of plan formulation, which seeks to find an allocation of resources – a plan – consistent with balancing supply and demand for at least the major product groups. Although it is well adapted to the assignment of priorities and the pursuit of simple, clear objectives, it is much less satisfactory when objectives become more complex and when the planners would like to examine alternative plans.

To meet these more recent needs, techniques such as input–output analysis and linear programming have been developed, and adapted for applications in planning. Both techniques can help in analysing some aspects of resource allocation at moderate levels of aggregation but neither is able to work out a complete plan. Even the fastest computers face quite low limits on the scale of problem they can solve, and aside from such computational constraints it is simply very hard to assemble all the information needed for a detailed planning model rapidly enough for the model to be used. Despite these limitations, models have proved useful in many areas of planning and computers have been especially helpful in the data processing field, recording and combining data for a variety of planning tasks. One should not, however, be deluded into believing that formal planning techniques offer any kind of panacea: the problems of the centralised model are far from purely technical.

The second category of reforms recognises the inherent limitations of central planning and seeks to construct a much more decentralised model. Proposals relating to such a model have arisen in Czecho-slovakia and Poland in the past, but only Hungary has successfully implemented and sustained reforms of this kind, since the introduction of the so-called New Economic Mechanism in 1968. In Hungary's case, the key feature of the reforms was the abolition, except in a few specified situations, of compulsory plan instructions from ministries to enterprises. The preparation of central plans went on very much as before, but instead of being implemented by means of instructions, they were implemented through a set of indirect economic regulators. These included price, tax and subsidy policy; credit guidelines; profits taxation and the wage regulation system; taxes and controls on international transactions (for a detailed review, see Marer, 1984; also Hare, Radice and Swain, 1981).

Enterprises were supposed to study, and respond to, their markets (including foreign markets) instead of relying on central instructions about their current production, though in the investment sphere a good deal of direct central control was retained. The aims were to make the economy more flexible and responsive to demand, more competitive in international trade and more receptive to innovation, while preserving the basic framework of a planned economy. As it turned out, these aims have been, and continue to be much harder to achieve than the reformers anticipated; though it is now generally accepted that the quality of production in Hungary, and the balance between supply and demand in most markets, have greatly improved.

In part, the continuing difficulties can be blamed on external problems such as the oil price increases of 1973 and 1979, both of which had severe adverse effects on Hungary; the decline in Hungary's terms of trade; and the recent Western recession. But there have been internal problems too, which have probably had more significant effects on the functioning of the economic mechanism since 1968. These include the lack of institutional change, the failure to limit investment, fears that the reforms may be reversed and the short-term character of the incentive system.

On the institutional side, neither the structure of central economic institutions – ministries and bureaux – nor the over-concentrated structure of enterprises was substantially changed. Thus hopes of the development of domestic competition proved to be over-optimistic in most branches of production and the persistence of the traditional institutions of economic management made all too plausible the suspicions of enterprise managers that the old system of planning might be restored. One effect of these suspicions was to make enterprises much more dependent on central institutions than the reformers intended. Even though no longer legally required to do so, many enterprises tended to seek ministry approval for their plans or accepted ministry suggestions, undermining the envisaged sensitivity to market signals. The fact that most enterprise managers were the same people who had operated the pre-reform system did not, of course, facilitate radical change; and in the face of day-to-day operating problems it was easy to find supporters for new central measures and controls. In the event, despite some recentralising moves in the early and mid-1970s, the reforms were never fully abrogated; and the reform process was renewed in the early 1980s, only this time accompanied by institutional reform as well (see Hare, 1983a).

The reforms provided that managerial and worker bonuses depended on profitability in the current year, imparting a short-run bias to the incentive system very much as before 1968. To be fair, it has to be conceded that a greatly superior system is not at all easy to devise, either in socialist or capitalist economies. For worker bonuses, current profits may be as good as anything; for managers, it may be better not to rely on any current performance indicator at all, but to motivate people through promotion prospects related to successful longer-term developments in their enterprise. For top managers, there is the corresponding prospect of transfer to a larger enterprise or the ability to attract investment resources, though this would require the allocation of investment funds to support successful managers rather than for expansion in branches pre-determined by the centre.

In Hungary's post-reform system, control over investment has not proved easy. Over half of investment has been initiated by enterprise decisions, financed from enterprise development funds, loans and grants from state bodies; the remaining investment, mainly infrastructure and very large projects being decided by the state as part of the plan. Pricing policy, enterprise tax rules and credit policy were expected to afford adequate powers to regulate enterprise investment, by acting on the cash flows needed to finance it. But in practice the controls were relatively ineffective. The pre-reform growth orientation remained strongly entrenched at enterprise level, reinforced by the knowledge that sanctions against ineffective investment were very weak since enterprises would not be permitted to go bankrupt. This is one aspect of the phenomenon referred to by Kornai as the soft budget constraint problem (Kornai, 1980b). Enterprises frequently act as if investment was virtually costless, and there has been a tendency for them to start projects with their own funds, then seek state support to complete them. The result of such behaviour, checked from time to time by centrally imposed freezes on investment starts, is that total investment has continued to exhibit cycles, just as before the reforms. It is worth remarking here that Western economies also experience investment cycles, though the causal mechanism is very different from that sketched above. In particular, fluctuations in business confidence appear to bring about periodic declines in investment, while government intervention, far from restraining investment as in Eastern Europe, is called for to stimulate it.

The question of soft budget constraints will not be resolved merely by further central exhortations about financial discipline. To a considerable extent, it is really a matter of the environment within which enterprises operate, especially the lack of competition. By this, I do not mean anything like the textbook-style perfect competition since there is no prospect of that in Hungarian conditions (or, perhaps, in conditions elsewhere for that matter). Interestingly, the latest round of reforms in Hungary does include some steps which should strengthen competition. For reasons of brevity, the recent changes are merely listed here:

(1)   A further price reform to align domestic prices more closely to world market prices; however, to be fully effective this measure would require fewer restrictions on imports and continued stimulation of exports. But CMEA transactions are still governed by the traditional model and Western trade could not easily be liberalised under present conditions.

(2)   Merger of branch ministries into a single Industry Ministry, partly to reduce day-to-day intervention in enterprise decision-making.

(3)   Break-up of several large trusts into their constituent enterprises.

(4)   Relaxation of procedures for establishing new producing units, especially small enterprises and co-operatives and various forms of working association. This also includes leasing out some state and co-operative shops and restaurants to private individuals.

Although they will not quickly account for more than a tiny fraction of aggregate production, the small units referred to in (4) could be most important in the longer term. The power to form these new units is no longer a monopoly held by the central ministries, and it should not be politically awkward to let some of them go bankrupt if they prove unviable. Thus they could make a useful contribution to the economy's flexibility, in time. As with other reform measures, the initial response might be quite slow until potential small entrepreneurs/managers are convinced that the new arrangements are there to stay.

While still dealing with Hungary, it is important to note that two special factors have contributed to the economic success of Hungary's reforms; one is political, the other is economic. The political factor is the aftermath of the 1956 uprising. Following the Soviet intervention and the installation of Kadar as Party leader, the regime embarked on a path of conciliation, seeking support wherever it could. This moderate approach facilitated the introduction of reforms, while the 1956 disaster encouraged caution as far as political change was concerned. The second factor is the success of reforms in agriculture. Collectivisation was basically completed in the early 1960s, but sensible pricing policies made compulsory delivery quotas unnecessary and the government was generally tolerant of small-scale private sideline activity engaged in by the agricultural workers. It is this kind of flexibility which is now being introduced in industry.

To sum up, we can say that Hungarian experience has shown how Eastern Europe can be reformed into a somewhat more open and decentralised system. However, the barriers to change – institutional, political, etc. – have been substantial and the degree of improvement in economic behaviour and performance, while significant, remains much less than the more hopeful reformers anticipated. Although other East European countries have shown some interest in the Hungarian reforms, they have not followed this example at all closely. While the 'unreformed' economies (or conservative reformers) face many economic problems, the pressure to undertake fundamental reform is not that great. These economies still manage a reasonable economic performance and administrative planning does have some points to its credit. For instance, the speed with which most East European economies have coped with the debt crisis does demonstrate that administrative planning is very effective in dealing with massive external shocks and achieving specific objectives in a comparatively short period of time.

3.2   France

The French economy has grown rapidly since the Second World War, overtaking Britain in terms of income per capita and becoming one of the most developed economies in Europe. Soon after the War, a planning system was introduced to aid the process of recovery and prevent any collapse to the depressed conditions of the 1930s. Once established, the planning system continued to formulate development plans for successive periods, usually five-yearly as in the centrally planned economies just discussed. The system was most influential, and was regarded as most successful, in the 1950s and early 1960s. By the late 1960s and for much of the 1970s, its rôle in French economic management was slowly declining, for a mixture of economic and political reasons. However, the new Socialist government under President Mitterrand, which came to power in 1981, has been trying to revive planning and restore its earlier prominence in the policy-making process. Under present conditions, this has turned out to be a good deal more difficult than the Socialists expected.

It would scarcely be possible to recount the full story of French planning in a short section such as this (for details, see Estrin and Holmes, 1983a and b, and Cave and Hare, 1981, ch. 4), but the principal developments are outlined so that we can assess how far the planning system contributed to French economic growth, what special factors facilitated the system's acceptance, and the recent circumstances that call for changes in its rôle and approach. All this is essential background material for an evaluation of the prospects and desirability of introducing the French type of planning in Britain.

French plans have not all emphasised the same objectives. Thus the first (1947–53) stressed reconstruction of the economy, while the next two (1954–7, 1958–61) paid greater attention to France's competitiveness in view of the increasing openness of the world economy and the formation of the EEC in 1957. Planning related to regional and social issues came to the fore from the fourth plan (1962–5) onwards; however, worries about inflation and the balance of payments have tended to dominate the planners' thinking since then. Nevertheless, despite this general emphasis, both the sixth (1970–5) and eighth (1980–5) plans incorporated aggressive industrial policies to foster industrial expansion from the supply-side.

The latter plan was abandoned in mid-1981 after the socialist government assumed power, to be replaced by a more expansionary, interim plan (1981–3). Meanwhile, work on the ninth plan (1984–8) is well underway. Its general aim is to seek the fastest domestic growth compatible with external equilibrium, indicating that an important lesson, with some parallel in the British situation, has been learnt: namely that France cannot yet expand demand rapidly enough to reduce unemployment without running into severe balance of payments difficulties. The plan focuses on 12 priority programmes ranging from the modernisation of industry to improving the judicial and security systems; it is hard to judge how fully these programmes have been co-ordinated. In common with several recent plans, the latest proposals display a marked reluctance to provide quantified forecasts or targets, on the grounds that there is considerable uncertainty about the rate of recovery from the present world recession. However, the socialist group in the National Assembly have insisted that some targets should be included in the plan, though it remains unclear how they are to be achieved.

The Planning Commission is the chief agency concerned with plan formulation in France. It has always been a small body, staffed mainly by senior civil servants; its position in the governmental structure has varied over the years, but since 1962 it has reported directly to the Prime Minister or his office (with the exception of the period 1981–3 when there was a separate Ministry of Planning). Aside from formulating plans, the Planning Commission also supervises plan execution and at times provides general economic advice to the government. In view of its smallness, the Commission could not itself undertake the entire burden of planning activity. Instead, it requests studies and reports from a number of other bodies, and has established commissions concerned with particular sectors or aspects of economic activity where plan proposals can be discussed and, hopefully, agreed by the economic agents most likely to be affected by them.

According to Cave and Hare (1981, p. 70), the planning process is usually decomposed into four stages, namely analysis, dialogue, formulation of the plan, and implementation. The first stage, analysis, has tended to be the most technical, since it is here that a variety of planning models has been employed. Whatever the particular model being used, analysis typically begins by extrapolating recent economic and social trends over the forthcoming plan period in order to reveal inconsistencies, imbalances and other difficulties likely to emerge then. Subsequently, alternative assumptions about government policy, and about exogenous factors such as the rate of growth of world trade, are inserted in the model to obtain a range of rather more satisfactory plan projections. As far as possible, these should show how to overcome the problems identified in the initial extrapolation exercise.

In the second stage, some of these projections are presented to the commissions mentioned above, and an elaborate dialogue ensues. Commission membership includes employer and trade union representatives, independent experts and some officials. The planners hoped that such groups would be able to reach a consensus about developments in their particular area of the economy and hence either accept or propose agreed modifications to one of the projections from the Planning Commission. But in most cases, the consensus approach proved to be unworkable because of the conflicts of interest within the commissions, especially between employers and trade union officials. In practice, employers' representatives took the most active part in commission deliberations, despite their antipathy to some aspects of the planning system; the unions often either declined to participate or indicated that they would not be bound by commission conclusions. Consequently, what at first glance appears to be the most remarkable innovation in French planning was unable to justify all the hopes that rested on it.

Nevertheless, the commissions were by no means a wasted initiative, being especially valuable in the informational sphere. The planners were enabled to report possible developments in the economy to the interest groups concerned with particular enterprises, sectors, regions, etc., while the latter also had an opportunity to put forward their own demands and raise issues not already allowed for in the plan calculations. To the extent that initial plan proposals were modified as a result of these deliberations, new inconsistencies were likely to be introduced and further central calculations, followed by another round of dialogue, would be required before a consistent plan could be formulated. Thus the second and third stages of the planning process tended to merge. From the fifth plan onwards, the result of these stages has had to be presented to Parliament, sometimes in the form of plan variants, for debate and final approval.

If the final plan had been in accord with consensus views expressed in the various commissions, the fourth stage of plan implementation should have been quite straightforward. Indeed, in theory, merely to publish the plan should have been sufficient to induce compliance with it, as all the agents in the economy took mutually supportive and compatible decisions, especially concerning investment. Unfortunately, the real world, even in France, is much too complex for such a simplistic approach to be viable.

As argued in the next chapter, price-type signals generated in the course of market interactions are rarely sufficient to enable firms to take the most appropriate investment decisions; this is the case whether or not the prevailing prices can be regarded as equilibrium ones. In this situation, therefore, an indicative plan of the French kind should be able to supplement the available market information by offering useful guidance about probable growth rates and hence investment requirements in the economy as a whole, and in some of its principal branches. This is what the plan was intended to do, but of course its success in this respect was always contingent on a number of key assumptions.

The most important of these assumptions have to do with uncertainty in the economy and the formation of expectations; in addition, the increased sensitivity of the French economy to fluctuations in overseas markets, with related concerns about the control of domestic inflation, have led to changes in the perception of France's planning problem. Taking the latter point first, it seems that the original approach to planning based on the identification and removal of anticipated bottlenecks has gradually become less and less useful, as it has become easier to circumvent bottlenecks as and when they arise, through foreign trade. As a result, some kinds of planning error or misjudgement are much less serious than they might have been, and so it is no longer essential for plans to be comprehensive. Reflecting this situation, planning in France has gradually shifted away from the production of co-ordinated branch plans covering the whole economy, towards macroeconomic planning, largely in financial terms, combined with special programmes to meet the particular needs of the coming plan period. Some of these special programmes covered individual industries, such as the plans for the development of the nuclear energy industry, high-speed trains and the telecommunications industry.

On the first two points, *uncertainty* about future economic developments and opportunities is just as pervasive a feature of the French economy as elsewhere. Hence agents considering making investments in some branch are compelled to base their evaluation on their *expectations* about the developments likely to affect them. It can easily occur that different agents have different expectations about any given subset of possible future events, and may therefore disagree about the merits of particular investments. Somehow or other, investments based on these disparate expectations come to be aggregated in the various commissions to arrive at a 'consensus' view. However, it is doubtful whether a great deal of practical significance should be attached to the resulting totals. Yet if this procedure is rejected, the alternative may well be the tacit acceptance of the initial proposals from the Planning Commission which, although internally consistent, might correspond to no one's expectations. This is certainly a cruel dilemma.

Limitations of technique as well as comprehension have meant that only one or at most a small number of alternative plan variants is prepared. In any case by the time the plan is approved, only a single variant remains. Consequently, if some major external event occurs which has not already been allowed for in the plan calculations, it can throw the whole plan out of balance. In France such events occurred with the 'events' of 1968, then again in 1973 and 1979 with the two oil-price shocks; the economy is still adjusting to, and recovering from the most recent of these. Since investors are all too aware that such shocks could occur again, they would be foolish always to act as if the latest plan was certain to be 'correct'. Instead, they need to use plan information quite selectively, combining it with other sources in order to build up their 'world view'. Thus even if nothing untoward happens to upset the official plan, it is impossible to rely on economic agents to fulfil it 'automatically'. It is therefore essential to make some organisational and economic arrangements to facilitate plan implementation, especially as short term macroeconomic policy may come into conflict with plan objectives.

In principle, one would expect the planners in France to achieve relatively firm control over public sector activities (including the nationalised industries), at least in the longer term through control over investment programmes. Private sector regulation, by contrast, would have to depend on the inherent 'logic of the plan' (Lutz,

1969, pp. 24–5), which, as we have already suggested above, can hardly be relied on; or on a variety of indirect tax and credit measures stimulating compliance with the plan. Perhaps surprisingly, Estrin and Holmes (1983a, ch. 6) suggest that the public sector paid the least attention to the official plan, most ministries displaying remarkably little commitment to it.

Compliance by the private sector has changed over time, as the range and power of the instruments available to the government has become more limited. In the early years of planning the government still controlled import licences and could influence much of investment through the allocation of Marshall aid. Subsequently, however, these channels of influence lost their significance: trade controls were relaxed or abandoned altogether and investment funding was increasingly provided by retained profits and from financial institutions. Hence regulation came to involve a combination of informal consultations and discussions (particularly with some of the major firms), some influence over the allocation of credit by the state-owned banks, and little else. The conservative French governments of the 1970s tended to be hostile or indifferent to planning and, although they did not go so far as to dismantle the planning apparatus, they were not averse to presiding over its decline. Also, the government wished to present an appearance of not interfering with the market, which forced what planning remained into a macro-mould (Estrin and Holmes, 1983a, p. 124). To some extent, the plan might have continued to sustain growth merely by its effect on confidence, by showing that continued growth was possible, but such a broad demonstration was clearly inadequate to implement detailed branch or sectoral projections.

From the above short account of French planning one has to conclude that its direct impact on French economic development must have been quite modest. However, its indirect effect on confidence and its rôle as a forum for interest groups to meet and exchange ideas were both extremely valuable benefits though most researchers have found it very hard to discern more concrete indications that plans for particular branches had much impact. Despite such limited efficacy, French planning was widely admired by outside observers during the 1960s, both for its (assumed) relationship with the then developing and rather elegant theory of indicative planning, and for its (assumed) connection with France's increasingly successful economic performance. As we have seen, neither connection was ever as strong as used to be assumed. (See also Section 4.1 for more on the theory of indicative planning.)

Now that planning is once again a favoured policy in France, it is evidently important to reconsider what functions it should and could fulfil. While doing this, we must bear in mind the favourable environment for planning which exists there. Thus planning institutions are already well established and still command broad respect from most groups of the population even after the decline of recent years. In addition, the traditional centralisation of French government and the country's business organisation are both helpful factors, as is the fact that French political parties are not divided on the question of planning or on the need for direct government intervention to restructure particular industries. Moreover it should be noted that these factors are substantially less favourable in Britain, a point we return to at the end of the chapter.

According to Estrin and Holmes (1983a, ch. 2), the planners should be seeking to provide or generate some of the information needed to guide investment decisions, which is not already provided by the market. Widespread uncertainty about the development paths which the economy could follow suggests that additional information could be helpful, but the complexity of the real economy prevents it from being enormously detailed. In practice, the planners have to confine themselves to the identification of prospective inconsistencies in the existing economic trends, the provision of macroeconomic indicators relevant for many agents, and, where possible, an assessment of those branches or projects in which the appropriate investment is relatively insensitive to the alternative realisations of currently uncertain economic variables. In other parts of the economy, the most that can be expected is the announcement by the planners of *conditional pre-commitments* (see Section 4.3). These would not commit the planners to definite decisions, but would outline their likely responses to a range of future economic situations. To the extent that favourable outcomes (e.g. rapid growth, low inflation, etc.) depend on co-operative private sector responses, pre-commitments can be used to induce such co-operation; otherwise, they simply give the private sector a better basis for predicting how the government will react to exogenous events (e.g. another oil shock, sudden recovery of world demand, etc.). In practice, of course, it would at best only be feasible for a small number of these commitments to be made; otherwise the government itself would feel too constrained (and knowing this, the commitments would become less credible to other agents) and the 'message' conveyed through the commitments would become too complex for reliable and clear comprehension.

This is perhaps what should happen under the French planning system, and it accords with much of the theory set out in the next chapter, as well as our subsequent discussion of a possible framework for British economic planning. Nevertheless, it remains rather remote from French planning practice, even under the Mitterrand government in power since 1981. Part of the problem is an institutional one. The Ministry of Finance (just as the Treasury in Britain) has always formed the focal point of the French administrative structure and in recent years the Ministry for Industry has also gained in influence. This leaves the planners, lacking an independent budget and with only modest formal powers, in a peripheral position in relation to many important economic decisions. Frequently, they are able to recommend but not to insist on action, with the result that the credibility and status of planning is slowly undermined.

The present government favours planning on ideological grounds, but is beset by apparently insurmountable short-term problems which militate against a firm commitment to strengthen planning. Not only has the planners' institutional position undergone little substantive change, but the government has proved just as reluctant as its predecessors to allow public bodies to publish medium-term forecasts which are deemed to be unacceptably gloomy. Moreover, as Cobham (1983) emphasises, even the nationalisation of the banks which took place in 1982 has not been accompanied by any real attempt to use the banking system to strengthen plan implementation. Accordingly, it is hard to see a rationale for the change of ownership, except in terms of political expediency; this is a point to bear in mind when we return to the question of nationalisation in a British context in Chapter 6. While the present constraints persist, it is hard to see how French planning can break away from the limited rôle it has been able to play in the last decade and a half (see Estrin and Holmes, 1983b and 1984).

3.3 Japan

There cannot be many people who are unaware of Japan's remarkable development success since the Second World War. This undoubted success is frequently attributed to the interventions of MITI, the Ministry of International Trade and Industry. It is argued that MITI selected the key sectors on which the development effort would concentrate, controlled imports to ensure a securely protected domestic market and thence launched repeated assaults on the world market. By adopting such a strategic approach to investment, and through its control over the economic levers which permitted these investments to make profits, first domestically and then overseas, MITI apparently acted as a highly effective planning body.

However, it is important not to exaggerate the rôle of MITI in Japan's success. In the first place, the combination of MITI's existence and Japan's successful development is clearly insufficient to establish any necessary connection between the two; other institutions and conditioning factors were involved in the development process and these must be allowed for both in understanding Japan itself, and in any consideration of the applicability of Japanese experience elsewhere. Secondly, MITI is by no means omnicompetent. A number of the industries favoured by MITI have not done well and even in some of the successful ones the eventual organisational framework was not always in line with MITI's proposals. Moreover, some branches grew rapidly without the benefit of MITI's patronage. Thirdly, it would be misleading to suggest that Japan's development has relied heavily on extensive protection from competitive pressures. It is true that there has been some protection from foreign competition, but within the country itself competition among the (usually) small number of domestic producers has tended to be fierce. The forms of competition, as elsewhere, are influenced by the institutional environment provided by the Japanese economy, in ways that we refer to again later on. Fourthly, the most effective Japanese companies have achieved their success by producing well-designed, good quality products and marketing them well wherever they saw worthwhile opportunities. MITI's intervention was probably helpful, but rarely decisive, in bringing about these results. Finally, it is quite possible that MITI's future rôle may, in any case, be somewhat different from what it has been in the past. The nature of the world economy has changed substantially since the 1950s and, unlike that earlier period, Japan can no longer rely on massive imports of tried and tested technology to underpin its continued growth. Let us now review these points in more detail.

Since Japan possesses almost no indigenous resources, its development has entailed enormous imports of raw materials, including oil, which has had to be paid for by means of corresponding exports of finished goods. This basic fact explains both the structure of Japanese trade with the rest of the world, and the extreme emphasis in policy-making on securing and maintaining international competitiveness. Nevertheless, despite all the controversy aroused by Japan's export performance in Western European and US markets, the country was only exporting about 10 per cent of its GDP by the late 1970s as compared to a typical European share of well over 20 per cent.

The government bodies most directly concerned with the economy are the Ministry of Finance and MITI. There is also an Economic Planning Agency which prepares long-term indicative plans, but according to Magaziner and Hout (1980, p. 31) it has a relatively minor rôle. The Finance Ministry is analogous to the British Treasury in that it is responsible for monetary and fiscal policy and hence the government's budget balance. Also, since most industrial policy measures have budgetary effects, they normally require approval from the Ministry. Within the Ministry, the Financial and Banking Bureaus are the most significant for our purposes. The former 'manages the Fiscal Investment and Loan Plan (FILP), which channels government trust funds into industrial sectors via public corporations [such as the Japan Development Bank] that offer loans and grants' (Magaziner and Hout, 1980, p. 32). The latter regulates the Bank of Japan and hence the commercial banks, providing one avenue for influencing the volume and structure of investment. Thus much lending to corporations was at preferential interest rates, and individuals were given strong tax incentives to save, with the tax rate on investment income being less than that on earned income (Hills, 1983, p. 71). However, in recent years the Finance Ministry has tended to adopt a fairly cautious and restrictive attitude towards new industrial subsidies, as a result of the increasing budget deficits that have followed the 1975 depression.

MITI was established in 1949 by merger of the Ministry of Commerce and Industry, and the Board of Trade. Its responsibilities cover most industries, though other ministries supervise telecommunications, railway equipment and the railways, and pharmaceuticals. Within its sphere of influence MITI has a remarkably broad and open-ended remit, summarised by Magaziner and Hout (1980, p. 33) in the following terms:

(i)   shaping the structure of industry and adjusting dislocations that arise in transition;

(ii)   guiding the healthy development of industries and their production and distribution activities;

(iii) managing Japan's foreign trade and its commercial relations;

(iv)   ensuring adequate raw materials and energy flows to industry; and

(v)   managing particular areas such as small business, patents, industrial technology, etc.

Of course, MITI does not intervene in all industries, but only in a selected few at any moment of time. Intervention assumes different forms in different industries, while in most cases MITI's action calls for agreement with other ministries such as the Finance Ministry discussed above, and consent from the Fair Trade Commission; in addition, political constraints are sometimes operative. The need to secure agreement and support can slow down policy changes but, when finally accepted, the new policies are likely to be well thought out; moreover, from industry's point of view, there are considerable advantages in a government policy which only shifts at infrequent intervals.

The various ministries in the Japanese governmental structure often appear to act in competition with each other. As a result, Hills (1983, p.69) argues that 'Coordination is a considerable problem, made more difficult by a weak political leadership structure'. On the other hand, it is easier to sympathise with Johnson's (1982, p.44) view that successful development needed a bureaucracy protected from all but the strongest interest groups, so that it could set and achieve long-range priorities. In this context, a weak polity may well have been positively helpful. Once co-ordination was achieved, it was then not easy to upset.

Given our concern with industrial policy here, we also need to comment on Japanese industrial organisation and its links with government agencies. Much of Japanese industry, notably the larger corporations, is grouped into conglomerates of firms based on the main banks. Since the bulk of investment has been funded from retained profits and bank loans, with relatively little equity, it follows that the leading banks in each conglomerate have possessed considerable power to influence the investment strategies of their dependent enterprises. At the same time, competition between conglomerates has been astonishingly intense, with each group seeking to have a leading company in each industrial sector. Sometimes, as Hills (1983, p.67) points out, MITI has complained of 'excessive competition' and in proposing rationalisations the ministry has sought to curb its alleged excesses to some degree. But this attitude neglects the possible benefits, in terms of more efficient production, that ensue from active competition. However, many MITI officials clearly appreciate this point as the following quote from a recent newspaper report indicates (Hamilton, 1983): 'The only difference between what we do and what you do in Britain,' says a young MITI officer, 'is that we tend to work with several private companies in competition with each other. You work with one company like ICL, and wonder why you are less successful.'

Aside from the conglomerates, each of which spans many branches of the economy, there are several business organisations devoted to the promotion of business interests in political circles. The most influential of these is the *Keidanren* (Federation of Economic Organisation) concerned mainly with big business, but other bodies (e.g. the Chamber of Commerce and Industry) also represent small business. In addition, there are numerous industry associations which maintain close relationships with the corresponding sections of MITI.

These links between business, politics and the bureaucracy are reinforced and sustained by the Japanese practice of *amukadari* (descent from heaven). The bureaucracy has long been held in high esteem in Japanese society; as a result, it generally attracts the best qualified graduates into its ranks, and these entrants gradually work their way up the hierarchy. As soon as one of a year's entry to some ministry reaches the rank of vice minister, it is conventional practice for the remainder of that cohort to retire from the ministry. This is what is meant by *amukadari*. The retiring bureaucrats are found positions in industry and politics, but retain links with their former ministry. Consequently, it is not surprising that business and government are well-informed about each other's needs and practices, so that co-ordination is somewhat easier to achieve than in countries where such connections are rather weak: Britain might well be a case in point, since such links are actively discouraged and tend to be regarded as 'corrupt'.

Even with the support of this effective communication system, it is not easy for MITI to determine its policy priorities and ensure that they are implemented. Support for a particular industry has both microeconomic (financial arrangements; availability of skills, markets; competitiveness) and macroeconomic (resource transfers between sectors; overall growth and productivity) implications. It is widely agreed that MITI, in consultation with all the interested parties, takes account of these implications in developing its own proposals, but it cannot then merely impose its 'solution' on the industry concerned. To a surprising degree, MITI relies on market forces to support its measures, and in some cases firms (or entire branches) have used their own independent market power to develop along lines contrary to MITI's preferred strategy. Nevertheless, MITI has developed a broad range of policy approaches and instruments to prod industries to develop in accordance with its strategic thinking, especially concerning the investment rate and structure of production; technology development; and export–import measures (Magaziner and Hout, 1980, pp.39 *et seq.*). Where it has succeeded in promoting industrial restructuring, MITI must have been assisted by the fact that large Japanese firms adopt a long-term point of view which includes the formulation of long-term product development strategies.

As emphasised by Hills (1983, p.73), 'MITI's involvement has been mainly in fledgling or depressed industries'. The ministry has encouraged concentration and rationalisation of production in order to 'stabilise' competition and base development on a small number of low cost producers. In those industries where rapid growth and easy profits allowed marginal producers to remain viable, MITI could do little to change the structure of production; it had most impact on industries that were initially highly fragmented, such as sewing machines and car parts.

While seeking to accelerate growth and investment in the emergent branches of the economy, MITI has also had to contend with the need to rationalise production in declining branches. In the past, MITI has promoted legislation permitting cartels to form in certain industries. More recently, however, the Finance Ministry has opposed this form of development, though MITI in turn responded by securing new legislation that permitted cartels to facilitate the rationalisation of depressed industries (the

Structurally Depressed Industry Law). But this legislation only takes effect for a particular industry if at least two-thirds of the firms in the industry request intervention. Since many firms naturally prefer short-term financial assistance, which they can still obtain from the banks, rather than inducements to retire capacity, it may well turn out that the new provisions are not often invoked.

In the area of technology, notably R & D, MITI is one of several governmental agencies involved. In the early post-war period, MITI and the Ministry of Finance jointly controlled technology imports estimated to have contributed 46 per cent of Japan's growth from 1947–73. Even in the late 1970s, Japan was importing considerable volumes of new technology, though in terms of new contracts, Japan has actually been exporting more than she imports for some years. Since 1971, Japan has been fourth in the world as far as R & D outlays are concerned. Moreover, only a minute fraction of these outlays has been committed to defence-related activities, and the Japanese government has consistently provided a relatively modest share of R & D funding, normally well under 40 per cent. The bulk of R & D funding comes from private industry, stimulated by generous tax incentives.

MITI itself does not control a large proportion of public R & D funds but it runs a number of research institutions with projects funded jointly by itself and private sponsors. Following some concern in the late 1970s that private R & D expenditure was not recovering from recession at the desired rate, these institutes have become the vehicle for promoting MITI's view that much more R & D was required in branches concerned with information technology. In addition, MITI envisages that Japan should now strive to become independent of the West in basic research. Some observers have questioned whether such a hierarchical and disciplined society will be able to exhibit the initiative and independence of thought required to promote such research successfully. However, as already pointed out, Japanese hierarchy and discipline exist within a remarkably competitive society. In this context, new ideas are likely to find financial support and, more importantly, alternative approaches to problems will often be supported. At the level of fundamental research rather than applied research and R & D, the fact that Japanese firms and the relevant parts of the bureaucracy are prepared to take a long term view of development should be conducive to solid and consistent support, at least in some fields. But of course Japan could not hope to be at the forefront of development in all spheres.

Turning to export–import measures, these have been very much what one would expect of a country poor in raw materials and striving to develop rapidly. Thus exports have been stimulated in various ways, including export-related accelerated depreciation and cheap long term credit for investments leading to higher exports. Conversely, manufactured imports have been restricted sharply, especially in those branches earmarked for rapid domestic development. However, all this was mainly in the 1950s and 1960s. Since then, Japan's very success has resulted in the abandonment of many of the earlier formal restrictions. As Hills (1983, p.79) puts it, 'MITI's rôle as carteliser and rationaliser has been eroded by domestic pressures, its rôle as research coordinator has been curtailed by monetary policy, and its rôle as protector has been diminished by international pressures'. The latter has resulted in a Japanese home market which is now substantially open to overseas competition, except in a few areas where closed procurement prevails, or where domestic political pressure demands continued protection (e.g. agriculture, retailing).

We now consider development in a number of branches some of which followed MITI's guidelines while others went their own way. It will then be possible to conclude this section by outlining what may be regarded as the key features of the Japanese development model. Magaziner and Hout (1980) surveyed six industries: two in which Japan had achieved remarkable success (steel and motor cars), two which are now undergoing decline after a period of success (aluminium and shipbuilding) and two which are still increasing in importance (industrial machinery and information electronics). In each case, I concentrate on MITI's involvement and the response by the industries concerned, without going into great detail about other aspects of each industry.

Taking steel first, this was quickly picked out as a key industry after the Second World War and the branch received substantial public support in the 1950s and 1960s. This tailed off in the early 1970s as the Japanese steel industry became a major world producer, with productivity estimated to be 15 per cent better than US levels. Following the second energy crisis of 1979, the industry has been in decline; MITI is discouraging further domestic investment, promoting rationalisation and even supporting overseas investment in steel production by Japanese companies. Despite this, Japanese steel-makers have recently increased their investment in high quality steels, as if to buy their way out of recession.

In the 1980s, MITI concentrated on mobilising financial resources and, with co-operation of the Ministry of Finance, provided a variety of tax incentives to stimulate investment and growth. Almost all of the new development was on greenfield sites and involved large-scale plants to benefit from economies of scale. About two-thirds of the investment funds came from loans, mainly through government financial institutions, but with some private support as well; as the government's rôle declined, the share of private funding steadily expanded.

MITI's Heavy Industries Bureau and the Japan Iron and Steel Federation have worked together to co-ordinate planned capacity expansion. Although the decisions embodied in the consensus plan were never formally binding on anyone, MITI disposed of some powerful policy instruments to help its views to prevail, such as control over imported raw materials (coal, iron ore) and foreign exchange import quotas. However, in the mid-1960s, Sumitomo went ahead with its expansion plans against MITI's wishes. Initially, MITI limited the company's import allowances, but demand soon expanded again, and the additional capacity was required to meet the demand. MITI and the Ministry of Finance have supported overseas raw materials developments, and have sometimes encouraged short-term cartels to form to manage production in a more orderly fashion during recessions. Overall, however, the actual flow of public funds into the industry has been modest since the 1950s, and the selective assistance that was provided has not blunted competition within the industry.

The same can also be said of the car industry, where domestic firms have been fiercely competitive. Shortly after the war the industry was in a very poor state, but in 1952 MITI formulated a policy package to protect the industry, stimulate imports of technology and foster growth. Import quotas on cars were applied in the 1950s and early 1960s, very high tariffs up to the mid-1970s, and most foreign investment in the industry was discouraged. The only exception was investment in production which was considered to help development of the domestic industry. In addition, royalties would only be paid on technology licensing deals if 90 per cent of the licensed parts were produced in Japan within five years.

This policy led to six applications by Japanese companies to assemble foreign cars under licence. MITI approved four and developments proceeded rapidly, with the Japanese firms soon improving on their imported technology, introducing new, superior models. Apart from some financial support and tax concessions to the motor car industry (e.g. reconstruction loans, accelerated depreciation), MITI has also sought rationalisation to facilitate higher volumes and lower costs. It had some success in the parts industry, but little impact on vehicle manufacture itself. In fact the rapid expansion of domestic demand encouraged new entrants to the market, though there was a little merger activity in the 1960s (largely unconnected with MITI initiatives) and some links with foreign firms in the 1970s when restrictions were lifted.

MITI's concern, however, was that Japanese producers should lower costs and produce a sufficiently high quality product to be competitive on world markets, in view of the increasing pressure on Japan to liberalise imports and hence, correspondingly, to achieve success in export markets. Although rationalisation of production never got very far, the government did better in the field of export promotion by subsidising market research, some tax assistance and export credits. Most of these special arrangements had ceased by the early 1970s as MITI withdrew from the now extremely vigorous and dynamic car industry. At present, the industry faces some degree of recession at home and significant restraints on its exports. As with the steel industry, its response appears to be one of improving product quality, particularly by incorporating an increasing range of electronic gadgetry into the latest models. So far, the car industry is one which was recognised early on by MITI as a potential winner (though initially opposed by the Ministry of Finance), but which nevertheless largely pursued its own course of development within the protective and very favourable environment engendered by the authorities. Very little direct intervention was needed (or would have been accepted) to generate a dramatic success – the large-scale production of low cost, high quality cars able to compete effectively in virtually any market.

Aluminium and shipbuilding present a rather different picture from the two previous cases. Despite their difficult situations, neither industry has invoked the Structurally Depressed Industry Law mentioned earlier to invoke MITI's help in developing stabilisation plans. In the case of aluminium, Japanese electricity costs and hence the costs of smelting aluminium are very high (four times North American levels) and the industry has accumulated enormous losses. Yet MITI and the industry seem unable to reach agreement on how to adjust. The former favours a permanent, market sensitive solution involving withdrawal of capacity, while the producers favour protection and subsidies; there is also disagreement about the level of imports that should be permitted. Meanwhile, little constructive is being done and since most producers belong to larger conglomerates with plentiful financial resources the existing stalemate could persist for some time.

Shipbuilding built up very quickly in the 1950s and 1960s so that by the late 1960s, Japan had become the world's lowest cost producer of ships. In the early 1970s, 50 per cent of the ships launched in the world were made in Japan and the industry earned substantial profits. Also by the same time, virtually all the earlier government support provided to the industry had ended. Yet after the 1973–4 tanker boom, Japanese shipbuilding started to decline; other lower wage countries also entered the market, exacerbating Japan's difficulties. But again, the industry cannot reach agreement with its supervising ministry (in this case the Ministry of Transport). Several of the smaller companies have gone bankrupt, but political pressure prevented a larger company from doing so, against MOT and Ministry of Finance wishes. However, the government approved the formation of a cartel to manage the contraction in demand and to retire some of the excess capacity; this lasted until March 1982. Since then, demand has continued to fall and future capacity requirements are still being revised downwards, within the framework of an informal cartel.

One aspect of adjustment in shipbuilding, steel and other industries in Japan, which would be different from the British situation, is the employment position, with many of the Japanese workers being guaranteed lifetime employment. In principle this means that workers cannot be made redundant when demand contracts, unless the whole enterprise goes bankrupt. An interesting consequence of such employment protection is that workers' representatives are frequently involved in discussions about industry and/or firm level adjustment policies; in addition, working practices tend to be highly flexible as workers are only guaranteed employment, not a specific job. Thus when demand for a particular product group declines, part of the problem faced by the affected firms is to find new areas to which workers can be redeployed. In some cases, workers are even 'loaned' to firms in other industries altogether. This protection only applies to workers and managers in the larger, well-established companies, which amounts to well under half the labour force; other workers do not enjoy such favourable conditions and hence bear the brunt of any sustained and general contraction of demand. However, the fact that the protected workers will still be used to produce something, and hence generate some demand for spare parts, components and other ancillary services, should mean that unprotected workers experience less drastic fluctuations in the demand for their services than they might otherwise expect to do.

After this short digression, let us now examine two industries which are still at relatively early stages of their growth cycle in Japan. Industrial machinery of various kinds has been in receipt of government support since the early 1950s, with a huge variety of tax relief, credit and loan schemes in operation from time to time, reflecting the real diversity of the industry's product range. In addition, MITI has supported rationalisation cartels in some parts of the industry. The home market was protected and measures were introduced to improve product quality and promote exports. By the early 1970s, much of the industry had become efficient enough to be competitive internationally, though it had not yet had a great impact on world markets. Nevertheless, much of the earlier government intervention was gradually withdrawn.

In recent years, the market structure has been changing in two important respects. The first is a strong trend towards the sale of complete plants, often including arranging installation, training workers, and installing appropriate control systems. This so-called systems business is supplanting sales of individual machines in many countries and is forcing producers to put much more effort into 'packaging' and marketing their products than previously. The second is the introduction of sophisticated new technologies to produce a generation of very high precision machinery. The technologies concerned include lasers, ultrasonics and integrated electronic circuits (microprocessors). MITI and other government agencies currently provide substantial funds to support the R & D effort needed to develop the new equipment. But after initial successes in numerically controlled machine tools and other machinery in the late 1970s and early 1980s, world market conditions have become tougher. The combination of world recession, a strengthening of protectionist sentiment in Europe and North America and more aggressive development strategies by producers based in these countries, makes the outlook for Japanese producers rather less rosy than it seemed only recently. It is too soon to be sure, but this may be an instance where Japan's attempt to achieve a dominant position could be thwarted by a vigorous response elsewhere.

Information technology is the other nascent industry to be discussed here. Its boundaries are actually rather hard to define since they are still changing rapidly, but as presently understood, the industry would include: the development of increasingly sophisticated electronic components, e.g. integrated circuits on chips; computers and other instruments using chip-based microprocessors; computer peripherals; equipment relying on computers and/or microprocessors, e.g. robots; telecommunications systems and peripherals. The government's principal contributions have been in supporting R & D, and in providing financial help to firms seeking to buy computers.

On the research side, the government (through MITI and Nippon Telephone & Telegraph Corporation) has combined with private producers to sponsor an ambitious research project, the VLSI (very large scale integration) project, to produce a 'super' chip. As a result of this collaboration half a dozen of the leading companies have produced prototype 256K chips and should soon be ready to market them commercially. Japan has also initiated recently a massive research programme to produce a so-called fifth generation 'intelligent' computer. In the short run, this will undoubtedly generate spin-offs allowing existing products to be improved, but the long term prospects are unclear since the basic design concept of the new computer is not yet firmly settled. As far as financial aid is concerned, Japan has facilitated the leasing of computers to many private users, through low interest loans and tax concessions. An advantage of this approach is that it encourages users to upgrade their models as soon as improved designs become available. At present, Japan appears to have an almost impregnable position in information technology hardware (i.e. physical equipment) but is much weaker in the production of software (computer programs to enable specific tasks to be carried out by a general-purpose computer). However, the deficiency has been recognised and more resources are being devoted to this area now. Finally, office automation and the introduction of electronic devices into telecommunications are both proceeding apace.

What can we learn about the Japanese approach to development from this highly compressed survey of organisational arrangements and case studies? According to Magaziner and Hout (1980, p.4), Japan's strategy rests on three main elements:

(i)   recognition of the country's need to develop a highly competitive manufacturing sector;

(ii)   the deliberate restructuring of industry over time towards higher value added, higher productivity industries. (The Japanese call them 'knowledge intensive');

(iii) aggressive domestic and international business strategies.

It appears to follow from (iii) that if Japanese companies are not sufficiently aggressive, or if they are met by strong challenges from US and European companies (among others), then they may not succeed; this has been the case in such branches as construction equipment, much of the chemicals industry, marine engines, etc. Conversely, when Japanese companies meet with a passive or weak response from overseas competitors they can quickly outclass the competition and dominate the chosen market. Moreover, it used to be assumed all too complacently that Japanese competition could only be effective at the lower quality, simpler end of any given product range. But element (iii) applied within rather than between industries soon dispelled that myth; the collapse of the British motor-cycle industry is a striking instance of the unfortunate consequences of misplaced complacency in the face of effective Japanese competition across an entire product range.

Taken as a whole, elements (i), (ii) and (iii) are not entirely consistent with each other and, while they clearly state one of the main requirements of Japan's development ((i)), and two of the means of achieving it ((ii) and (iii)) they cannot be regarded as an adequate explanation of Japanese success. Elements (i) and (iii) are essentially market oriented, while (ii) implies some form of government intervention without specifying how it should be conducted. Thus at the very least, (ii) concedes that the market mechanism calls for some central 'guidance' but provides no clue as to the proper limits and conditions of this guidance.

Johnson (1982) provides a fuller account of what may be termed the Japanese model in the course of his discussion of MITI and its rôle in promoting post-war Japanese development. He would certainly accept the need to achieve and improve competitiveness (element (i), above) and stresses the approach usually adopted: a combination of superior organisation, labour peace and cost-cutting. Three approaches to industrial policy are seen to be possible, namely bureaucratic control, civilian self-co-ordination, and administration through inducement (these are literal translations of the Japanese terms). Experience in the 1930s and during the war showed that neither bureaucratic control nor self-co-ordination (essentially, *laissez-faire*) alone could be relied on to achieve rapid development that was reasonably well-balanced and co-ordinated at the macroeconomic level. Hence after the war, MITI and other economic ministries gradually developed the techniques of administration through inducement.

The Japanese model is based on an incentive structure geared to developmental goals such as maintaining employment, raising productivity and reducing costs by means of investment, as opposed to short term profitability. The model then requires:

(1)   A small, élite bureaucracy to select the industries to be developed most rapidly (e.g. by choosing to produce and export goods with a high income elasticity, using the strong domestic market base to achieve economies of scale); to choose the best means of development; to supervise competition in these areas. Having selected the priority sectors in each period, non-strategic sectors of the economy are more or less ignored and left to their own devices;

(2)   A political system which leaves the bureaucracy relatively free to take long term initiatives and operate effectively;

(3)   The development of *market-conforming* methods of intervention as far as possible;

(4)   A 'pilot organisation' such as MITI, which may be regarded as a kind of economic general staff.

The difficulty, of course, with the last point is partly to determine the appropriate mix of powers; in the Japanese case the post-war MITI, by combining responsibility for both industry and trade, was considerably more effective than its pre-war precursor, which lacked power over international trade. Partly, also, the problem with (4) is to show that MITI or something like it was necessary for Japan's success. However, the alternative is a much more pluralistic structure in which different supervisory bodies would be involved in preparing development plans for different branches. But at some stage, overall co-ordination has to be brought about, both between total savings and planned investment, and between imports and exports, as well as in other macroeconomic balances; in addition, in cases of conflict, priorities need to be established and enforced. It is rather hard to see how this could be done effectively without an agency such as MITI with powers that span a high proportion of the country's economic activity.

3.4   Some Lessons for Britain

What can Britain learn from these very diverse experiences of planning? We have discussed a very centralised system and market oriented reforms that have taken place within it; a market-type economy which has operated a fairly loose form of planning, principally to guide the allocation of investment (France); and another market economy which has developed investment programmes for selected industries through reaching consensus between private firms and government agencies, while nevertheless functioning exceptionally competitively (Japan).

Let us begin by noting some implications of the individual country discussions. From the discussion of Eastern Europe it is clear that there is little to be said in favour of detailed production planning, with its output targets for individual branches and even enterprises. Decentralised economic systems seem to be perfectly capable of matching the supply and demand for most goods, though it is possible to construct arguments for the use of output targets in certain limited spheres (e.g. where increasing returns to scale are important). Secondly, despite persistent difficulties in the area of investment, the East European countries do furnish some examples of the beneficial effects of investment planning, particularly in fostering the rapid development of key industries. Thirdly, devising effective budget constraints (or resource constraints in general) for enterprises remains one of the most intractable problems of central planning. Lastly, an economy with full employment achieved through the East European type of planning may not be very attractive for consumers; hence it cannot simply be assumed that ordinary citizens would necessarily be in favour of planning.

While Eastern Europe does not, therefore, provide an overwhelming case for centralised planning, French planning is also not a convincing demonstration of the advantages of indicative planning (discussed in the next chapter). Despite the strong theoretical case that can be made for indicative planning, its benefits are not borne out by the experience of French planning. Nevertheless, the piecemeal industrial planning that occurred in France can be credited with some worthwhile achievements, such as developments in nuclear energy and telecommunications. On the other hand, it has also resulted in some miserable failures, as in the attempts to foster an indigenous computer industry. However, the French case does show that industrial investment planning can bear fruit provided it is followed over a long period of time. It also shows that a limited degree of non-tariff protection (e.g. preferential ordering by public sector bodies) can have beneficial effects in certain cases; the infant industry argument is not completely irrelevant for advanced industrial economies.

The Japanese example demonstrates that planning need not be an exclusively governmental activity, the effectiveness of strategic product planning depending crucially on firms' own attitudes towards internal and external planning, and the time horizon with which they normally operate. As argued in the last chapter, for a country like Britain the success of official industrial planning would be highly dependent on the quality of planning at the level of individual firms.

For all three examples it has been recognised that successful development requires proper co-ordination of the volume and composition of investment. While the unaided market mechanism may not always generate the right signals to guide these decisions, a purely centralised, administrative system is evidently not very satisfactory either. For although such a system is capable of mobilising resources to sustain a high investment rate, it does not appear to be conducive either to high levels of productivity or to the rapid absorption and diffusion of new technology. The constant problem is to devise the proper mix of market forces and government intervention.

Virtually all societies find that political pressure develops around threatened, declining industries, seeking to protect jobs and preserve traditional specialisms. The result is frequently a massive subsidy bill which does virtually nothing to transform or modernise the economy concerned, including the particular branches in receipt of subsidy. In this regard, the Japanese have been fortunate in possessing a highly competent bureaucracy capable of taking a long term view of prospective developments in new branches, and a relatively weak polity. Consequently, rather few branches have had the political clout to demand and get subsidies other than short term ones to facilitate desirable adjustment. Both France and Eastern Europe, including Hungary, have fared considerably worse in this respect, as indeed has Britain itself.

Other fields in which there are possible lessons for Britain include the conduct of macroeconomic policy, labour relations, short run and long run incentives, management of the external balance and government–industry relations. The main problem with the first of these, as well as with the external balance, is to arrange the regulation so that it conflicts as little as possible with other policies relating to investment (see Section 4.3). As far as labour relations are concerned, the importance of peaceful, co-operative relations between management and labour (and government agencies) and the involvement of worker representatives in major decisions about restructuring or developing particular branches can hardly be over-emphasised. Where relations are less good, institutional and other means have to be found to circumvent areas of conflict and avoid damaging stalemate (see Chapter 5).

On incentives, it is clearly essential to avoid undue concern with immediate profitability provided that long term policies for development are concordant with market influences and result in profitable outcomes in due course. It is hard to neglect profitability altogether without falling into the East European trap of inefficient production, with poor choices often made about the most appropriate areas in which to specialise.

Finally, there is the question of government–industry relations. Both France and Japan have something to offer here. The key to success seems to involve a mixture of wide-ranging consultation with industries in which public intervention might be called for, a serious effort to reach agreement on the most suitable forms of intervention, and then little or no day-to-day interference in the industry's activities and decision-making. As was pointed out in the section on France, Britain's record in this sphere has not been very satisfactory.

These points have been expressed here extremely briefly, because most of them will be taken up again and addressed more fully elsewhere. By themselves they are not sufficient to explain why one or other country has done well compared to Britain, but they do provide some pointers to the kinds of policy and planning structure that would have a good chance of working in Britain.

4
Theoretical Approaches

Having now discussed some of the salient issues that arise from Britain's past forays into the field of economic planning, as well as the experience of several other countries, we have reached a point where it would be useful to examine planning in more theoretical terms. This is done in this chapter and the next, in order to provide a firm basis for the more concrete proposals relating to a possible planning structure for the British economy which are presented in Chapters 6 and 7. While Chapter 5 deals with what is really the political dimension of planning (forms of workers' participation, and related issues), the present chapter confines itself to the economic aspects of planning. Naturally, it would be absurd to suggest that economic and political aspects could ever be fully separated in practice. Thus although a formal separation is convenient for expositional purposes, these two theoretical chapters should be read as a whole.

The present chapter begins by considering the theory of indicative planning which argues that, for a variety of reasons, a market economy cannot be relied upon to generate all the information required for firms to take efficient investment decisions. The second section looks at planning from something closer to a Keynesian perspective, and suggests that the volume of investment is likely to be too low in an economy like the British; moreover, for a mixture of political and economic reasons, its composition is unlikely to be conducive to rapid structural change and growth. From these two sections, therefore we can conclude that there is a rôle for some form of economic planning in improving information flows relevant to investment decisions, and in providing guidelines on the desirable pattern of investment.

The third section of the chapter examines the linkages between the planning system called for by Sections 4.1 and 4.2, and conventional macroeconomic policy. It is argued that, as far as possible, macroeconomic policy should be conducted in such a way as to minimise any adverse impact it might have on investment, though past experience in Britain does not suggest that this would be at all easy. Section 4.4 concludes the chapter by surveying various ways in which the economy's overall planning problems may usefully be decomposed. Some such decomposition is essential, of course, given the complexity of the overall problem, and the inevitable dispersion of relevant economic and technical information throughout the economy.

4.1 Indicative Planning

Most analysis of indicative planning sets out from the view that resource allocation through markets is generally desirable and conducive to economic efficiency. The analysis recognises, however, that the agents who trade in various markets, whether they are households, firms, or departments of government need to be adequately informed to be able to take sensible economic decisions, notably about investment. It is then suggested that market signals in themselves cannot or at least do not provide agents with sufficient information for this; hence the state can play a useful role by organising a system of indicative planning to improve the flow of economic information (cf. Johansen, 1978, Section 7.2). This approach implies, therefore, that the market economy basically functions well except for certain imperfections to do with information flows. If this view is correct, then it would be appropriate to confine government intervention to the informational sphere (on the theory of indicative planning, see Meade, 1970 and 1971; for an excellent, recent analysis, see Estrin and Holmes, 1983a, chs 1 and 2).

Such a line of argument evidently begs a lot of questions, both about the underlying theory of a market economy and about its connection with the realities of a specific market-type economy such as the British. To see this clearly, let us begin by sketching the relevant theory.

The theoretical basis for indicative planning is a competitive, general equilibrium model of the economy (for a thorough, technical treatment, see Arrow and Hahn, 1971, and Debreu, 1959). In this kind of model, the economy is viewed as a collection of interacting markets in which all agents are assumed to treat prices as given. Effectively, this means that individual agents, whether firms or households, regard the ruling prices as beyond their control. Consequently, demands and supplies in each market can be shown to depend only on these parametric prices, the relevant prices including those for products as well as factor input prices (such as wages). By the same token, whenever prices change, demands and/ or supplies in some or all markets will also change. What we mean by an equilibrium in this situation is a set of prices at which supply equals demand in every market.

It was a remarkable theoretical achievement to show that this competitive model is internally consistent, in the sense that with suitable assumptions we could be sure that it would always possess an equilibrium set of prices. For from a planning point of view, the model apparently implies that all the economy's information and incentive problems can be resolved once the right prices, namely the equilibrium prices, are somehow determined. To be more specific about this, the equilibrium prices have the following properties:

(1)   Firms treat the prices as given and organise their production activity in order to maximise profits. Similarly, given prices and incomes, households determine their demand for consumption goods and services (as well as their labour supplies) to maximise their resulting satisfaction (utility).

(2)   Apart from the equilibrium prices, firms and households need no other information about the rest of the economy. In other words, the price system *alone* is sufficient to co-ordinate economic activity: thus the decisions taken by self-seeking firms and households turn out to be *socially* coherent. Individual self-interest is quite compatible with market equilibrium.

(3)   At a competitive equilibrium, assuming that there are no externalities (explained later in the section), the allocation of resources is technically efficient; moreover, it achieves full employment (see Koopmans, first essay, 1957).

The first property is really just a restatement of the usual behavioural assumptions associated with general equilibrium theory, while the second and third properties are rather striking and attractive features of the resulting equilibrium. Unfortunately, although the model's elegance and simplicity are appealing, there are many reasons why the model has to be regarded as inadequate as a description of any real economy such as the British one. Nevertheless, much of the available analysis of indicative planning seeks to explain how the real economy can be 'patched up' in certain respects, to make it fit this 'ideal' model more closely.

Given the inadequacies of the model, it might be argued that it should be rejected altogether and replaced by something different. One possible alternative, which is actually just a neat way of expressing some of the basic ideas contained in the general equilibrium framework, is outlined in sub-section 4.1.1, below. Another alternative is process analysis, which is highly critical of the above approach to economic analysis based on an apparently static view of equilibrium. As the name suggests, process analysis regards the economy as a set of ever-changing processes, the spur to change being the recognition of previously unexploited economic opportunities (see, for instance, Kirzner, 1973). Thus the theory does recognise that agents possess differential information and it focuses a great deal of attention on the 'entrepreneur', the agent or agents who try to recognise new opportunities for profit. While this is clearly sensible, process analysis, at least as presently developed, provides no models sufficiently well worked out to provide a useful set of policy implications. At the same time, on the basis of admittedly interesting but often fairly loose analysis, it exhibits an astonishingly strong preference for resource allocation through market forces and offers little guidance about market failures and imperfections. Consequently, for all its defects, the general equilibrium approach remains a useful starting point for our analysis.

From the point of view of a theory of planning, the principal shortcomings of the general equilibrium model outlined above include its treatment of uncertainty and intertemporal transactions, the neglect of transactions costs and externalities, and the assumption that everyone in the economy behaves competitively. In principle, the model has to take the view that equilibrium is determined in all markets simultaneously, 'all' here including both the markets for currently available goods and services, and futures markets for goods and services available at any date in the future. This is because some of the decisions taken in the current period, notably investment decisions, depend on the prices fetched by the resulting additional output in future years. Thus even though, at equilibrium, price information is sufficient for all agents, this must therefore include information about the prices that will prevail at all dates relevant to current and indeed future investment decisions. In practice, of course, these futures markets do not actually exist except for a limited range of commodities (e.g. wheat) and financial securities, and even then only for very limited forward periods, which implies that even a well-functioning market economy is likely to fail to provide agents with adequate information for their investment decision-making. Hence this line of argument suggests one possible rôle for an indicative plan, namely to fill this informational gap.

The future path of development of an economy is always associated with considerable uncertainty about the likely pattern of demand, the rate of technological development in various branches including the rate of appearance of new products, the demand and supply functions that may be faced in export and import markets, and so on. If we were only concerned to forecast the future, then such pervasive uncertainty might not greatly matter, since it would merely result in forecasting errors. But this uncertainty is more important than that because the alternative development paths that the economy might follow have a bearing on the economics of current investment decisions, which in turn has an important bearing on the current state of the economy. To some extent, and this is the approach suggested by the orthodox theory, the uncertainty might be mitigated by means of various forms of insurance, though the scope for this is bound to be rather limited (see Arrow, 1970). A second possible rôle for an indicative plan, therefore, is to provide information on the alternative feasible development paths for the economy, and the circumstances under which any particular path would actually be followed.

The standard general equilibrium model neglects the costs of establishing and operating markets and assumes that market transactions are costless (for a useful survey of the theory of transactions costs, see Ulph and Ulph, 1975). In fact, however, substantial resources are devoted to the business of making a market economy function properly; these resources are employed in several different ways, including:

advertising (including the preparation and distribution of price lists);
bidding and tendering for contracts;
marketing and selling effort;
legal and institutional arrangements for enforcing contracts, and

for setting up and terminating businesses;
setting up trade associations;
establishing and maintaining quality standards.

Some of these points are concerned with the general environment
within which market transactions are conducted, while others have
more to do with specific items of business. The implication of all
this is that even in the theoretical world where price information is
sufficient, it is costly to prepare and transmit this information in
such a way as to make it available to all potential customers.
Moreover, transactions are not usually anonymous as assumed by
the theory, for the identity of the parties involved does frequently
matter, and agents are not trading with an abstract market, but
with specific partners; this is recognised by law, in which contracts
are always between a specified pair (or group) of agents.

This point can be accommodated in the theory by making a
distinction between traded and non-traded goods. In this case, the
non-traded goods would be specific bundles of information and
managerial skills characterising individual firms. Then the theory of
general equilibrium outlined above applies to the traded goods,
including the conclusions about the efficiency of resource allocation
in respect to these goods. However, not much can be said about
overall efficiency, since there is no way of judging (within the
theoretical model) whether the non-traded resources (managerial
inputs) are efficiently allocated. But the approach does have the
merit of according firms a rôle in the theory, and it does explain
why most contracts are not between 'anonymous' traders. In
contrast, in the version of the general equilibrium model in which all
goods are traded, nothing at all can be said about the organisational
structure of the economy, though efficiency results are stronger.

If there are increasing returns to scale in the production and
transmission of certain types of economic information relating to
current transactions then a system of indicative planning might be
able to reduce the costs involved in this by centralising the procedures
for dealing with these information flows. In particular, it might be
able to help firms identify possible trading partners by establishing
a form of information network.

Turning to externalities, these can arise either in production or
consumption. When production by some firm or consumption by
one or more households affects the production possibilities of at

least one other firm, then we have a production externality. When such an externality is unfavourable, as is the situation with pollution when it raises the production costs of a non-polluting firm, it is often called an external diseconomy; conversely, a favourable externality is an external economy. Similarly, when consumption by certain people either makes others worse off (for instance noise, pollution by private car exhausts), or raises firms' costs (for example excessive alcohol consumption leading to irregular work habits), then we have a consumption externality. These, too, can be either external economies or external diseconomies. The fundamental problem with externalities is that they cause a divergence between the private and social costs and benefits of various activities. Hence private agents responding to the price system by seeking to maximise their own private gain will not at the same time act in accord with the social interest. As a result, competitive, general equilibrium will no longer allocate resources efficiently from a social point of view. It is essentially in order to combat this problem that post-war British governments have operated various forms of location and pollution controls. In addition, regional policy can to some degree be justified in terms of externality arguments.

Finally, we must consider the assumption that all agents behave competitively. In discussing this, it is important to examine price determination, various forms of imperfect competition, and the rôle of non-price signals in the economy. The competitive assumption itself, by postulating that all agents are price takers, leaves completely unexplained the questions of how prices are set and who is supposed to set them (see Arrow, 1959).

Needless to say, most prices are actually fixed by the firms producing the various products, with reference to their costs, as well as to their observed market position. Away from equilibrium it is hard to understand how else firms should behave, and equally, it is not plausible to suppose that their behaviour suddenly changes radically at equilibrium. Apart from any other considerations, equilibrium is a property of resource allocation at the level of the economy as a whole, and many individual firms will simply have no way of knowing whether or not the economy is at equilibrium. In particular, for individual firms it will often not be at all clear whether a given price is an equilibrium price or not. Naturally, the importance of information about this will depend on the economic decisions likely to be affected. In the short run, firms will quickly adapt what they produce to what they can actually sell. In the longer term, however, where some investment may be involved, firms need to make judgements about future prices, and current prices are often the only information available to guide them.

To allow time for other agents to respond and adapt to a given set of prices, firms are likely to adjust their prices periodically rather than continuously, and once prices have been determined they will endeavour to meet whatever demand is forthcoming. Interestingly, this is almost the exact converse of the competitive assumption, since what we are saying is that firms actually set prices and meet the market demand, instead of taking prices from the market and choosing a profit-maximising output level at those prices. It is only at equilibrium that these two stories are equivalent.

Many markets are only served by one or a few firms – the cases of monopoly and oligopoly respectively – and in these situations the competitive assumption is unreasonable even at equilibrium. For the firms serving a particular market are bound to perceive that they possess some market power and that the extent of this power is constrained by competitors' reactions. Thus firms are aware of their mutual interdependence, ensuring that the price signals emphasised in the competitive model are insufficient for their economic decision-making: in addition, firms need information on demand and some estimate of their competitors' behaviour. A similar situation arises when production costs hardly vary as the level of output in some industry changes. For then there is no optimum size of firm, so that the structure of the industry is indeterminate, and whatever firms are established are likely to find themselves behaving like the oligopolists just discussed.

In other circumstances, too, non-price information is important for firms. Consider, for instance, an increase in demand for some product. According to the conventional market model, this would be reflected in a higher price, to which firms would respond by raising output. In practice, however, it is more likely that prices would initially be unchanged, but firms would either experience a fall in their stocks of output or a lengthening of their order books. These non-price signals are the more usual ones inducing firms to raise output to meet the new demand (for an extended analysis of the economics of non-price information, see Kornai, 1980b).

Another, and perhaps more significant example concerns invest-ment. It has already been noted that firms need information about future prices, in order to evaluate investment opportunities. For any opportunity to be realised, however, it must first be perceived and then acted upon by one or more firms (the resulting informational problems have been emphasised in Loasby, 1976 and 1981). A possible difficulty here is that the improvements in economic information brought about by indicative planning may make some opportunities known to too many firms. One advantage of imperfect information is that often only one or very few firms will be in a position to recognise and respond to a given investment prospect. If many firms know about it – perhaps because its viability depends on certain government prepared and hence public price forecasts – and each knows that others possess the same information, then it is not easy for them to decide on a proper response. If none respond, then the opportunity remains unexploited; if all respond positively, then most probably none will succeed in making a profit. This argument suggests that there should be some 'optimal' degree of imperfection of information, a point which it would be unwise for an indicative planning system to ignore. The problem arises, however, when certain types of information enter the public domain, so a possible solution might be, rather paradoxically, to restrict access to it, for instance to those firms willing to pay an appropriate fee. Alternatively, it might be appropriate for some public agency to limit the number of entrants, especially as economic efficiency may be better served by encouraging certain firms to enter in preference to others, rather than by relying on fairly arbitrary informational imperfections to determine the pattern of entry.

In this section, some of the arguments for indicative planning have been outlined. It has been suggested that the following types of economic information could be provided in such a system:

(1)   Estimates of future prices (needed for investment decisions)
(2)   Guidance about the alternative development paths that the economy might follow (to help accommodate uncertainty)
(3)   Demand and supply information: an information network to help firms identify possible trading partners (to reduce transactions costs)

One would expect the first two of these to be interrelated, in that future prices will depend on the development path to be followed. But the third could stand alone, and represents a much more micro-level approach to planning. It does not seek to impose or suggest any particular allocation, but merely takes the view that a market-type economy will function more efficiently if information, particularly non-price information flows are improved. However, to avoid or mitigate the problem mentioned in the preceding paragraph, it may be important for the envisaged information network not to offer a wholly free service. More details about this proposal are provided in Section 7.2.

A final question to raise here concerns the role of the private sector in the informational sphere. If, as argued above, there are substantial economic gains to be made from the provision of information not generated automatically by the unaided market, then surely it should be profitable for someone to engage in the business of information production. This is quite correct, of course, and quite a diversified private industry exists, including such activities as: model-building, with solutions available to subscribing firms; market research and a whole range of business consultancy; the production of trade journals, and so on. Given our interest here in state-supported indicative planning, it is therefore essential to identify those areas where information production and provision is judged to be socially, but not privately, profitable. In my view, this could include much of the third and some aspects of the first and second types of information mentioned above, notably those aspects related to the public sector, and overseas transactions where the government may have access to more and/or better information than the private sector, and possibly establishing the information network if the available technology so dictates. Again, some detailed proposals will be discussed more concretely later on, in Chapters 6 and 7. In addition, it is not at all uncommon for firms to enter into information agreements, whereby they may agree to exchange information about prices, proposed investment and other matters of common interest where some co-ordination may be advantageous.

4.1.1 An alternative approach

Some readers may find it helpful to see some of the points discussed in the above section analysed more formally; this is the aim of the present sub-section. However, rather than setting out the technical details of general equilibrium theory, I adopt an alternative approach. This involves a specification of the factors affecting the returns to a given investment project, in combination with the net present value investment criterion. In the interests of clarity and brevity, the discussion will be conducted with the aid of algebraic notation; throughout, prices will be denoted by row vectors, corresponding quantities by column vectors.

Let us consider a typical investment project, with investment outlays taking place over m periods (years, say) and producing a marketable product or service over the ensuing n years. During the construction phase (years 1–m), let Z_t be the vector of investment inputs required in year t, measured in physical units; so $Z_t = (Z_{1t}, Z_{2t}, \ldots, Z_{Kt})$, where Z_{it} is the quantity of the ith good required in period t (e.g. tons of cement, number of workers of a given type, etc.) and K is the total number of goods. The corresponding price vector is p_t, so that *investment outlays* in year t are given by:

$$I_t = p_t \cdot Z_t \qquad (t = 1, 2, \ldots, m) \tag{4.1}$$

Once the project comes into operation, it gives rise to a vector of outputs $y_t = (y_{1t}, \ldots, y_{Lt})$, where L is the number of distinct products ($t = m+1, \ldots, m+n$). The corresponding price vector is q_t, so *revenue* in year t is:

$$R_t = q_t \cdot y_t \qquad (t = m+1, \ldots, m+n) \tag{4.2}$$

Disposing of these products entails marketing costs, as well as the production costs themselves. These costs require the vector of resources $X_t = (X_{1t}, \ldots, X_{Mt})$, where M is the number of distinct inputs into the production or marketing process. With π_t as the corresponding price vector, *costs* in year t are:

$$C_t = \pi_t \cdot X_t \qquad (t = m+1, \ldots, m+n) \tag{4.3}$$

In considering investment from a social point of view, this is really all that we need to know (except for the discount rate – see below). However, from a firm's point of view, the net effects of a project on its financial and tax positions are also of importance, since these can influence both the timing and the total effective cost or benefit resulting from the project. Consequently the firm can be expected to evaluate new projects net of these tax and financing effects. Let

T_t = net tax effect in year t $\qquad (t = 1, 2, \ldots, m+n)$

F_t = net financing effect in year t $(t = 1, 2, \ldots, m+n)$

In both cases, a positive number represents a net contribution to the project in the relevant year (a subsidy, or a loan) while a negative number represents a net withdrawal from it (a tax, or repayment of a loan).

Taking all these factors together, the present value of the proposed investment project,

$$\text{NPV} = \sum_{t=1}^{m} \frac{I_t}{(1+r)^t} + \sum_{m+1}^{m+n} \frac{R_t - C_t}{(1+r)^t} + \sum_{t=1}^{m+n} \frac{T_t + F_t}{(1+r)^t} \tag{4.4}$$

where r is the appropriate discount rate. The first term in (4.4) represents the investment outlays, the second operating surpluses or losses, and the last term incorporates the tax and financing effects just mentioned.

Now, equations (4.1) to (4.4) indicate quite clearly the kinds of information about which firms need to take a view in order to evaluate a proposed new investment, such as building a new factory or developing an additional market. Apart from information about the technology, in the form of relationships between the vectors, Z_t, y_t and X_t (essentially, production functions) firms must estimate the likely size of their market (y_t) to determine a suitable scale for the project and forecast all the prices contained in equations (4.1), (4.2) and (4.3). Finally, they need to know about or forecast the tax and financing implications.

Since much of the price information is not available from observations of currently operating markets, firms must either estimate it themselves, make use of some private sector consultancy or forecasting agency, or rely on guidance from an indicative plan. An indicative plan should also be able to provide information on the most likely directions of government policy, to the extent that this would affect the tax effects, T_t, and via its impact on financial markets, the financing effects, F_t. Government policy will also influence the general economic environment and hence the firm's estimates of its market size and share, and detailed aspects of public policy such as decisions about particular items of expenditure obviously determine directly the demand for the goods and services concerned. The appropriate discount rate r (assumed the same for all periods, for simplicity) depends on the returns available on alternative dispositions of available funds, such as from financial securities; again government policy influences what these returns are likely to be.

The above formulation should not be taken to imply that firms will only invest if they are certain about all the numbers needed to evaluate the present value, (4.4). In practice, there will always remain substantial areas of uncertainty about the technology, prices, available markets, government policy, and so on. Even the time periods m (for construction) and n (for operations) must be regarded as highly uncertain except for the simplest and most routine of projects. The extent of uncertainty means that in evaluating investments it is often helpful to carry out sensitivity analysis in order to identify those few, key factors to which its success is most sensitive; these factors can then be investigated more closely. At a more fundamental level, the uncertainty is frequently so severe that investment decision-making is little more sophisticated than 'backing a hunch'. While a system of indicative planning would seek to mitigate certain areas of uncertainty, it cannot realistically hope to eliminate it.

4.2 The Allocation of Investment

Many reasons have been advanced to explain Britain's low growth, most of which have little immediate bearing on the proper conduct of economic planning in Britain, though they might well constrain its likely efficiency. Such reasons include:

(1) The rigid class structure of British society which often inhibits co-operation between workers and managers/owners;

(2) General attitudes in Britain inimical to industry;

(3) The failure of the education system to move very far in the vocational/technological directions;

(4) An adversarial political system not conductive to operating economic policy with anything other than a rather short time perspective.

(5) A lack of entrepreneurs, entrepreneurship;

(6) A highly unbalanced research effort, with too much pure reseach to the neglect of applied work, and an excessive emphasis on military R & D.

(7) The dominant place of the 'City' and finance capital, to the detriment of industrial capital;

(8) Distortions in the tax system which tend to encourage financial and property investment, discourage investment in industry;

(9) A banking system geared to short-term lending; relatively little long-term lending and a lack of direct involvement by the banks in business affairs;

(10) Organisational factors which limit the effectiveness with which existing resources are used in production, and inhibit the recognition of investment opportunities.

The first four of these factors and to some extent the seventh may be classified as social or political. Whatever government is in power it would be unreasonable to expect rapid change, though one would naturally expect a Labour government to take some positive steps at least in relation to the first three factors. Nevertheless, especially in its initial stages, any system of economic planning that we might envisage for Britain would have to function in the presence of these factors; they could not merely be assumed or wished away *a priori*, but operating the planning system might help to overcome them. In any case, it would be wrong to use such factors as an excuse for inaction.

The remaining six factors are more immediately economic in character. The balance of research could certainly be improved dramatically by a sufficiently determined government, since much of the research in question is government funded. Within a five to ten-year period, the share of British GDP devoted to civilian, applied, industrial R & D could be raised towards the levels of our major competitors. Similarly, the distortions in the tax system which were so devastatingly attacked by the impressive, but now quietly ignored Meade Report (Meade, 1978), could be remedied quite speedily if a government so chose. To the extent that inadequate entrepreneurship may partly be a consequence of weak or misdirected incentives, these improvements in the efficiency of the tax system can only improve matters there too. Again, however, any change in economic behaviour is unlikely to be especially rapid.

Finally, there remain factors (7), (9) and (10), concerned with the role of the 'City' and finance capital, short-term lending by the banking system, and organisational weaknesses. These factors jointly determine the allocation of investible financial resources in each period. This includes both the allocation of these resources between financial and real assets, which involves concrete institutional issues best left to the appropriate section of Chapter 6, and the determination of the branch and project structure of real investment, to be reviewed in this section.

The emphasis on investment here is quite widely supported in the recent literature on growth in general, and Britain's slow growth in particular. Thus Scott (1981) argues that growth in any economy depends above all on the volume and quality of investment. He is especially critical of studies such as Denison's (1967, 1979) well-known work, which seek to separate the effect of investment on economic growth, from that of technological progress. In Scott's view, these factors cannot legitimately be separated since technological change is virtually impossible in the absence of investment.

Pollard (1982) substantially agrees with Scott that investment is decisive for growth, arguing that other factors, whether social, institutional, political or whatever are at most contributory, but cannot be regarded as crucial for growth. While accepting that trade union-supported restrictive practices and aggressive wage demands are not helpful, he takes the view that this behaviour is largely a consequence of decades of slow growth and underinvestment. Hence much of the criticism for Britain's present predicament must be directed at the Treasury and the kinds of macroeconomic policy it has pursued, rather than at the unions or other organised groups. As Pollard (1982, p.118) puts it:

It is not the least indictment of Treasury policy that it has converted the potentially positive force of British trade unionism into an agency that inhibits growth, embitters social relations and brings long-established working class ideals into disrepute.

This viewpoint contrasts interestingly with that of Brittan (1978) who apparently believes (p.268) that:

The [British] disease is that of collective action by special interest groups preventing a reasonably full use being made of our economic resources.

The disease is regarded as a stage of political and economic development through which all countries may expect to pass, and in the British case it does not have much to do with Treasury policy. Given the general tenor of Brittan's argument, this is rather a surprising claim; for he is extremely critical of government intervention in other areas such as industrial policy and incomes policy. The relevant interest groups in his analysis include trade unions as well as various producer groups seeking special privileges from the state. In my view, however, this type of explanation for Britain's economic weaknesses lacks conviction because it does not really differentiate Britain from other countries which might be expected to face similar problems.

Macroeconomic variables such as the rate of investment are also played down by Williams *et al.* (1983), largely because they reject attempts to explain overall economic performance in aggregate terms. Instead, their explanation operates in terms of what they refer to as four national conditions. These concern enterprise control over the labour process, market structure and the composition of demand, the linkages between manufacturing firms and financial institutions, and the relationship between these firms and government departments and agencies. The four factors operate differently in different sectors and for this reason, much of the book is devoted to case studies. Nevertheless, although it is not hard to accept the importance of these factors, their principal impact on enterprise behaviour appears to be in the area of investment behaviour, especially conditioning the type of investments which particular firms will find profitable. It is investment which determines the quality, volume and range of production in the future and hence sets the conditions for firms' future viability. Thus the preference expressed by Williams *et al.* (1983), for a more disaggregated approach to the study of Britain's manufacturing performance, does not fundamentally conflict with my own emphasis here on the investment process.

Other studies which broadly support the same point of view include those by Carrington and Edwards (1979) and Stafford (1981). The former emphasises the practices of financial institutions in Britain as exercising the principal constraint on productive investment. The problem is said to be the lack of assured long-term funding, since British banks' traditional concentration on short and medium term loans, usually with quite stringent security requirements, effectively demands extremely high rates of return from projects relying on bank finance. It is true that loans are normally rolled over and hence converted into long term finance, but a firm has no absolute guarantee that its loan will not be called as soon as it is due and so must seek to protect itself against the resulting liquidity problems. Now it is quite clear from the standard theory of investment that an insistence on high rates of return, and rapid returns too, is very likely to depress the volume of investment below what would be desirable if longer term and cheaper funds were available. To this extent Carrington and Edwards are making an important point. However, the Wilson report on the functioning of Britain's financial institutions (Wilson, 1980) was far from convinced that the supply of funds to industry could be regarded as a severe constraint on investment, particularly as a very high proportion of investment in Britain is financed by depreciation provisions and retained profits. But in times of inflation, depreciation based on historic cost accounting principles (which have certainly been the British practice) severely underestimates the cost of replacing worn out assets and in any case the high effective cost of borrowing (interest plus repayment of principal) could still be deterring considerable amounts of investment at the margin. Hence the Wilson report may have been rather too complacent about this issue.

The second study, Stafford (1981) draws attention to the effect of demand on investment. It attributes Britain's slow growth to the relatively sluggish expansion of exogenous demand, notably exports. Hence in Stafford's view, faster growth is contingent on policy changes to stimulate exogenous demand, including measures to protect the balance of payments and some agency like the National Enterprise Board to facilitate a major restructuring of manufacturing industry. While agreeing that investment will only be undertaken when the investments concerned foresee adequate effective demand for the resulting output, it is far from clear that the direction of causality is quite as Stafford implies. For world trade has expanded since the Second World War at a much faster rate than Britain's own trade. Hence what needs to be explained is not so much the growth of world demand for exports (which has been remarkably rapid), but the poor response of the British economy to the available demand. Thus the demand is there, but our apparently inefficient and sluggish private sector has not taken advantage of what, for most of the post-war period, have been very favourable external conditions. Given this, Stafford is probably correct to argue that some additional public sector involvement in the investment process could be beneficial. For even allowing for the inevitable inefficiences and errors associated with public intervention in industry, the outcome may nevertheless be superior to what results from the existing pattern of private sector decisions. However, I am less convinced than Stafford about the merits of trade controls to protect British industry; this issue is pursued further in Chapter 7.

Considered in macroeconomic terms, investment has two essential functions. The first, and perhaps the most familiar in view of the post-war ascendancy of Keynesian economics, is that investment is one of the principal components of aggregate demand. Hence conventional fiscal and monetary policy can be directed towards investment and then, via the multiplier, affect the equilibrium level of national income generated in the current period. This type of interaction between short-run macroeconomic policy and the investment process is explored more fully in the next section. The second effect, surprisingly neglected until the advent of growth models, is the effect of investment in creating new capacity, thereby raising the economy's potential output in the future. The precise effect of such investment depends both on its overall *volume*, on its *composition* between branches, and on its *productivity*.

Taking the volume first, real investment in Britain could be too low because of inadequate savings, or because an excessive proportion of the economy's savings are pre-empted by other demands such as funding the government's deficit (though this may be financing public sector investment, of course), or purchasing property or overseas assets.

It has often been argued that in a predominantly market-type economy, the aggregate volume of savings that results from individual savings decisions is likely to be sub-optimal. Marglin (1963), for instance, suggested that people would be willing to save beyond the private optimum provided they had some assurance that everyone else would also be making a corresponding further contribution to savings. On this view savings, at least that part devoted to public projects of various kinds, is seen as possessing the standard properties of a public good, with its attendant free-rider problems (for a full discussion of public goods, see Brown and Jackson, 1978). Hence some form of taxation would be required to enforce a fair division of the burden of extra savings, but such taxation would command popular support.

The evidence that the private sector does behave in this way is actually rather weak. Empirical work generally finds that personal savings are substantially determined by the level and structure of after-tax incomes (including the provision of state welfare benefits), and by wealth effects dependent on the rate of inflation (see

Cuthbertson, 1982), while the allocation of savings funds undoubtedly responds to the tax treatment of different forms of asset (pension fund contributions, building society deposits, etc.). If the public good aspect of savings was significant, it would imply that people were also willing to submit to higher taxes to finance public investment. However, studies of wage determination have found that higher income taxes tend to be compensated by higher nominal wage demands, indicating that workers seek to maintain or improve their net, after-tax income. Given such 'real wage resistance', therefore, at least with our present institutional arrangements workers are not willing to save more through the medium of higher tax rates (see Fallick and Elliot, 1981).

In the British context, a more cogent reason for believing that savings may be too low concerns the distribution of income between profits and wages. Normally, the share of gross profits which is saved by companies, in the form of retained profits plus depreciation allowances, is far higher than the savings rate out of the income distributed to individuals (wages and salaries, plus unearned income). Hence for any given level of total income (GDP, say), the volume of savings will be higher if the share of profits in total income is higher. Since the share of profits in British GDP has fallen sharply in the last two decades, one would have expected from the above argument that private sector savings should have fallen. In fact, the fall has been somewhat less than expected, because the inflation of the 1970s seems to have stimulated personal savings, as people sought to restore the eroding value of their assets. However, savings could well fall further as inflation comes under control (assuming people are confident that there has been a long term improvement), unless the share of profits is permitted to recover to former levels.

Thus any government seeking to raise Britain's rate of investment must find a way to increase the share of profits in GDP. In the medium term, as Desai (1983) and others have emphasised, this means that personal consumption levels, and hence the real wages of those in work, cannot be permitted to rise substantially. This need not, and indeed should not preclude further measures to improve income distribution, or some improvements in public consumption. But it does point to a very clear conflict of interest between workers' understandable desire for higher real incomes 'now' as against the need for more investment to raise productivity and generate new jobs 'in the future'. At the same time, it must be stressed that higher profitability is a necessary but not a sufficient condition for achieving the higher investment required in Britain.

Various aspects of the conflict between present and future consumption are investigated more fully in Chapters 5 and 7, but it is worth asking immediately whether the conflict could be evaded altogether merely by accepting current rates of investment and allowing wages and other incomes to rise in line with growth in GDP as a whole. In other words, could Britain achieve and sustain a return to full employment with renewed economic growth without an increase in the rate of investment, especially that part of investment financed out of profits?

To answer such a question, the analysis needs to be set out a little more formally than before. It is useful to begin by recalling the well known national accounting identity between total withdrawals from the circular flow of income and expenditure, and total injections into the flow. Withdrawals comprise private sector savings, S, out of profits and distributed income, taxes net of social security payments, T, and imported goods and services, M. The last item appears because the national accounts always have domestic economic activity as their point of reference, whereas M clearly represents demand for output from countries other than the UK: hence it counts as a withdrawal. Injections comprise the sum of public and private investment, I, the government's current demand for goods and services, G, and exported goods and services, X. In terms of this notation, the identity asserts that:

$$S + T + M = I + G + X$$

or, rearranging to put this in a more convenient form:

$$I = S - (G - T) - (X - M) \tag{4.5}$$

Now we have already argued that there might be some resistance to increases in S that came about as a result of a shift in distributional shares from wages to profits. However, (4.5) also implies that real investment could be increased by a fall in $(G - T)$, such as would result from cuts in G or further increases in T; or a fall in $(X - M)$, the balance of trade surplus. While the former of these might well prove unacceptable to a government of socialist inclination, the latter should be eminently acceptable, since there is no point in accumulating overseas assets indefinitely when some increase in imports would allow domestic investment, and hence domestic job creation to proceed at a faster pace immediately. So equation (4.5) does point to one practical means of loosening the savings constraint on domestic investment: it would be important to prevent the extra resources from flowing into consumption.

At present, Britain is at best only investing enough to permit sustained GNP growth of around 2 per cent per year. Since, as a result of extensive structural change in various branches of the economy, the trend rate of productivity improvement is probably closer to the range 3–4 per cent per year, it is immediately clear that total employment in the economy will fall by 1–2 per cent per year. Hence unemployment can be expected to rise, albeit much more slowly than in the past few years. In order to return to full employment within a reasonable period, say 4–5 years, we would have to grow at a rate of 4–6 per cent per year to generate the required jobs, settling down to growth in the 2–4 per cent range once we were back at full employment.

Part of the additional growth could be achieved by increasing the capacity utilisation of already available fixed assets, but much additional investment would be needed as well. That, fundamentally, is why the question raised earlier must be answered negatively: it is extremely doubtful whether we can sustain a return to full employment without much higher rates of investment. The dilemma we have to face can perhaps be seen more graphically in terms of the following relationship. To explain this we need some additional notation. So let E = employment and R = replacement investment.

Then the new jobs resulting from gross investment, I, are given by:

$$\Delta E = b(I - R) - (a - b)R \qquad (4.6)$$

where a is the average number of workers needed to operate one unit of old capital, and b is the average number needed to operate a unit of the new. Although very crude and oversimplified, the second term of (4.6) makes clear that replacement investment will normally reduce employment in the economy, since we expect a to exceed b, that is a unit of old capital will typically have higher manning levels than what replaces it. It is the first term of (4.6), net investment, which actually generates new jobs: this is what must be increased sharply in the coming years, as argued above.

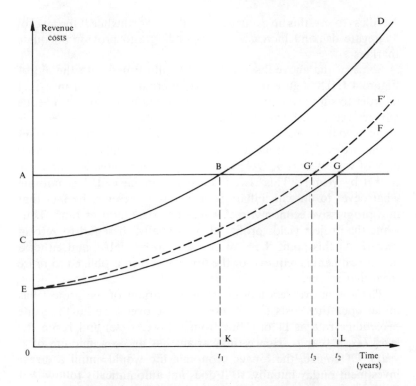

Figure 4.1 *Economic life of alternative investments*

Equation (4.6) has another interesting implication worth mentioning here, which concerns the coefficient, b. If this is high, so that new investment is typically quite labour-intensive, then a given volume of investment creates far more jobs than when it is low. However, this should not be taken as an argument for seeking to choose a pattern of investment with high b. Labour-intensive investment, which tends only to be viable at relatively low wage rates, should not be regarded as any kind of solution to Britain's problems assuming that we expect real incomes to resume an upward trend in the not too distant future. Another aspect of the same point is that if technology is changing quite rapidly, so that b is low and $(a - b)$ is large, then the substantial job losses from replacement investment (the term $(a - b)R$ in (4.6)) will call for very high rates of gross investment in order to prevent overall employment from falling.

Needless to say, this investment will only be worthwhile if the level of aggregate demand increases correspondingly to provide adequate markets.

Some of the above discussion can be illustrated with the aid of Figure 4.1. The figure represents two alternative ways of investing in order to supply a market which is expected to generate a revenue OA per year; the horizontal line AG indicates that this revenue is unchanged from year to year. With the more labour intensive variant of the project, operating costs (assumed, for simplicity, to consist only of wages) start at OC in the first year of production, and rise to KB by year t_1. This rise, it must be emphasised, has nothing whatsoever to do with inflation; it merely represents the fact that in a progressive economy, real wages rise steadily over time. Thus while the project yields profits of AC initially, these fall to zero in year t_1. At this point the project ceases to be viable, and either a new investment is required or the firm concerned is obliged to retire from that market.

The alternative, less labour intensive variant of the project has initial operating costs OE. These also rise over time (at the same percentage rate as before, but from a lower base) and reach the level LG in year t_2. Hence this variant has an economic life of t_2 years. Of course, the longer economic life would entail a larger investment outlay initially, so it does not automatically follow that the most capital intensive variant is to be preferred; equally, however, there is no justification for a general preference for labour intensive variants.

This analysis has assumed that the path of real wage rates would be the same irrespective of the kinds of investment choice being made. But in practice that is surely unlikely. It is more probable that selection of more capital intensive variants would be compatible with a somewhat faster rate of increase of wages, such as that shown in Figure 4.1 by the dotted line $EG'\,F'$. Economic life of the illustrated project falls to t_3 years, which is obviously still well above t_1.

Interpreting the figure in macro- rather than microeconomic terms, we can infer that correct investment choices depend on the level of aggregate demand and the expected growth of real wages, the former influencing principally the volume, and the latter the most appropriate capital intensity of new investment (when considered in conjunction with other factors such as required rates of return and the rate of technological development, and so on).

From the argument up to this point, we can conclude that Britain needs higher real investment, though just how far it should rise must rest on more detailed analysis and calculation beyond the scope of this book. It is also essential to take proper account of the productivity of this investment, as measured for instance by the extra capital investment needed to make it possible to produce an additional unit of output. This number, generally referred to by economists as the incremental capital–output ratio or ICOR, is on average a good deal higher in Britain (suggesting lower investment productivity) than in many of the other advanced economies. Hence there must be some scope for improvement in this sphere. However, to a substantial degree, the ICOR depends on the technology employed in particular sectors. Thus Britain's apparently unfavourable ICOR may partly reflect our product mix. Nevertheless, to the extent that our ICOR does fall, less investment is called for to generate a given amount of output growth. On the other hand, such investment is likely to involve higher capital-labour ratios than are usual in Britain (in terms of equation (4.6), this implies that b will be small). Consequently, to achieve any desired reduction in unemployment, more investment will be required the more productive the investment process becomes in terms of generating additional output. This line of argument merely reinforces what we have already said about needing to raise investment.

Let us now consider what can be said about the composition of this investment, and the role of government intervention through planning, in its determination and control. The most important point to make here is that the investment going on now and in the near future is intended to satisfy future demand; and the same should be true of any additional investment stimulated by an economic planning system. It is a complete waste of resources to invest in order to preserve jobs, or for any other allegedly 'social' reason, if demand for the resulting output is not forthcoming. So how can future demand be assessed, and who is in the best position to make the required assessment?

Obviously, in a predominantly private enterprise economy firms themselves are often in the best position to do this, since they know their suppliers, customers and the likely trends in technology. Also, financial institutions, consultancy firms and a variety of other private sector agencies are engaged in the same kind of exercise, either on behalf of specific clients or in the process of considering the investment prospects in particular branches of the economy. In many instances government intervention is unlikely to be capable of improving on this situation. But there are some situations where a system of economic planning could improve the structure of investment, and help to raise its overall volume, by overcoming the organisational impediments referred to near the beginning of this section (factor (10)). This is in addition to the informational factors referred to in the previous section. The areas in which planning could help include the following:

(1) Large, technologically, sophisticated projects in which the risks or simply the required financial commitment are too large to be borne by a single private sector firm, or a small group of such firms.

(2) Support for newly developing branches of production which the planning agency believes are being undertaken too cautiously by the private sector as currently organised.

(3) Support for branches of production in which the planning agency believes Britain possesses the appropriate skills to produce competitively, but where the private sector as currently organised is either losing ground in export markets, or failing to meet competition from imports. This could occur for a wide range of reasons and hence entails a corresponding variety of solutions.

(4) Projects whose success depends wholly or mainly on public sector demand for the resulting output of goods and services.

(5) The identification of small and medium scale projects to meet domestic demand for goods and services currently being met from imports or not adequately satisified at all; in other words, the identification of market opportunities not currently perceived and acted upon by the private sector in Britain. This overlaps with the informational aspects of investment discussed in the previous section.

In making these suggestions, it is implicitly assumed that the private sector left to itself would fail to generate adequate levels of investment activity in the areas mentioned. Assuming this to be the case, we could nevertheless take the view that market outcomes are inherently desirable, and should therefore not be interfered with. Such an extreme position might perhaps follow from the most over-simplified forms of general equilibrium model of the economy though certainly not from the highly qualified version of the model discussed earlier. The alternative is to establish a planning agency to undertake some of the functions neglected or poorly fulfilled by the market. In adopting the latter position, it is not of course necessary to insist that the agency should undertake all these functions, or to claim that its activities will always yield outcomes superior to the unaided market. All organisational mechanisms for allocating resources, however they combine elements of planning and market behaviour, are costly to operate and are bound to make some mistakes. What is being claimed here is that there are certain types of economic decision where, for a mixture of organisational and informational reasons, a planning agency would have a good chance of peforming better, on average, than the market.

The tasks of this proposed planning agency would involve efforts to reduce or share the risks borne by the private sector (points (1) and (4) above), promotion of reorganisation within the private sector (points (2) and (3)), setting up joint public–private or purely public enterprises to undertake new projects (points (2) and (3)) and the identification of promising branches or projects (all points (1)– (5), though less important for (4)). There is actually no reason why all these activities should be carried out by a single centralised planning agency and a lot to be said in favour of some degree of decentralisation of the planning process, as discussed in Section 4.4. below. Details of the institutional implications of these proposals are covered in Chapter 7.

4.3 Planning and Macroeconomic Policy

The conception of planning built up in the last two sections envisages that it would:

(1) Improve economic information flows, especially those relevant for investment decisions,
(2) Facilitate economic change and adjustment, through organisational and other measures to improve the volume and structure of investment.

The emphasis of planning therefore falls on various aspects of the investment process, and rightly so. For the Keynesian tradition which has guided British economic policy-making for most of the post-war period merely treats investment as a component of aggregate demand, largely neglecting its longer term effects on our capacity to produce output in the future. Moreover, the Monetarists have done little better in recent years since investment and growth are not especially central elements of their theories either. The present recession has witnessed an extremely sharp fall in investment and it is not yet clear whether the conditions for a sustained revival are being created. In this context, planning is additionally important for Britain to serve as a counterweight to the Treasury's traditional concentration on short term macroeconomic policy.

As explained in Chapter 2, past attempts at planning either foundered on the rocks of a deteriorating balance of payments or failed for some other short-term reason. It is not possible to guarantee that such problems would be avoided in the future, though the institutional proposals of Chapter 7 should help to reduce the risks. Even with these proposals, however, it remains important to discuss the interrelations between planning and short-term economic policy (some of the issues discussed below are referred to in Johansen (1978), various sections). This is the subject to the present section.

At first sight it might appear that we should simply distinguish between short-run policies concerned with demand management, the control of inflation, the balance of payments, and so on, and the long-run policy of economic planning concentrating primarily on the investment process. Unfortunately, such a neat distinction is impossible to maintain in practice, for the inescapable reason that most short-run policy has longer term effects, while resources currently allocated to meet planning objectives evidently have a short-term impact on the economy as well. However, the fact that such policy interactions have to be taken into account does not of course imply that planning is either impossible or undesirable, merely that it is more difficult than it would be in their absence. Planners may be constrained in their options by short-run problems, and perhaps more importantly, the conduct of traditional (mainly short-run) macroeconomic policy may need to be modified to assist planning. Many of the theoretical and empirical issues that arise in this context are discussed thoroughly, albeit rather technically, in Hughes Hallet and Rees (1983).

From the planning point of view, especially given our emphasis on investment, it is most useful if macroeconomic policy can be operated in such a way as to minimise its impact on the investment process, except to the extent that a long-term change in the level and structure of investment may be called for. One reason for taking such a view is that in an economy where most investment is and will remain a matter for private decision-making, it is important to maintain an economic climate favourable to investment. An additional reason is based on the arguments of the previous section, namely that investment in Britain is currently far below its most desirable level. In such a case, it is appropriate to regard consumption as the economy's 'cushion' or 'shock absorber' when adjustment is called for, since the marginal social value of investment exceeds that of consumption.

Now, it is easy enough to suggest that short-run policies should seek to 'protect' investment, but how can this be done and how far is it feasible? In the public sector it is often politically simpler to allow investment to fluctuate in response to changing economic circumstances and private firms are often in a similar position. Moreover, a general restriction of consumption will have its greatest impact on those products with higher income elasticity of demand, and these are likely to be the newer, technologically progressive products with potentially fast growing markets. Bearing in mind these difficulties, we examine the question of protecting investment by first summarising the main forms of macro-policy, and then considering the factors which determine investment in order to see how to identify appropriate policies for supporting investment activity.

Traditional macroeconomic policy comprises monetary policy, involving regulation of the money supply, interest rates and the exchange rate subject to the relevant market constraints; and fiscal policy, which comprises government decisions about public expenditure and taxation (including all aspects of the social security system). Monetary and fiscal policy are necessarily intertwined, since the latter determines the public sector deficit, which must in turn be financed by issuing new money into the system, or by selling government bonds. Decisions about these financial operations are at the heart of monetary policy. However, this is not the place to go into the details of monetary and fiscal policy: it is enough to note their principal elements as above (on the conduct of policy, see Blackaby, 1978, and Grant and Shaw, 1980; on the theory, see Levacic, 1976 and Sayer, 1982).

Theories of investment generally argue that private sector investment depends on four essential factors, namely:

(1)   Company profitability (current and expected).
(2)   The level of (real) interest rates both now and prospectively.
(3)   The prospective level of demand for the output.
(4)   Expected changes in costs (innovation).

The first two factors basically determine the availablity and cost of internal and external finance, respectively, while the third implies some expectation about the likely future market. It is interesting to note that all four are unfavourable to investment in 1985, with low company profits (although recovering sharply from their lowest levels), interest rates that are still rather high both in real and nominal terms by historical standards, and a depression from which recovery is at best very slow. In these circumstances, it is hardly surprising that investment levels have been so low since 1980, especially in industry. Naturally, public sector and nationalised industry investment may be determined by different sets of factors, but these are discussed in Sections 6.1 and 7.1 below.

The question of raising private sector profitability is discussed in Chapters 5 and 7, though it too could be influenced to some degree by macro-policy, such as company taxation. The next two factors – interest rates and the level of demand – are clearly determined by monetary and fiscal policy. The overseas component of demand is largely the result of policies exercised in other countries. In order to encourage higher real investment in the domestic economy, what is needed is a deliberate policy to keep interest rates low: particularly long term (real) interest rates payable on commercial and industrial investment loans. Such a policy might require support from a new exchange control system, and some constraints on credit to the personal sector, as we consider in Chapter 6. In addition, and this is undoubtedly a good deal harder, expectations about the future level and growth of demand, which are currently quite pessimistic in my judgement would have to undergo a sustained improvement. Otherwise, firms would be unwilling to invest a great deal more even if funds were almost costless. From this point of view, the stop-go type of monetary and fiscal policy is rather harmful since it creates uncertainty about future levels of demand and its short-term impact has often fallen on investment. As Nickell (1978) has argued, a relatively stable policy environment is likely to be more conducive to investment than one subject to frequent change. This is the case both for public and private investment.

However, some form of macroeconomic policy is needed for the standard reasons of maintaining internal and external balance. Naturally, if the conditions and circumstances affecting these balances are unchanged there is no call for any change in macro-policy instruments. However, the economy is often subject to external and internal shocks of various kinds, for instance shifts in relative world prices or the level of world demand, or autonomous wage and price increases (cost inflation), to which some adjustment must be made. Another type of shock is more microeconomic in character; it relates to the fourth factor listed above, expected changes in costs. These can arise for many reasons, but innovation is perhaps the most important. Investment by an innovator can force other firms in the same industry to invest themselves in order to match the new cost levels. Hence the volume of investment, via competitive pressures, is closely related to the rate of cost-reducing innovation going on in the economy. The appropriate adjustment to a macroeconomic shock naturally depends on whether the shock involves a temporary or permanent shift in economic conditions. In the former case it may be quite sufficient merely to draw on reserves or stocks, without changing the basic parameters of economic policy. In the latter case, the shift in conditions will require:

(1) The exercise of short-run macro-policies to maintain or restore internal and external balance,
(2) Some change in the volume and/or composition of investment, in order to bring about and sustain a longer term adaptation to the new circumstances.

The difficulty is to find policies which satisfy the requirements of (1) and (2) simultaneously. Without some attempt to do so, the most likely outcome is a series of policy manipulations seeking to satisfy the short-term constraints of (1) (but not necessarily succeeding), in which the effect on investment is more or less accidental and only by chance corresponds to (2). Price signals themselves induce part of the required adjustment in investment, but if macroeconomic policy depresses aggregate demand (for instance, to protect the balance of payments), or permits interest rates to rise sharply, then the initial rate of adjustment could be slow or even in the wrong direction. This is why it is so important that macroeconomic policy should be based on the long term considerations referred to under (2), as well as on the more conventional and familiar (1).

One way of reconciling (1) and (2) was suggested in Estrin and Holmes (1983a), namely the use of conditional pre-commitments as a means of reducing uncertainty about future policy changes. A similar notion is discussed in Hughes Hallet and Rees (1983, ch.7) who show that contingent policy rules are generally superior to rules which do not attempt to revise policies in the light of events. The two approaches are essentially the same if the contingent policy rules are communicated to private sector agents, such as firms contemplating investment. Then although these agents are not assured of a completely fixed policy environment, they do at least know the circumstances under which macroeconomic policy may be changed, and how it would change. This surely provides a better basis for planning than the present position, though of course some uncertainty would always remain since the policy calculations could never allow for all possible contingencies.

Aside from reducing private sector uncertainty about the government's policy response to certain kinds of exogenous shock, conditional pre-commitments may also be employed to influence private sector behaviour directly. For instance the government may undertake to reduce certain taxes if wages settlements fall within specified limits, or it may agree to undertake some additional infrastructural investment if private sector investment in particular areas/branches rises sufficiently. Such conditional policies, which are a form of implicit bargaining, are discussed further in later chapters.

However, fairly detailed economic models, covering several time periods, are needed in order to investigate the concrete policies that might come close to meeting all these requirements; there is no space here for such a detailed study, though we shall have more to say about possible long term/short term conflicts in economic policy later on (see also Hughes Hallett and Rees, 1983). While commenting on economic models, it is worth drawing attention here to a serious defect of all the macroeconomic models currently employed to make forecasts about the British economy. This is their failure to allow for the capacity creating effect of new investment, the models merely representing its effect on aggregate demand. Capacity is generally treated merely as a long term trend, substantially unaffected by the economic variables in the model and hence not susceptible to change through deliberate policy intervention. At the same time, existing models do not contain any constraints to force output to be less than or equal to capacity (though aggregation problems might make such constraints hard to interpret). Thus output is largely determined by aggregate demand, capacity by a long term trend and there are no particular constraints on the relationship between the two. The basic point, then, is that available models are not yet equipped to perform the kind of analysis suggested in this section, since longer term considerations have not been incorporated into the analysis.

4.4 Decomposition of Planning

It would obviously be inappropriate to construct a planning system in which all planning tasks were undertaken by a single central agency (such as a new Economic Planning Agency, based in London), not least because of the existing dispersion of economic and technical information throughout the economy. A natural question, therefore, concerns the most suitable allocation of planning tasks to different levels/sub-sections of the national economy. The object of this section is to investigate that question.

What needs to be considered, therefore, is a variety of ways in which the national economy may be decomposed into smaller sub-units, and the forms of planning organisation that would correspond to these alternatives. To keep the discussion within reasonable bounds I do not, in this section, pay any attention to mechanisms for regulating wages, or to the issue of work-place democracy in relation to planning, as these are both treated in later Chapters (7 and 5 respectively). Study of planning elsewhere, such as in Eastern Europe (see Chapter 3), suggests four rather natural principles according to which the national economy may be classified; these are based on: (i) activities, (ii) organisations , (iii) markets and (iv) regions.

It is an unfortunate fact that the bulk of economic theory is based on a complete neglect of the distinction between (i) and (ii), since firms are generally assumed to produce a single product. In that case there is a perfect correlation between *activities* (producing particular products) and *organisations* (firms). In practice, however, most firms produce numerous products or types of service, often running into the hundreds and spanning several distinct product groups. Despite this complexity, it is administratively simplest to collect statistics about economic activity from the individual producing units that operate in the economy. Firms are then classified into industries according to their major product or product line. Naturally, industries defined in this organisational way will always include firms producing many things which, in a classification based on activities, would have been assigned elsewhere. By the same token, industries defined strictly in terms of activities would have to include contributions from many firms whose output was sub-divided among several different industries.

To some extent, the centrally planned economies circumvent this ambiguity in industrial classification by specifying rather narrowly the permitted product range for each enterprise, its so-called production profile. But such control is surprisingly unsuccessful and from an economic point of view it seems to be a remarkably costly and inefficient means of enforcing a production structure whose only justification is its administrative convenience. In market-oriented economies such as the British, the problem is somewhat reduced by collecting data from establishments rather than entire firms. This is likely to ensure a higher degree of technological homogeneity in the products assigned to any given industry, an evident advantage if technical change is one of our concerns. But a snag with either of these classifications is their lack of emphasis on *markets*.

For instance, the market for packaging materials is supplied by firms making tin cans, paper and cardboard containers, plastic containers, and no doubt others as well; and some of the firms serving this market will be producing more than one of the main types of product. Similarly, firms which see themselves in the entertainment industry may reasonably have hotels, cinemas and drink production among their activities, involving totally disparate technologies. Different establishments would be assigned to different branches, as appropriate; thus a technically-based economic classification inevitably masks certain market relationships such as complementarities which, at the level of the firm, are absolutely crucial.

After packaging and entertainment, a third example illustrates an additional point, the impact of new products on both technologies and markets. This is the production of equipment to assist with small-scale calculations. The traditional products were mathematical tables (logarithms, etc.) and slide rules; these were then supplemented by mechanical and then electro-mechanical calculators, but in the last decade these have all been superseded almost completely by small, powerful electronic calculators. The market being served is much broader than the traditional one, largely because the new products are not only cheap, but also much easier to use, particularly for those with limited mathematical training: calculators are therefore used in many day-to-day applications where no one would have considered using a slide rule. So in this example, the new products involved a complete shift in the standard technology and dramatically expanded the market for the products. For the most part, the shift was brought about by firms with expertise in the new technology spotting the market opportunity, traditional suppliers to the market losing out completely and being quite unable to meet the competitive challenge. This kind of change is hardly discernible in a description of the economy based on branches defined in terms of product groups, unless the level of detail is unusually fine. It would, however, be reflected in a description based on organisations through the appearance of new firms; but an approach operating in terms of markets should represent it most satisfactorily.

What these examples show is that the location of firms in the economic structure is not merely a matter of the technology they use, as tends to be implied in the standard approaches to economic classification, but also involves markets: that is, the needs being served and the customer group or groups on which each firm chooses to concentrate. What we might call this *information matrix* is partly a subjective matter as far as individual firms are concerned, but it is nevertheless known (or, more accurately, perceived) in great detail at the level of the firm. However we choose to aggregate this information, something is bound to be lost; if we are lucky, or sufficiently skilful in selecting an aggregation scheme, the loss of detail may be compensated by an enhanced ability to take a wider view of certain aspects of economic change and development. In other words, we might hope to understand something about the 'forest', while the individual firm must rest content with information about itself and a few of the neighbouring 'trees'.

An important means of avoiding too much loss of information is to aggregate in several different ways; for instance, by markets for particular types of product, or by producers possessing particular technologies. A further direction of aggregation brings in the regional type of classification mentioned earlier, namely regional subdivisions of the economy. This involves treating defined geographical areas as the basic units of analysis; it focuses attention on the internal structure and characteristics of each such area, usually to the comparative neglect of the interrelations between them. If the regions are properly determined, the internal relationships should be strongest, with interregional transactions either negligible, or co-ordinated by a higher level of the planning structure. This kind of point about separability is discussed in Johansen (1978, Section 3.50), where he suggests that as far as possible, the partitioning of the economy should ensure that the policies available to one sub-division (in this case, region) should be independent of the specification of policy in others.

This section has so far pointed out a number of ways of classifying, or aggregating, economic information into manageable units, but without expressing a clear preference for one structure against another. The absence of preferences is quite deliberate. One lesson from Eastern European experience is that a simple organisational structure, such as one based on branches (a branch being defined in terms of product groups, but comprising all producing units whose principal product(s) belong to a given product group), as is most usual, creates an amazingly inflexible economy. Too many linkages and opportunities which should be seen are not, because they do not 'fit' neatly into the pre-ordained structure; moreover, very strong interest groups develop which are both dependent on and extremely defensive towards the given structure. In order to avoid this kind of situation, I would favour an organisational framework recognising the economy's real complexity, facilitating flows of relevant economic information between potential partners (i.e. avoiding the mistake of assuming that economic efficiency might be enhanced merely by swamping everyone with all the available information – that is simply nonsense!), and fostering change. Figure 4.2 below indicates what I have in mind, showing the main elements of the structure. The location of particular planning decisions within this structure will depend primarily on who is likely to be affected by the decision and who is likely to possess, or have access to the relevant information. Examples are given in later chapters to explain what this would mean in practice.

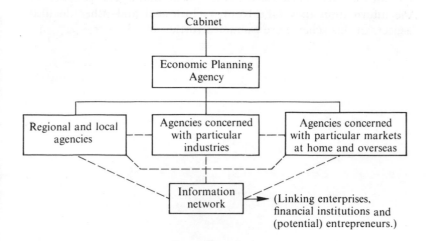

Figure 4.2 *Outline structure of proposed planning system*

In many cases, where these elements already exist in some form or other, the development of planning would then merely entail improving the co-ordination between various parts of the structure. Where elements do not exist, they would have to be established. One should not, however, infer that the advent of planning would necessarily have to be accompanied by an array of new, supporting organisations. To some extent, planning functions could be tacked on to the range of activities of existing bodies, and to quite a substantial extent I suspect, it would be found that private sector bodies such as trade associations were carrying out all the co-ordination that was required, as well as disseminating market and technical information. Thus even within the proposed structure, planning would have to be highly selective: we shall have more to say about this in Sections 5.2 and 7.2. Finally, I envisage the information network as being decentralised and voluntary, though possibly with some financial incentive to encourage participation, on the grounds that the social benefits from improved economic information flows might well outweigh the net private benefit to many individual firms. To reconcile this with remarks about the need for charges at the end of Section 4.1, it may be appropriate to pay for information supplied to the system, and to charge users for the information they take from it. Technical and other detailed aspects of this scheme are examined further in Chapter 7.

5
Planning and Democracy

The previous chapter outlined a number of relatively formal economic issues, largely to do with information or the volume and pattern of accumulation, in order to construct a case for economic planning in a developed, market-type economy such as the British. By discussing, in addition, some aspects of macroeconomic policy and several possible directions of plan decomposition, we were able to sketch some of the features of available planning systems. However, we have so far resisted the temptation to investigate the political framework within which this decentralised planning could or should be conducted. The principal task of this chapter is to remedy that important omission.

I begin the analysis at what is in some respects the most difficult and controversial level, that of individual firms, by examining workplace democracy. It will be argued in Section 5.1 that some form of workplace democracy is desirable in itself, quite irrespective of any connection that such a system might have with economic planning. Democracy at enterprise level is not necessarily a precondition for planning; indeed it can either impede or facilitate the operation of a planning system, as we shall see below. Section 5.2 studies the connections between local, regional and national planning and considers the forms of democratic control and accountability that would be required in each case. Finally, Section 5.3 looks at the types of decisions made at various levels, and discusses the scope for democracy within the planning system as a whole. It also outlines the steps by which a new planning system could be introduced, and the political conditions for its success.

5.1 Workplace Democracy

There has been a great deal of debate about the most appropriate forms of workers' participation in the British economy, and about the management role that may be exercised by workers. Some useful proposals emerged from the Bullock Report (Bullock, 1977) discussed in Chapter 2, and more recently Tomlinson (1982, chs 3 and 7), Crouch (1983) and Hodgson (1984, esp. ch. 9) have analysed the general principles of workers' participation, and some practical steps that would take us in the direction of greater, and more effective participation. Much of this analysis sought to make out a case for workplace democracy on its own merits, with little or no reference to economic planning. However, planning and democracy have been linked together in some proposals for economic reform in Eastern Europe, notably in Czechoslovakia and Poland, while Yugoslavia has been characterised for a long time by a high degree of worker self-management at enterprise level in combination with a variable degree of central planning (see Wilczynski, 1983, ch 5). In British discussions, only a few contributions have insisted on tying the two issues together, notably those based on or sympathetic towards the Alternative Economic Strategy (AES). Thus Aaronovitch (1981) and London CSE Group (1979) both see an advanced level of workplace democracy as an essential prerequisite for successful socialist planning, and as a key element in a broadly based strategy to bring about the transition from a substantially capitalist to a socialist type of socioeconomic system in Britain. While rather less explicit about ultimate goals, and apparently more compatible with established, market-based economic relationships, the TUC–Labour Party Liaison Committee took a very similar view before the 1983 general election (see TUC–Labour Party, 1982).

Nevertheless, the fact that a case for workplace democracy was made out before planning entered into the picture, indicates that the two things can be separated, at least conceptually and most probably in practice as well. From a political point of view such a separation is most desirable, since linked issues normally suffer the same fate. Keeping the questions of workplace democracy and planning apart means that each can be treated on its own merits and if one falls out of favour (e.g. through a change of government), the survival of the other is not automatically prejudiced.

It is possible, however, that there has been a political element in the recent attempts to link the two issues. Following the failure of the last Labour government to strengthen worker participation at enterprise level (as reported in Chapter 2), there is an obvious temptation to tack such measures on to the coat-tails of planning.

For some form of planning would almost certainly be introduced by a new, possibly more radical Labour government. Nevertheless, this is a risky tactic, because the constituency that strongly supports both workers' participation and planning may be rather narrow. For reasons set out below, it is not obvious why supporters of workers' participation should automatically favour planning, or conversely why supporters of planning should necessarily favour substantial participation. Consequently, linking the policies in the way that is sometimes done can actually undermine support for both of them.

In order to justify these remarks, it is essential to begin by defining the relevant concept of workplace democracy. It can, of course, take many different forms, from modest arrangements for worker–management consultation, through direct participation by workers or their elected representatives in certain management functions, all the way to workers' partial or complete ownership and hence control over their place of work (cf. Wilczynski, 1984, p.98 and Hodgson, 1984 p.131). For the present discussion, I assume that we should pay greatest attention to those forms where the workers possess some decision-making power within their enterprise. This is not to deny the practical importance of advisory and consultative arrangements of various kinds, but their relevance to the question of economic planning which is my prime concern is quite minimal.

Decision-making itself also encompasses an extensive array of possibilities, depending on the type of decision involved and the extent of worker representation on the decision-making body. In view of my emphasis in the previous chapter on planning in relation to investment, it follows that I am most interested in those bodies which have the power to take investment decisions. For the great majority of enterprises such powers are normally the prerogative of the board of directors; though in the case of multiplant firms, some authority over investment may be delegated to plant-level management, and for large multidivisional firms the divisional boards are likely to have some investment powers. Essentially, however, we are concerned with worker representation at board level.

As for the procedures surrounding this representation, it is quite apparent that direct democracy is simply not feasible in any but the very smallest enterprises. The notion of 'popular planning', which has arisen in some recent discussions (e.g. at GLEB – the Greater London Enterprise Board; also referred to in Wainwright and Elliott, 1982, p.258), is not easily generalisable unless it makes considerable use of existing organisational networks such as trades councils or the trade union structure, or establishes some mechanism of representation. For any large organisation, workplace democracy must be a representative democracy.

In normal practice, therefore, the work-force in a given firm must choose a number of representatives to occupy the seats on the board allocated to the workers. These representatives can be chosen in many different ways: for example, nomination by management or by the non-worker members of the board, nomination by the relevant trade union branch(es), election by the local trade union(s), or election by the entire work-force of the firm concerned. Given the lack of trust which sometimes characterises worker–management relationships in Britain, the first of these methods can hardly be recommended. Trade union nominees would be somewhat better since one could have more confidence that they would try to represent workers' interests as they perceived them. Also, although such nominees would presumably be chosen by union officials, most of these would have been elected themselves; hence this is a form of indirect election. An election by the relevant union branch(es) opens up the selection process a little more but is still open to objection. For on the one hand, many firms have workers belonging to several different unions so that choosing representatives via the union structure could be both complicated and a source of disputes; it would, however, pose the useful question of what the most appropriate union structure would be. And on the other hand, many workers belong to no union at all and would therefore, in effect, be disenfranchised. Consequently, an election by the entire work-force is surely the most effective mechanism for choosing board representatives. Candidates for election would not be restricted to trade union members (indeed, one can even envisage a situation in which some candidates might not even be employees of the firm concerned). Paradoxically, this could actually strengthen the position of trade unions within a firm and broaden their base of support. Given their experience, it is more than likely that a substantial proportion of candidates, at least in heavily unionised firms, would be union members. Their election by an electorate including non-members of the unions must help to raise the trade unions' standing within the firm, not only with regard to planning, but also other issues.

Many other procedural matters remain to be considered, like the frequency of elections, possibilities of recalling representatives, the range of decisions in which workers' representatives on a firm's board have voting or veto powers, the treatment of subsidiaries and other components of larger units, special arrangements (if any) for multinational companies, provisions to disseminate management information, and so on. However, different solutions will be needed for different cases and space limitations prevent me from elaborating the details. But within the general framework outlined above, the extent of work-force representation could vary a great deal, and this does call for some comment here.

At one extreme, it could be insisted that the entire board of directors should be elected by the work-force. Formally this would come close to the Yugoslav system of workers' self-management (see Estrin, 1984), though in that instance there is a variety of external rules and controls to constrain managerial behaviour, and enterprise assets are in any case state property. In a substantially private enterprise economy like the British this arrangement would evidently raise serious questions about shareholders' rights and the significance of private ownership. These questions do need to be asked, of course, but it must be emphasised that under present conditions any practical proposal concerning planning will have to take as given a large part of the organisational environment. For this reason, what may be called *laissez-faire* workplace democracy cannot be regarded as a realistic option. Even in nationalised industries, where the ownership issue would not arise in quite the same way, it is not clear why the work-force should occupy such a privileged position. Thus in the ensuing discussion, I shall exclude *laissez-faire* workplace democracy from further consideration, despite the fact that some accounts of the AES tacitly assume something very close to this case.

At the other extreme, the work-force might only elect one or two representatives to a board of, say, 20 members. Such nominal representation affords little opportunity for the workers to play a decisive part in decision-making but it would provide access to management information, including that concerning future development of the firm by means of investment decisions. Thus workers would be better informed and could make their views known at the highest level of the firm prior to major decisions being taken. This is clearly an improvement over the position without board representation, and a system that may function well in some firms where the general atmosphere of worker–management relationships is one of trust and constructive co-operation, or where the firm is not too large. In other firms, an intermediate position with stronger but still minority work-force representation may function more satisfactorily. Such a position would be compatible with the majority recommendation of the Bullock Report (Bullock, 1977; and see the discussion in Ch. 2) and except where otherwise stated, it will be the form of workplace democracy assumed in the remainder of this chapter.

Let us now review some aspects of workplace democracy, in a planning context. There are three main aspects to consider, two of which really present no problems at all and fully deserve to be supported. The third is rather more complicated. The three aspects are: first, the encouragement of worker initiative in the elaboration of plan proposals; secondly, establishing procedures for consulting workers about proposed new investment projects, whatever the source of the original ideas; and thirdly, allowing the work-force a measure of decision-making power in relation to investment decisions.

Now it is hardly possible to object to plan proposals from groups of workers, or from anyone else for that matter: popular participation in that sense can only be welcomed and encouraged. But that does not mean, of course, that the resulting proposals must automatically be accepted by anyone, only that they should form part of the pool of ideas to be considered. Similarly, the consultation of workers about new investments is clearly desirable in order to improve their understanding about new developments, and to elicit co-operation.

The third point is more contentious, in that it concerns the degree to which workers should be able to insist that particular projects be carried out, or to veto the implementation of projects they disapprove of. I would argue that such powers should be quite limited. Naturally, this does not mean that workers' views are immaterial to those taking investment decisions. For instance, with investment proposals opposed by the work-force concerned, the relevant board of directors would be foolhardy not to take such opposition into account, possibly to the extent of amending or even abandoning their original ideas. Nevertheless, the final decision would normally remain a matter for the board, and given my assumptions this would be able to outvote work-force representatives if necessary.

My insistence on this position rests on arguments about information and incentives, managerial risk-bearing and responsibility, and the supply of investment funds. In addition, wider considerations of investment allocation and the importance of restructuring in an era of unusually rapid technological change are relevant; finally, the elusive concept of social need calls for some critical comment.

Investment decision-making requires above all some ideas about possible projects. To evaluate these, firms need information on the available technological alternatives, the potential markets, the supply of inputs including labour of various skills, and the prices and costs expected to prevail when a project is realised. Given their position in the economy, workers are likely to be best informed about technology and working practices, and least well-informed about prices, costs and markets. Undoubtedly, forms of worker participation in the management structures within firms can be devised to ensure that workers learn about these latter issues as well. But in conventionally organised firms in a capitalist economy the incentives, or basic interests, of workers as compared to managers/shareholders/ directors are often assumed to be so much at variance that they would tend to have different preferences about investment, even if the same information was available to everyone. Specifically, groups of workers would be most likely to favour projects protecting their own jobs or even expanding employment at their establishment, paying rather less attention to productivity and profitability than managers would. Since workers do not usually provide risk capital, nor have any contractual responsibility to the shareholders, or to the financial institutions providing loans, for the profitability or otherwise of investment projects, this potential bias is not so surprising. Nevertheless, we need to consider how far this rather pessimistic standpoint would be justified in present British conditions, and how its implications might be mitigated.

West Germany and the Scandinavian countries have had workers' participation at board level for a long time, without any indication that worker–management differences are irreconcilable. Indeed the access to management information afforded by such participation, together with strong social pressures to take a long term view of the firm's interests probably helped to ameliorate the differences.

Similarly in Yugoslavia the areas of disagreement between workers'
representatives and management are normally quite small. Hence
the available evidence strongly suggests that the above pessimistic
view may not be justified in practice. While there is always some
scope for conflict, the long term interests of workers, shareholders
and other interested parties are not obviously incompatible, for all
groups share an interest in the long term viability and development
of their particular firm. However, even with this broad consensus
on objectives some disputes would arise, especially in multiplant or
multidivisional firms where the allocation of investment (as well,
perhaps, as its volume) could prove to be contentious. But the really
essential question is not whether there would be disputes between
shareholders' and workers' representatives on the board, but whether
they would be more frequent or more intractable with a system of
workplace democracy than otherwise. Personally, I doubt whether
they would be. In the British case, in view of our sparse experience
of democratic forms of management, it may take some time for
workers and managers to learn to work together effectively at board
level, but I can see no real reason why they should not succeed.
However, it should be added that doubts and fears about participation exist both on the trade union and the management sides, the
former sometimes resistant to incorporation in management because
that is seen (probably correctly) as undermining their traditional
position in wage negotiations, the latter afraid of losing some of
their power and authority. Thus effective participation entails change
on both sides.

In a mature socialist economy, or in a capitalist economy with
well-developed profit-sharing schemes and established arrangements
for worker participation in management, much of this conflict might
simply be avoided since worker and management interests ought to
be more in harmony then. Although Britain is not in such a
favourable position, it would be unfortunate if developments in the
area of planning had to await these institutions. In their absence,
the only workable resolution of the underlying conflict requires the
bulk of decision-making responsibility to be assigned to those
who provide or control investment resources – retained profits,
depreciation allowances and borrowings. As far as some individual
firms were concerned, this approach might merely suppress a
permanently incipient conflict, but for the economy as a whole
success in improving investment and achieving some growth should

help to make the terms of the resolution quite widely acceptable. Moreover, aside from promoting worker representation on company boards, government itself could greatly reduce the scope for conflict by acting as a kind of insurance agency for workers. This would not guarantee to preserve particular jobs, but it might, for instance, protect workers by providing state funded retraining programmes. Such a programme should obviously be geared to meet the needs of expanding parts of the economy, in so far as these can be identified in advance; and it would not be very expensive provided that the economy was operating much closer to full employment than it has been in the last few years. Some people might reject all the above as just 'buying off the workers', but the lack of constructive and viable alternatives makes it hard to take very seriously such a scornful dismissal.

Unless some government itself undertook to direct most investment funds towards approved projects, a great deal of reliance has to be placed on private sector institutions forming their own assessments of projects and placing their funds in those which promise a sufficient return. Funds would simply not be placed by these institutions in firms unable to offer some prospect of good profits, whether this inability was due to poor marketing, high costs compared to competitors, or any other reason. Naturally, some mistakes or misjudgements are bound to be made however investment decisions are organised, but it is surely best that these should be made by those who bear the principal financial risks. However, this principle should also allow for the risks assumed by workers when they accept jobs in a particular firm.

In the last chapter, I argued that there should be some government involvement in the investment process, through the instrument of a form of economic planning agency. However, I emphasised the limited spheres within which it should function. This was partly because in many areas market signals are likely to provide a perfectly adequate guide to investment decisions, and partly because, even where these signals are deficient or ineffective, government intervention will not automatically lead to improved resource allocation. Experience in the planned economies where the investment process is highly centralised suggests that even there (and one might even say, especially there), it is remarkably hard to achieve satisfactory co-ordination of investment and secure efficient outcomes in terms of the additions to productive capacity actually installed (see Chapter

3). Hence, although welcoming *guidance* from the planning agency over some aspects of investment, it is important to proceed quite cautiously towards any form of direct, comprehensive *control* by central agencies.

Nevertheless, since the principal argument for planning was that the market sometimes allocates resources very poorly, there are certain to be cases where more active intervention is desirable. For instance, it may be judged that one or other traditional branch or product group should be phased out of domestic production while others are expanded; or the organisation and structure of domestic production in some area may need to be modernised involving transfers of production between plants, some closures, some expansion. Naturally, if market forces are apparently failing to induce the required adjustment, it is important to study the reasons for that failure (which may include policy errors) and also to consider whether the planners' judgement itself might be mistaken. Leaving aside the latter possibility, the adjustment involved is an essential part of the economy's adaptation to new and ever-changing technological and market conditions. In this context, planning should be seen as a valuable instrument of change. Such change can be resisted or slowed down, especially to protect jobs in the short term; or alternatively, the social costs of change can be reduced by subsidising individuals and firms who lose out from it, for instance through generous redundancy payments.

Unless these subsidies were extremely generous (and it can easily be argued that they should be), this is just the kind of change which would be, and often is, most strongly resisted by the workers affected. Such resistance could be more effective, and consequently more damaging economically, if workers in particular plants had a decisive say over investment decisions. They would not often be willing to support transfers of funds and other resources away from their own producing unit to support development elsewhere, either in other parts of the same enterprise or holding company, or in the case of a declining industry, in other branches altogether. Thus their perceived private interests might lead them to adopt an unduly parochial view of investment alternatives, in relation to what might be socially desirable. While this obviously creates some practical difficulties for a combination of workplace democracy and decentralised economic planning, it is not clear, as we argued above, that the resulting disputes would be any more severe than in the absence of democracy. However, an alternative means of giving workers some direct influence over investment, by developing workers' investment funds, is referred to in Section 6.2. This scheme does not suffer from the problems discussed here in relation to workplace democracy.

Let us now examine the over-worked concept of social need, which is referred to in Blazyca (1983), Trades Councils (1980) and at greater length in Walker (1984), but all relatively uncritically; CSE (1980) takes a more critical standpoint as does Hodgson (1984), while Nove (1983) is the most sceptical of all about the usefulness of the concept of social need for economic planning. Supporters of planning frequently claim that market-type resource allocation is not only prone to various kinds of inefficiency, but that it leaves some important social needs unsatisfied. That is undoubtedly so, but there is little evidence to indicate that planners are much better than anyone else at identifying these needs, whether they are planners based at national level or groups of workers at enterprise level. The problem here is that social need, broadly interpreted, is practically infinite and without prices and costs or some other means of evaluation there is no natural and consistent way of determining relative priorities. Thus it becomes easy for people with strong, well-formulated views to promote their own priorities, while claiming that social need is what they seek to satisfy; this kind of distortion is quite familiar from Eastern European planning practice.

Similarly, at the level of the individual firm, it is natural for workers formulating 'alternative plans' for their plant or factory to propose to make new products using existing or at least familiar technology. As in the case of the Lucas Aerospace plan (discussed extensively in Wainwright and Elliott, 1982), the products concerned may be designed to meet various apparently unmet social needs, but without much attention to the product markets likely to be available in practice. Consequently, it is not too surprising if the management fail to act on all the ideas put forward. Such a reaction does not imply that the neglected ideas are bad ones, merely that the managers are either unfamiliar with the new markets they would need to enter or are not convinced that there would actually be an adequate market. Perhaps the solution would be for the workers to seek financial backing elsewhere, or to sell their ideas to firms already operating in the right markets; in effect, this means that the workers concerned would find, and hire, their own managers. It hardly seems fair to criticise firms for failing to produce products for which there is supposedly a social need, but either a market where they have no expertise, or no effective market at all. As emphasised in CSE (1980, pp.82, 83), proposals for 'socially useful' production cannot constitute an alternative to some form of state intervention. For if the proposed products would be supplied to the public sector, then their viability depends on the level and structure of public expenditure. While if they would be sold privately, either at home or overseas, then the proposals are basically just a critique of the market research already carried out by management, especially if production would actually be profitable. Finally, if production could not be profitable, then subsidies are called for, so again sustained production is only possible with the help of state intervention.

On the other hand, since social needs are potentially so limitless, it is evidently absurd to allow the economy to run for substantial periods of time with high levels of unemployment, as in Britain in the early 1980s. Even though it is next to impossible to rank social needs in any unambiguous manner, it must be better from a social point of view to satisfy some needs rather than none. However, the way to ensure that resources, notably the labour force, are fully utilised is through macroeconomic demand management policies, substantially a government responsibility. Firms, of course, should also be playing their part by developing new products or seeking to expand their existing markets but they can only be expected to do this to an extent adequate to maintain and expand employment if the general economic environment is favourable, offering reasonable profit prospects and steadily expanding aggregate demand. It is the latter conditions which have been absent in recent years and which a more appropriate macro-policy should be providing. When that condition is fulfilled, suggestions about preserving, or even expanding employment in certain areas in order to produce goods and services for which there is allegedly a 'social need' will no longer be heard.

The important point that comes out of this is that both the private and the public sectors should be concentrating their efforts on producing goods and services for which there is, or is likely to be a market. Price and income relationships, as well as the mechanisms for the supply and allocation of publicly provided services should ensure that there is a satisfactory correspondence between 'need' and effective 'demand'. In practice, there will always be gaps in the market where no entrepreneur has yet spotted particular opportunities, as well as obsolescent products which some firms continue to turn out in the face of declining demand. Similarly, it is always easy to think of potential products (or services) not currently in production, though that is not at all the same thing as identifying a viable market opportunity, or indeed a social need.

Perhaps ironically, what seems to follow is that those best placed to take sensible planning decisions are those best informed about potential or actual markets. In most cases this would not be the work-force at an individual plant or enterprise; it is more likely to be management, potential customers, or planners working outside the enterprise. Consequently, the interests of all these groups need to be represented at board level. Thus from the argument so far, it appears that planning can be compatible with the limited form of workers' participation envisaged at the start of this section. Much more serious difficulties would arise, however, if we sought to combine planning with something closer to the *laissez-faire* model of workplace democracy, with the workforce in full control.

Another issue over which there might be some conflict between workplace democracy and efficient investment allocation through planning has to do with the arrangements for regulating incomes. At its most extreme, rather than simply preferring investment in their own workplace instead of elsewhere, the work-force in many firms might favour increases in their current income – wage and salary increases – over investment anywhere. This could happen partly because they might have a shorter time perspective than managers or others contemplating investment, partly because they might not see current profits as a binding constraint on investment. Hence it might be assumed that they could have both higher personal incomes and more investment, by making use of external finance. In a sense this view is often correct for an individual firm, but for the economy as a whole, the rate at which wages and salaries increase affects the prospective profitability of investment proposals as well as the overall availability of credit for investment purposes. Thus unless prices rise *pari passu* with wages, hence negating the original attempts to push up the real wage, there will be a trade-off in the short-run between increases in real personal incomes and the volume of investment. Even in the inflationary case (prices and wages rising together), a similar trade-off is likely to arise to the extent that inflation engenders uncertainty about future relative prices and the price level which in turn inhibits investment.

How serious this area of conflict would be in Britain is not very easy to judge. However, as with the earlier discussion of investment choices the essential question is not so much whether there would be conflict, but whether it would be sharper or milder under a regime of workplace democracy. Since it is not clear why workers' propensity to ask for higher incomes should be greater under such a regime than at present, the problem may not be too serious. Also, if the propensity to seek wage increases is unduly strong, then the remedy, surely, is not to reject the notion of workplace democracy, but to formulate some other mechanism to regulate incomes, such as an incomes policy. The question of income regulation is pursued further in Section 7.3. Similarly, if a system of workplace democracy leads to just as much underinvestment as our present arrangements and institutions, then the proper remedy is surely to be found in the field of government intervention in the investment process; this was, after all, one of the arguments for planning adumbrated in Chapter 4.

It is worth remarking here that incomes policy actually provides an area where there may well be some useful complementarity between workplace democracy and planning. In general some kind of incomes policy is a necessary condition for planning, for as was implicit above, the planning of incomes is merely the obverse of the planning of investment. Now Britain's past experience strongly suggests that a centrally imposed incomes policy is bound to fail, ultimately perhaps because it undermines the *raison d'être* of the trade unions. For an incomes policy to succeed, therefore, it has to pay attention to the rôle to be played by the unions and more specifically, it has to find a new rôle for them. Workplace democracy is a possible mechanism for doing this, since it offers the work-force in each firm (including, but not exclusively, the trade union members) the opportunity to take part in decision-making over a much wider range of issues affecting the firm, than the conventional wage-bargaining process would allow. However, as the submissions to the Bullock Committee made clear, there are considerable divisions within the trade union movement about the form of workplace democracy, and, as noted earlier, some unions evidently would not welcome the opportunities it could offer, for fear of incorporation into the management structure. This is an important additional reason for not basing concrete proposals for workplace democracy solely on the existing union structures; at the same time, it means that the change in union rôles envisaged above might not be easy to bring about in those branches where the unions opposed the whole idea.

A further aspect of complementarity is based on an informational argument. In the absence of workplace democracy, informational asymmetries between management and workers are very likely to produce inefficient employment contracts (for details of the argument see Hart (1983), Azariadas and Stiglitz (1983)). Azariadas (1981) provides a useful survey of the theory of implicit contracts while Williamson *et al.* (1975) investigates the same problem in an organisational failures framework. The form of workplace democracy proposed above would certainly provide workers with information on product markets, demand, company profitability and suchlike matters. It may also provide managers with better information about the relative productivities of different groups of workers. Hence it is possible that workplace democracy may facilitate the development of employment contracts that come closer to meeting the conditions for social efficiency.

In this section, I have argued that economic planning of the sort envisaged in the last chapter is likely to be compatible with a limited form of workplace democracy, along the lines of the Bullock proposals. Thus supporters of more comprehensive forms of workplace democracy, such as the *laissez-faire* model referred to earlier, cannot also consistently support the approach to planning favoured in this book. Likewise, those who would prefer a more centralised type of planning, for whatever reason, can hardly support any but the most nominal degree of worker representation on company boards. To this extent, there is a trade-off between certain characteristics of the planning system (especially its decentralisation, though precise definitions of this concept remain controversial; see Heal (1973, ch.3); Cave and Hare (1981, chs 5 and 6); Hurwicz (1971); Johansen (1978, Part 1)), and the most viable pattern of workplace democracy.

5.2 Local, Regional and National Plans

The last section only favoured quite modest developments in the sphere of worker participation (workplace democracy) within an economic planning system. But this must not be taken to imply that the proposed plans would then largely be drawn up and implemented by a single central agency staffed by remote technocrats with no accountability. The previous chapter (Section 4.4) has already suggested, mainly on informational grounds, that the activity of planning needs to be decomposed in various directions. In this section that argument is extended to incorporate political considerations that go beyond the arrangements for managing individual enterprises that were explored above.

The question of accountability raises a number of delicate, and at times intractable issues. It is understandable and entirely proper that a range of interest groups in society should wish to be involved in some way in planning decisions, and in reviewing the results of earlier decisions; the difficulty is in designing a supervisory structure which allows for local autonomy and initiative while simultaneously achieving adequate control and accountability. Most probably this conflict is inherent in the situation we are discussing, even with the best of organisational frameworks. The pervasiveness of the problem is illustrated both by Eastern European experience and by our own experience in attempting to regulate nationalised industries. Nevertheless, it would be useful to consider what form of planning organisation might minimise these difficulties.

The simplest organisational structure would have a Department or Ministry responsible for economy wide planning, and a number of lower level agencies dealing with individual regions or types of investment project. The lower level bodies would be accountable to the Ministry in the sense that the latter would issue operating guidelines and receive regular reports, while the Ministry itself would be responsible to Parliament. In other words, this structure embodies the conventional doctrine of accountability to Parliament, and really recognises no other forms or levels at which accountability may be exercised. This is the same practice that is adopted in relation to the nationalised industries, and it is subject to the same practical limitations (cf. Tomlinson, 1982, ch.4).

The two main limitations of this structure concern the inability of Parliament effectively to exercise its prerogative, and the 'division of labour' between Ministry and lower levels.

Reliance on Parliamentary supervision is based on broad claims about the sovereignty of Parliament, derived from its representation of the various interest groups that comprise the British political system. But representation is not at all the same as effective democratic control. Also, it must be remembered that the bulk of Parliamentary time is taken up quite properly with legislative matters and that the various committees of the House of Commons, although fulfilling a limited supervisory role in relation to the implementation of policy and the behaviour of public sector bodies, have very broad remits. Consequently, it is unreasonable to expect them to investigate thoroughly any given area of policy – such as planning, in the present context – more than once every few years. *De facto*, this relegates effective control and supervision to the relevant Minister, or to the cabinet in the case of the occasional, very big decisions that have to be taken. Although Parliament might be quite content to delegate such powers to Ministers and the cabinet, other social groups may not regard this as an adequate framework for democratic control. Hence there is clearly a need to devise something more effective *and* more democratic (in a sense to be specified). What this might be is considered below, after some comments on the second limitation, concerning the 'division of labour'.

Within a hierarchical structure such as that just proposed as a possible planning structure, the allocation of tasks between levels would either be laid down in the relevant legislation or it would be established by the Ministry. In either case, however, it is inevitable that the Ministry would retain some powers to intervene in lower-level decision-making, since there are no other bodies in the system that could do so. From the point of view of the Ministry itself, such interventions can be defended on a number of grounds: they ensure consistency in practice between lower level agencies; they help to make planning activity more consistent with other national policies; they are the only mechanism for checking abuses and correcting errors; they give the centre considerable influence over resource allocation, especially concerning investment; and they enable the centre to prevent or control excessive competition between different lower level agencies.

In my view, although these arguments are frequently advanced in relation to planning, they nevertheless have little merit. Their serious drawbacks include the introduction of unnecessary uncertainty into the decision processes of lower level bodies and the assumption that the centre is capable of making correct judgements about lower level proposals. The latter point is completely contrary to all that was said in the last chapter about information in planning systems. Moreover, informational considerations also suggest that consistency is not as desirable as the hierarchical approach presupposes. Now, the imposition of consistent practice is certainly justified when we can feel confident that the best practice has been identified. Lacking any assurance of that, it must be better to encourage each agency to develop its own practice subject only to general guidelines and constraints emanating from the centre. These restrictions should be sufficient to facilitate effective communication between lower level agencies and between the agencies and the centre. The lower levels of the system could then learn from each other's mistakes and successes, without waiting for ministerial permission or instruction. In addition, there is no clear reason for wishing to control lower level competition, provided that the main terms and conditions under which financial assistance may be offered to firms wishing to invest are subject to definite constraints. Such constraints need not be identical for all areas or branches.

This scepticism about the possibilities for Parliamentary supervision, as well as about both the effectiveness and the desirability of detailed ministerial control over lower level planning agencies invites us to consider an alternative planning structure. This would seek to avoid most of the shortcomings of a formal hierarchy while also allowing the interests associated with each unit of the system to be reflected in the accountability provisions: in this way, it would operate more democratically. The proposed alternative involves substantially the same set of planning agencies or organisations, but with different arrangements for their supervision and accountability. Figure 5.1 illustrates the structure I have in mind. For consistency with the previous chapter (Figure 4.1) I have labelled the Planning Ministry the EPA (Economic Planning Agency).

It is evident from Figure 5.1 that what remains of a hierarchy in this system would be very loose indeed, entailing little more than exchanges of information, particularly of guidelines, advice and reports, but generally not instructions. The centre would also provide funding to the other agencies in the system in the form of budgeted totals set for some years ahead (as in a system of rolling plans) rather than on an annual basis. In addition, local authorities might wholly or partly fund the lowest tier of the system.

Aside from the absence of authority relations between different levels in this structure, it would also be loose in another important sense, namely its incomplete and variable character. Although

Figure 5.1 *Planning structure and accountability*

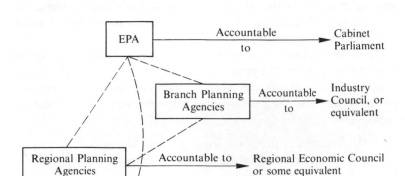

Note Dotted lines denote flows of information (reports, guidelines but *not* normally instructions) and resources (mainly financial).

branch, regional and local agencies are all shown in Figure 5.1, there is no presumption that a complete set of these agencies would ever exist. Branch agencies, in particular, would only need to be set up for those branches where the private sector was judged by the centre to be lagging behind the real demands of the economy, where there were problems of co-ordination between private and public sector developments (e.g. energy, transport, housing); or where the government wished to establish a new branch or develop previously unexploited links between existing branches.

Similarly, it may not be necessary to establish regional agencies for all areas, and certainly not local planning agencies under every local authority. It all depends on the economic problems identified in each area, and the extent to which active participation in the planning system would contribute to their solution. In some areas, especially those with relatively low unemployment, and only mild problems of structural adjustment to face, a planning agency might have relatively little useful work to do. Whether these problems were present or not, the various local and regional agencies would also be engaged in the process of raising the overall volume of investment in Britain, an objective emphasised in the last chapter (see Section 4.2).

To make the discussion more concrete, some examples to show how this system could operate may be useful at this point. These will also serve to clarify the relative powers of the various agencies in the system, and the relationships between them. We consider in turn:

(1)　An investment proposal from a large overseas company (cf. the recent decision by the Japanese company Nissan to build a factory in Britain).

(2)　A computer software company (educational and business software) as an example of services not tied to a specific location.

(3)　A flat-pack furniture company to illustrate medium-scale domestic manufacturing.

(4)　Public sector investment, distinguishing between infrastructure (roads, water supply, etc.) and nationalised industry investment (gas, electricity, public transport, etc.).

Investment by foreign companies, especially multinationals often arouses controversy because of its scale, as well as the power of the companies concerned to attract the maximum possible financial support from public agencies by playing off one region against another, or even one country against another. Especially when unemployment is generally high, different regions can be expected to compete actively for such large projects, tempted by the additional employment that would be generated directly or indirectly.

Within the planning framework envisaged in this chapter, an investment proposal from a large overseas company would be directed initially at the EPA, but would involve negotiation with the relevent branch agency (if any) and with the regional agencies. The branch agency would carry out an economic evaluation to assess the likely viability and profitability of the project, and hence determine the maximum subsidy (inducement) that it would be worthwhile to pay to attract it to locate in Britain. If the branch agency or the EPA judged that the project was unlikely to be an economic success then it could not proceed; at most there could be further discussions with the company concerned to re-examine the assumptions on which its own calculations had been based. Following a favourable assessment, the project would be referred to regional agencies while the company itself also investigated a number of possible locations. A regional agency that sought to attract the project would obviously need to have a suitable site. In addition, it would decide on a package of other supporting measures such as capital grants and other direct subsidies (which would be constrained by EPA guidelines and regional budget limits), related infrastructural investments (linking roads, drainage, port facilities, electricity supply, etc.), and help with relocation and training of the required manpower. Other regions might be going through a similar procedure, but the company itself would normally make the final selection, while the various support packages on offer would all be restricted by EPA guidelines as indicated above. In major decisions of this kind, it is probably inevitable that in practice a great deal of political pressure would be brought to bear on the EPA as well as the incoming company, either to go ahead with a particular project even when there are economic reservations about it (cf. the ill-fated De Lorean car plant in Belfast), or to favour certain locations over others. Nevertheless, the above outline of procedures concentrated on the economic aspects of the decision-making process, since these are my prime concern.

In the case of a computer software company, if this involved the planning system at all it would almost certainly be one or more of the local planning agencies. The software business is highly competitive and risky, demand mainly being satisfied by a large number of smallish firms; the product range (the available packages of special purpose computer programs) is growing rapidly both in scope and sophistication, reflecting the application of computers to new fields as well as the introduction of new models of cheap, fast microcomputer. Since rather little fixed capital equipment is required to begin operations and since there is an active second-hand market for computing equipment, it would appear that entry and exit costs should both be very low. Hence the case for public intervention and support for this industry, aside from the provision of general grants available to all investors in specified categories, is extremely weak.

The only qualifications to this position concern the shortage of skilled manpower facing this industry, environmental considerations, and the identification of specific, and perhaps exceptionally complex software needs not currently being met. In addition, the public sector may have a role in developing appropriate software standards. Thus a new software firm might approach a local planning agency for assistance with training, or there may be a regional or national training programme in force. Also, given the high skill profile of such firms it would probably choose an environmentally attractive location, with good scenery, infrastructure, culture and so on, since these features would help recruitment. Conversely, areas wishing to attract such firms would have to provide a suitable environment. So one role for local and regional planning agencies would be to undertake environmental improvement schemes, though again bearing in mind their overall budgets. For software standards and the development of complex software, a branch agency is a more appropriate instrument if the private sector is otherwise unable to co-ordinate these areas. The recently announced Alvey programme (Alvey, 1982) concerning developments in information technology, now being implemented by a directorate supported by the Department of Industry, is a good illustration of the kind of initiative required in this field.

Flat pack furniture is now well established at the cheaper end of the furniture market. The technology is well known though there is scope for product variation through the use of new designs, and for quality variation depending on the materials used and the organisation and control of production. There is no compelling reason to locate firms manufacturing flat pack furniture in any particular region, though their low risk (assuming competent management) and moderate labour intensity may make them relatively attractive to regions of especially high unemployment. A small project of this kind would initially approach the local planning agency covering the preferred location, while larger projects would involve the regional planning agency as well ('small' and 'large' would be defined for different branches in the EPA guidelines). In either case, general grants would be available, as well as any infrastructural support which the agency concerned agreed to provide.

Tacitly, the last two examples have assumed that private sector initiatives would generate an adequate volume of investment overall, with the planning agencies providing some financial assistance and infrastructural support but otherwise not intervening. However, investigations carried out by the EPA or lower level agencies might reveal that import penetration in, say, flat pack furniture was rising rapidly, without any offsetting expansion of exports. If a particular cause could be pin-pointed, such as unattractive product design or high costs due to the use of unduly labour intensive equipment, then the firms concerned could be encouraged to restructure themselves with the help of a suitable package of temporary subsidies. The highest cost firms would be encouraged to leave the industry, while others undertook modernising investment to lower costs and improve their competitiveness. Also, since the problem presumably arose at least partly because existing management failed to perceive and hence counter a competitive threat from overseas, it may be necessary to make financial support conditional on management changes. Since the adjustment envisaged here covers the whole industry, it would be organised and monitored by the relevant regional (if the industry was largely concentrated in one region) or branch agency. Notice that import controls were not among the adjustment assistance measures just discussed. This is largely because the high domestic prices they permit are harmful to consumers while also failing to provide strong incentives for desirable restructuring (for a detailed account of arguments concerning import controls, see Chapter 6; for an interesting discussion of adjustment assistance, see Wolf, 1979). Note also that this example is a microeconomic illustration of the broader problem of underinvestment encountered in the previous chapter.

Finally, let us turn to public sector investment. Some reference has already been made to infrastructural investment in association with the private sector projects just discussed. However, much of this investment is not tied to specific private investment projects in that way, but depends much more on general demographic and economic trends. I imagine that both this, as well as investment in the nationalised industries, would be organised very much as at present except that the EPA would play a co-ordinating rôle where appropriate, as would regional planning agencies within their own areas. Moreover, assuming that a combination of economic policies, including the active use of planning, succeeded in shifting the British economy on to a faster growth path, then the existing administrative arrangements and economic criteria would also yield higher volumes of public investment.

These illustrations have so far made little allowance for disputes between different agencies in the planning system. What happens, for instance, if a local agency wishes to approve a project which the relevant regional agency regards as unwise? For the most part, such argument can be avoided if EPA guidelines to lower level agencies are sufficiently clear. For instance, they could specify that projects in certain branches and/or falling below specified financial limits would be the exclusive responsibility of local planning agencies (where these exist; otherwise a regional agency would have to be involved instead). Projects in some other branches (possibly only those costing more than some specified financial limit) would be dealt with by branch agencies, while everything else would be directed through the regional agencies. Then higher level bodies would only have veto powers in respect to lower level decisions, in accordance with the published guidelines; similarly, they would have powers of compulsion in the same circumstances. Funding arrangements for the various levels in the system could also provide a source of conflict, but this aspect of my proposals is discussed more fully in the next chapter.

It might be thought that the dispersed responsibility for investment envisaged here might complicate the overall co-ordination and macroeconomic control of the economy. However, this is surely rather unlikely, since in the absence of planning, investment decision-making in a private enterprise economy is already highly decentralised and only enters macroeconomic calculations via surveys of investment intentions and econometric estimates of aggregate investment functions. As already stressed, the planning system would be used to raise the volume and quite probably change the branch structure of investment in Britain, but always within a framework of financial and resource constraints determined by the EPA. Hence, although there are certain to remain some problems of macroeconomic co-ordination (recall Section 4.3) in our proposed system, I cannot see why they should be more severe than those that we already experience.

Another aspect of the system that may be queried is its administrative cost, since all the new agencies would require appropriate staffing and in view of the agencies' functions many of these staff would inevitably be quite highly paid professionals. Nevertheless, fears of an uncontrolled proliferation of bureaucracy are hardly justified, especially as many of the required staff are already in place, in one guise or another. At the regional level, our proposals are not dissimilar to those introduced by the 1960s Labour government, though as we reported in Chapter 2, the regional bodies introduced then were hardly established before planning fell out of favour following the abortive National Plan. Several government departments, such as the Industry and Employment Departments already maintain regional offices to collect data of various kinds and to facilitate the study of economic trends and problems at a more disaggregated level than the national economy as a whole. At least in the early stages of planning it ought to be possible either to amalgamate these regional offices to form the planning agencies or, more plausibly, to draw a substantial proportion of the staff needed for the agencies from the existing offices, without actually merging the latter.

Branch agencies already exist to some degree as divisions within the Industry Department and other government departments and ministries. Hence again, the formation of the agencies discussed in this chapter entails few new staff, merely the hiving-off of certain activities from existing bodies, with only a small number of completely new agencies. In some respects, the formation of branch agencies can be regarded as analogous to the development of industrial associations in Eastern Europe and the Soviet Union, a reform that was outlined in Chapter 3. In both cases, the aim is to improve the co-ordination of investment while also decentralising the upper levels of the planning system. Certainly in the British situation, there is no reason to suppose that such specialised agencies need employ more than a handful of people each, given that their principal concerns are with industrial liaison, investment appraisal and the preparation of branch plans.

Let us now consider the question of accountability in relation to the structure shown on Figure 5.1. The treatment of the planning ministry at the top, and the local agencies at the base is sufficiently self-explanatory to require no further comment. However, the industry and regional councils referred to at the intermediate levels do call for some explanation. Each council would serve as an arena where the interest groups concerned with the associated agency would be represented. Thus the councils would receive regular reports on agency activities, would propose new activities and review the effectiveness with which existing functions were being fulfilled. Council decisions would largely concern matters of investment strategy and structure, rather than individual projects. However, in practice this implied separation between general strategy and its detailed implementation via specific investment decisions would be difficult, if not impossible to sustain. For it is almost inevitable that discussions of strategy would be informed by reference to particular projects while, conversely, one of the principal determinants of strategy is the set of investment opportunities perceived as being available. The relevant planning agency would obviously have the task of studying and exploring the boundaries of this set and the resulting information would be used by the council in selecting a strategy. Given this dependence on agency information, therefore, councils would not normally be in a position to formulate completely independent investment strategies.

Nevertheless, it would be wrong to infer from these remarks that councils would merely rubber stamp agency proposals. For the councils would be able to consult outside experts who might be able to suggest investment options not already under consideration. In this way, the scope of the planning agencies' investigations may be widened, though the councils would not go so far as to duplicate the agencies' work. Moreover, in the process of approving an investment strategy, councils should be able to bring to bear a range of expertise and knowledge of industry or regional conditions sufficient to enable them to review it thoroughly and critically. In addition, a good deal of both agency and council business is neither strategic nor strictly operational: for instance conducting surveys of particular industries or areas, considering the criteria that should be used to discriminate between acceptable and unacceptable projects, developing statistical services to support the kinds of analysis the agencies need to perform, and so on. All these areas would provide the councils with important business, as would their general responsibility to oversee the activities of their respective planning agencies.

How would these councils be set up? First of all, it is essential to identify the economic interests that ought to be represented, since these will be different for different agencies. Secondly, representatives of each interest group need to be appointed or elected. In Britain, there are now several public bodies of tripartite character, on which there are members appointed by the central government, trade unions and industry, the latter two groups of representatives being provided by the TUC (Trades Union Congress) and the CBI

(Confederation of British Industry); an important example of such a tripartite body is the National Economic Development Council (NEDC) referred to in Chapter 2. While it is of course important to secure the co-operation of the TUC and the CBI with the government in any planning exercise, it nevertheless seems to me highly undesirable to retain this rigid pattern of representation on the proposed planning councils. Representation should not be determined in the traditional way, and nor should each interest group appoint all its own representatives.

Since these remarks envisage a clear break with currently accepted practices, I must pause here to justify my position, and spell out a viable alternative. As far as justification is concerned, the task involves understanding the origins of existing tripartite arrangements and then noting their shortcomings. There have been consultations between government, business and trade union interests for many years, though usually of an occasional and informal character. Relationships between the three interest groups were somewhat closer and more formal during the Second World War but as soon as traditional wage bargaining was resumed again wartime restrictions relaxed the more usual disunity prevailed. However, by the late 1950s it was becoming increasingly clear that the combination of active Keynesian demand management to sustain the economy at or very close to full employment, with free collective bargaining in the labour market and cost-plus pricing in many product markets, was generating more and more inflationary pressure. True, this was still in a situation where price increases scarcely in excess of 5 per cent per year were regarded as a serious matter rather than as a cause for congratulation; nevertheless, in comparison with the pre-war and early post-war years the position was evidently deteriorating. Now, as we observed at the end of the last section, one requirement for improving this situation is to find a new role for the trade unions, either supplanting or at last supplementing their usual role in wage bargaining. At the level of a firm, the workplace democracy that we discussed earlier could begin to fulfil this function, but in the 1950s and early 1960s, policy-makers were more concerned with macroeconomics and the national economy. Consequently, the notion of involving trade union and business leaders in the national policy-making process emerged, in the hope that such participation might inject greater realism and responsibility into wage negotiations. As we discussed in Chapter 2, the specific institutional form taken by this participation was the National Economic Development Council (NEDC) and the associated office (NEDO). The tripartite formula used for NEDC soon spread to the various 'little Neddies' and subsequently to other agencies such as the Manpower Services Commission. This tripartite approach is now well established at national level in Britain.

Nevertheless, both in its existing forms and especially if it were extended to the proposed planning councils, it suffers from a number of shortcomings. First, the accepted practices merely reflect the existing institutional structure in Britain, according little or no weight to other interest groups such as consumers, either at home or overseas. It is more than likely that the tripartite form of representation would result in councils striving to protect existing production arrangements to an excessive degree, at the expense of new ventures and new types of organisation. Secondly, both the CBI and the TUC can only claim to represent at most a modest proportion of the business community and workers respectively. Many firms have no voice in CBI affairs and a high proportion of workers does not belong to unions. Accordingly, it would appear to be highly unjust to both groups to insist that their only representation should be through CBI or TUC channels.

Thirdly, I cannot see why the central planners themselves should be formally represented at all at intermediate levels of the planning system. At the local level, it makes sense for planning bodies (where they exist) to be accountable to local authorities; and at the national level, something like the existing tripartite structure, while not ideal in principle, has the advantage of familiarity, while also keeping the number of distinct bodies engaged in consultations and negotiations down to a manageable level. But since the national level planning body (the Economic Planning Agency) will provide intermediate, and perhaps lower levels of the system, with guidelines for their operations and since planning legislation will in any case provide what should be regarded as national constraints on planning practice, additional central representation at intermediate levels surely has no justification.

Having outlined my reservations about relying on the standard tripartite formula for the proposed planning councils, let me now sketch an alternative procedure. Although I am convinced that parts of Britain's institutional structure must undergo some change before our economic performance can be expected to improve greatly, such change will only come about gradually. As in France, it will take time to build up support for a planning system and for this reason it would be unwise to introduce all features of the system straightaway. Also, it would be desirable, wherever possible, to build on the existing institutional framework while also allowing for some experimentation with alternative arrangements to learn more about what would work best under British conditions.

Now, the simplest way of initiating a planning council is certainly by appointment from existing bodies or interest groups. For instance, in the case of a regional planning council it would be natural for representatives to come from the local authorities in the region concerned, as well as from trades councils, chambers of commerce or other business organisations, consumer groups and so on, perhaps supplemented by a number of independent members, expert on economic, financial, environmental and other relevant matters. This is close to, though rather broader than the now traditional tripartite approach, but in any case I would only regard this as the starting point of a process that could eventually become considerably more democratic. Even at the start, the formation of a regional council would be guided by the EPA, in order to ensure that each council possessed the range of skills judged to be necessary for the effective conduct of its business. I would not expect the EPA to have the power to veto the appointment of representatives proposed by the interest groups mentioned above, but it should be able to appoint some independent experts to provide inputs not already covered adequately.

For a branch council, the initial procedure could be quite similar to this, except of course that the relevant interest groups are more narrowly defined. Consequently, a formula comprising management and trade union representatives, together with a few independent experts, should provide a perfectly satisfactory starting point.

To progress much beyond this stage depends on a number of preconditions. First, if planning was to become a more democratic process, the way in which this could be achieved would depend a great deal on the attitudes of the main political parties to the activity of planning. In France, for example, although political parties disagreed about many things there was a surprising unity on the question of planning, all parties accepting the need for state guidance to modernise and restructure the economy in the post-war period. In Britain despite the experience of wartime planning introduced by the National Government, and the renewal of planning in the early 1960s at the instigation of the then Conservative government, support for economy-wide planning now seems to be a monopoly of the Labour party, with limited support from the smaller parties in Parliament. Hence one might suppose that the arguments in this book should be addressed most forcefully to the Conservative party, to convince it of the merits of economic planning. However, even in the presence of fundamental disagreements about planning it is possible to operate the system reasonably democratically, as we shall see. The main drawback of continuing deep disagreement between the parties is the uncertainty it would create about the survival of the planning system in any form at all, a serious matter in view of the long term character of the investment process. The design and operation of the system would have to take account of this uncertainty and seek to mitigate its effects.

Secondly, it would be important to arouse popular interest in planning. Since economic planning is often conceived of as a rather dull, dry business, there is a great deal of popular prejudice to overcome. At the same time, investment decisions taken by both private and public sectors can radically transform whole areas within a decade or so, so that the practical effects of planning are not at all remote from everyday life. However, many of the details of current planning practices such as the procedures for obtaining local authority planning consents; the various kinds of public enquiry; compulsory purchase, compensation arrangements and other legal aspects of planning; as well as decision-taking by government departments, are so complex that they are almost opaque as far as most people are concerned. Thus one way of facilitating the development of more democratic planning would be to make planning a more transparent process, perhaps through some simplification of existing procedures; public information and education campaigns could also play a useful role here. Inevitably, however, the planning system would remain quite a complicated one.

Thirdly, the range of individuals and interest groups represented on the planning councils would have to be widened considerably beyond the conventional tripartite pattern. To achieve this, the following procedure could be employed. Every so often, say annually, advertisements in the press and on television would invite interested members of the public to apply for membership of a planning council, presumably the one in the area where they lived, or one dealing with a particular branch of the economy in which they have some interest or expertise. An appropriate selection system would have to be developed to ensure that the resulting councils were properly balanced in terms of the skills and interests represented on them, including some representatives of management and labour, of course. Most likely, the councils would include a high proportion of members with some experience of business affairs, or with related knowledge and experience. Even so, I imagine that council members would need to undergo some form of initial training to enable the councils to function effectively. How often they would meet and how they would organise their business would vary considerably depending on the nature of the area covered by a given regional council or particular characteristics of the industry represented by a branch council. Hence it does not seem useful to make any general suggestions about this here. Also, at this stage of the argument I have not suggested using elections as a means of selecting council members. This question is considered fully in the concluding section of the chapter.

5.3 Democratic Planning

A reader of the previous two sections might infer that I only favour a fairly limited exercise of democracy in relation to economic planning. The aim of the present section, therefore, is to explain why that is nevertheless an incorrect inference. It is true, of course, that I only supported a restricted form of democracy at the level of the workplace. This was because of my conviction that a *laissez-faire* type of workplace democracy would impede rather than foster the development of ideas and attitudes conducive to successful planning. For the same sort of reason, the last section emphasised accountability, and the proposed planning councils were to be filled by a rather complex process of appointment.

So where does democracy fit into all this? In the first place, I would claim that the proposal to encourage popular participation in the planning process, both through the various planning councils and at enterprise level is itself an important advance in democracy. Instead of appointing a selection of those who apply to sit on the councils, however, it might be argued that some form of election should be held. Several points could be made for and against this idea, though on balance I am not convinced that it should be supported. Nevertheless, it is not a matter about which my views are either strong or finally settled.

An important advantage of holding elections is that they would provide a convenient vehicle for publicising and popularising the idea of planning the economy, as well as informing the electorate about the candidates standing for office on the planning councils. Against this, I suspect that many people who could make, and should be encouraged to make, a valuable contribution might be unwilling to take an active part in the conventional kind of public election campaign. This point might make it very difficult to establish councils encompassing a sufficiently broad range of experience and interests in the general population.

Secondly, it is essential to consider the kinds of social decision-making which are amenable to democratic procedures. As far as planning is concerned, there are several levels of decision-making, which we list and then discuss: these levels involve decisions about:

(1) The aims and organisational framework of the planning system;
(2) The shape of the national development plan, broken down by region/branch; to a large extent this involves determining at least in outline the structure of investment (how this might be done is examined in Chapter 7);
(3) The structure and priorities of investment at branch/regional level;
(4) Selection of, and detailed financial arrangements to support individual investment projects;
(5) Changes in practice resulting from reviews of earlier decisions and any other pertinent information.

Decisions in category (1) would obviously be taken by Parliament and embodied in the legislation that set up or modified the planning system. The Economic Planning Agency would be responsible for category (2) decisions, subject as usual to Cabinet approval and the occasional Parliamentary debate. These decisions are then used to determine the guidelines – in terms of priorities and overall budget limits – to be issued to the lower level planning agencies. The framework within which the various agencies' decisions are taken is established by category (3), and this is one of the principal responsibilities of the planning councils, though naturally they would be constrained or influenced by the guidelines determined under (2). The planning councils would also deal with the main issues arising under (5).

The remaining decisions, those in category (4), would be taken by the appropriate level of the planning system, depending on the nature and size of the projects concerned, rather as we outlined in Section 5.2 through a number of specific illustrations. For reasons of commercial confidentiality it would not generally be desirable for the details of individual projects to be debated openly, though it would clearly be necessary for planning agencies to provide their respective planning councils with some information about the projects being supported. Small projects, and a few larger ones where the market and/or the principal inputs were substantially local, would naturally fall within the remit of local planning agencies. Most larger projects would be dealt with by the other branch/regional agencies; at times projects would be considered by more than one agency, generating a certain amount of competition. As emphasised earlier, such competition is to be encouraged, provided that agencies are working within definite budgets, and that there are clearly defined limits on the maximum support permitted for any single project.

For a variety of reasons, certain projects would also be submitted to national level for approval, and just as at present a few would be reviewed in a public inquiry. A particularly important group of projects likely to require higher level (e.g. EPA) consultation, if not necessarily approval, would be those involving a major contribution from a multinational, non-British registered corporation. Such corporations possess the resources not only to play one region off against another, but also one country against another. They are able to do this, not just because of their resources, but also because regions are fighting for projects to help alleviate their unemployment problems. Consequently, projects which might be regarded as mobile, either inter-regionally or internationally, are likely to be scrutinised much less severely than more local projects, and are often offered stronger financial inducements. This problem is especially significant within the EEC since locating a plant anywhere in the Community affords access to the whole area, and at present there is only limited Community-wide regulation to govern relationships with multinational corporations.

What these remarks imply, therefore, is that in the investigation of individual projects (category 4), there should be no attempt to introduce democratic procedures. The protection of commercial confidentiality, and the need to engage in often protracted and highly complex negotiations before the detailed formulation of a project is accepted, are almost certainly incompatible with formally democratic decision-making. Hence the preparation of this kind of decision should normally be left to an agency with some executive authority, as suggested above. However, there is no reason why a particular project recommendation should not be submitted to a council for approval; or even a shortlist of alternatives, for that matter. In contrast, a democratic approach is both feasible and appropriate for deciding on the basic principles and organisation of the planning system, for approving or reviewing recommendations from the EPA about the structure and general priorities of the investment programme, and for reviewing the outcomes of past choices (categories 1, 2, 3 and 5). Thus the area for debate should focus on the precise way of introducing or developing democracy in relation to these decisions. In this chapter I have put forward one quite specific set of proposals. Needless to say, other structures and mechanisms could certainly be devised, and some may well be superior to what has been suggested here. My own immediate aim was merely to open up the question of democracy and planning for wider discussion, and to clarify some of the issues which must be taken into account in such a discussion.

6
Institutions: Developing the Existing Structure

This chapter and the next one are concerned with the institutions associated with the type of planning system that I envisage for Britain in this book. The rôles of certain, already existing, institutional forms, and how they might need to be modified or developed, are studied in this chapter. Chapter 7 then extends the discussion by considering a number of new institutions or arrangements that would improve the functioning of the proposed planning system. Throughout the two chapters, much of the detail will refer to specifically British institutions or, in the case of new institutions, to forms most likely to succeed in British conditions. Nevertheless, much of the argument should also apply to other developed, market-type economies. In addition, since other recent proposals about planning have themselves made reference to the need for changes in our institutional structure, I shall comment on these proposals in the appropriate sections.

Four quite distinct institutional issues are tackled in this chapter. The first is the treatment of nationalised industries which is a controversial matter under any government nowadays. The second concerns the financial institutions and their rôle in planning. Since some supporters of planning also favour nationalising some of the banks, our discussion of this topic overlaps to some extent with the first section of the chapter. Next we turn to an examination of local enterprise boards and regional development agencies. Some of these already exist, the boards being established by several Labour-controlled local authorities, the agencies by the last Labour government. In view of the argument of the last chapter, it is important to consider how far these bodies fit into the organisational framework suggested there. The fourth issue has to do with the regulation of international transactions. Since 1980, of course, since the Conservative government abolished exchange controls shortly after it came to power, there has been virtually no official control over such transactions on capital account, and there was already relatively little control over current account transactions. Nevertheless, the Labour Party, the TUC and others writing about planning in particular or the Alternative Economic Strategy (AES) in general seem to favour some form of control over imports and the outflow of capital. Hence the institutional arrangements that would be required to exercise this control, and the arguments for and against it are reviewed at the end of the chapter.

6.1   The Rôle of Nationalised Industries

As they are presently organised, most of Britain's nationalised industries assume the legal form of a public corporation (see Tomlinson, 1982, ch. 4; much of this section is based on Hare, 1984). In practice this means that the assets are in public ownership, hence conferring some supervisory powers on the government, but that in most respects the management structure and internal organisation tend to be quite similar to what one would expect in a private corporation. Since these industries account for 11 per cent of GDP, 8 per cent of employment and 17 per cent of fixed investment in Britain, it is not surprising that they attract considerable attention and concern from economists and politicians. Moreover, nationalised industries are bound to be of central importance in any comprehensive planning exercise, and further nationalisation has been suggested by some as an important precondition of planning.

The last two points invite us to pause briefly to consider nationalisation in the broader context of economic policy as a whole. In this context, nationalisation would be regarded as one of a range of possible instruments of industrial or investment policy. As such it should be assessed alongside other instruments capable of achieving the same ends. Such alternative instruments presumably include various forms of regulation (the setting up of regulatory agencies, legal restrictions, etc.), taxes and subsidies, and the use of the power possessed by the public sector as a purchaser of commodities. At present, this last power is exercised by the Ministry of

Defence in the procurement of defence equipment, and by the DHSS in procuring drugs and medicines. However, it is a power which could be used more systematically as an element of industrial and anti-monopoly policy (though subject to the qualifications mentioned in Chapter 2).

Considered as an instrument of industrial policy, nationalisation suffers from a number of disadvantages. First, it is extremely time-consuming. For instance, the nationalisation of the steel industry and the shipbuilding industry (to mention but two cases) took a long time and the long drawn out process of nationalisation itself has a debilitating influence on the industries concerned. Secondly, it can be very costly. Since, at least in the short run, it reduces the funds available to the government for investment, nationalisation is misguided if its ostensible objective is to raise the volume of investment. This point is of some importance for a government facing a tight budget constraint, as would be the case for the British government in the foreseeable future.

Thirdly, even though nationalised industries are meant to be autonomous, their decisions are always associated with considerable political scrutiny and controversy. In itself this is not a bad thing, and it is even desirable where the industry is a statutory monopoly. But in many cases, the politicisation of economic decisions has an adverse effect on efficiency. This point would assume greater importance in the case of any further nationalisation, for all the industries which are candidates for that produce internationally traded goods and thus exist in a highly competitive environment. The point is much less significant for natural monopolies, for which nationalisation offers certain advantages, but all such industries are already in national ownership.

Let us now outline the arrangements for managing and regulating the present collection of nationalised industries in Britain. Each nationalised industry has a sponsoring ministry to which it is directly accountable and which has to approve its financial targets and investment plans. Management arrangements are set out in the relevant nationalisation Acts. The detailed powers and duties vary substantially from branch to branch, but on the whole the industries are expected to try to operate on a commercial basis, having regard to other, social obligations laid down and usually subsidised by the sponsoring ministry. Since the Acts were never specific enough to determine all aspects of policy, they have often been supplemented by other forms of control such as ministerial instruction. Also, the relations between the nationalised industries and their sponsoring ministries have often been characterised by informal understandings and politically motivated pressures, a point to remember in any assessment of the merits and demerits of further nationalisation.

In addition, various aspects of pricing and investment policy, the associated financial and other performance indicators, and guidelines for ministerial intervention have all been set out in a series of White Papers. These papers were issued in 1961, 1967 and most recently in 1978 (HM Treasury, 1961, 1967, 1978). In 1961 the emphasis lay with the financial performance and commercial operation of the industries but by 1967 attention had turned more towards economic criteria: marginal cost pricing, and investment decision-taking using discounted cash flow (DCF) methods and a test discount rate (TDR) (on the theory of these techniques, see Rees, 1976).

Prior to the 1967 White Paper, investment decisions in the nationalised industries were not often based on formal investment criteria, appealing instead to such non-economic arguments as 'essential for the maintenance of the system', or 'the latest available technology', or 'required to sustain a steady flow of orders to supplying industries' and so on. Where formal criteria were used, they were usually of the payback period type, i.e. working out how long it would take for the additional net revenue generated by some investment project to cover the initial investment outlays. Such criteria are biased against projects where the returns build up over a long period. DCF methods consider the cash flows generated over the whole expected life of a project. Cash flows arising in different years are discounted using the TDR and then screened to arrive at what is called the project's net present value (NPV). If the NPV is positive, then the project should be approved; otherwise it should be rejected. In these calculations, the TDR was intended to reflect the real rate of return expected on comparable, low-risk private sector projects. On this basis, it was initially set at 8 per cent but this was subsequently raised to 10 per cent.

How far did this more formal approach to investment decision-taking affect the nationalised industries' practice? First, opening up a discussion about investment criteria and investment efficiency probably stimulated the industries to re-examine what they were doing and to try to improve their procedures. Secondly, however, it proved to be very difficult to implement the new methods in some industries, because for a high proportion of projects there was apparently no way of separating off the effects of an individual project from the system as a whole. Thirdly, for very large and long term projects like power stations, the main factors affecting the returns to a given project are the level of demand ten to thirty years in the future, and the prices at which this demand is met. These depend on so many imponderables, including future changes in government policy, that even the most sophisticated investment criterion has to contend with enormous uncertainties. Finally, there is scope for considerable debate around the treatment of inflation, depreciation and replacement, taxes and subsidies and the most suitable discount rate, so that an acceptance of the new approach to investment still left a lot of problems to be resolved. Overall, therefore, the new methods only found immediate application in a few areas, though the ensuing debates about investment appraisal probably had beneficial spin-off effects on practice in most of the State industries (for some examples of the practice, and a useful review of the theory, see Bates and Fraser, 1974).

Financial targets were another issue in the 1967 White Paper, though they were emphasised more strongly in 1978. In an era when inflation was more pressing than in the 1960s, it was understandable that financial controls should receive attention, partly as a means of ensuring managerial accountability, partly to minimise the industries' contribution to the public sector borrowing requirement (PSBR). Two forms of financial control were envisaged: cash limits (subsequently known as external financing limits, or EFLs), and medium term financial targets. These were supplemented by a requirement to earn a real rate of return of 5 per cent on the investment programme as a whole, replacing the earlier project-by-project approach, and a reiteration (actually amounting to a weakening) of the 1967 view about prices.

The medium term financial targets were intended to cover three to five year periods, and by 1980 targets had been agreed for most nationalised industries, the parties to each agreement being the relevant industry board and its sponsoring minister. Most targets aimed for a certain rate of return on net assets over the agreed period, but that for the Post Office sought a specified return on turnover, and for British Steel and British Leyland it was impossible to do much more than aim to break even in the not too distant future. The status of these targets is not as clear as it should be: in particular there is room for doubt as to whether they are intended to represent merely the industries' aspirations, or whether they are plan targets with sanctions against any shortfalls in their fulfilment. This is an interesting point since similar doubts also arise in connection with the planning agreements as proposed by the last Labour government (see Chapter 7 for more discussion of such agreements).

A further problem with the medium term targets concerns their relationship with the EFLs, these being agreed annually for each industry with its sponsoring department and the Treasury. External financing limits form part of the government's programme for controlling public expenditure in general, introduced under the last Labour government but strengthened considerably since 1979. The approach involves setting annual cash targets for various components of government expenditure, and EFLs are just the particular cash limits that apply to the nationalised industries. Since in operating these limits, no distinction is normally made between current and capital expenditure, some observers have argued that their recent stringency has contributed to a fall in the industries' investment (see tables in Chapter 1), that being easier to cut back than current costs in the short run. This could make it difficult to achieve rapid productivity gains in the future and, more significantly, it could impede the industries' efforts to meet their medium-term financial targets. Within a planning framework, even if the cash limits system continued to be used, I think it would be important to treat investment and current expenditures by the nationalised industries separately. This would make it possible to maintain investment at higher levels than at present.

Heald (1980) critically evaluates the 1978 paper in relation to its predecessor, while Redwood and Hatch (1982) examine some of the wider issues of controlling the nationalised industries. Within the existing institutional framework, the main difficulty has been, and continues to be, that of providing a control environment that stimulates efficient production; accountability to ministers (and hence to Parliament), the work-force and customers; and fulfilment of financial and other obligations simultaneously. This key issue is still not satisfactorily resolved.

One might have expected the nationalised industries to provide a test case, or model, to illustrate the potential benefits of economic planning, especially in the fields of transport and energy. These sectors are important candidates for planning because each contains several nationalised industries, as well as a significant element of private sector activity. Also, many of the more attractive investments in these sectors are on a huge scale and take many years to put into effect (e.g. the motorway programme, constructing a new power station), and there are well-established linkages both within each sector (e.g. coal used in electricity generation, competition between road and rail) and with other branches (e.g. energy and transport are both essential inputs for almost all other economic activity).

There must of course be some planning in these sectors even if it hardly goes beyond ministers' powers to approve or reject particular investment proposals. It would be interesting to know how far such decisions are based on an overall appraisal of the most desirable lines of development in the sectors concerned, and how far they merely reflect the views and influence of the individual industries. I suspect that a more concerted effort by the government, through the Departments of Energy and Transport, to impose more realistic output, employment and investment targets would have yielded rather better outcomes. It seems that there is a need for better co-ordination within the nationalised industry sector of the economy, which is only partly fulfilled by the existing control arrangements. The next chapter considers some ways in which this situation could be improved.

Some recent proponents of planning have suggested that further nationalisation would be desirable in Britain, either to facilitate, or simply at the same time as, the development of some planning machinery (e.g. CSE, 1980, pp.74, 75, which is fairly cautious, and TUC–Labour Party, 1982, which is much less so). Targets have included some or all of the clearing banks (see the next section for a discussion of this), a selection of Britain's largest companies, as well as certain profitable and/or technologically progressive branches such as pharmaceuticals. The last of these is proposed at least partly because the National Health Service is its principal domestic customer. Some of the new nationalised companies would be established by agencies such as the now defunct National Enterprise Board (NEB – see Section 6.3, below).

Quite a number of arguments can be put forward in favour of such extensions of nationalisation, but there are also weighty counter-arguments and on balance I am not convinced that a compelling case has yet been made out. Briefly, further nationalisation could be justified in terms of employment protection, structural adjustment, strengthening government control over the economy, restraining monopoly, ensuring that certain technologically very sophisticated branches remain under UK control, or securing the domestic development of an essential industry. The last point is relevant when major rationalisation and modernisation is called for, if the private sector is unable or unwilling to undertake the task (e.g. British Leyland, or British Shipbuilders); or where an important private firm has suffered a financial collapse (e.g. Rolls-Royce) and the government is unwilling to allow the normal processes of liquidation and bankruptcy to proceed. However, Redwood (1984) is very sceptical about the desirability of intervention in such cases as these.

One might imagine that one or other of these arguments would apply to most branches of industry and that, as a result, much more of British industry ought to have been nationalised by now. Against this, however, it is not certain that nationalisation is an essential precondition for improved or stronger government control. As we remarked earlier, other policy measures are available or could be devised to achieve most of the objectives referred to above as possible reasons for nationalisation. Secondly, even for private sector industries in difficulty, the government may well not have access to superior information about the likely market development than the private firms themselves. Consequently, a government induced rationalisation (via nationalisation) might not be superior to what would have happened as a result of normal market forces. Given the large job losses in several nationalised industries in recent years, it is not even clear that the social costs of structural change are much reduced by nationalisation.

Thirdly, as we argued earlier, experience in running state industries suggests that there are serious problems in devising an effective organisational framework and suitable incentives to stimulate efficient operation. Foster (1971) provides a useful and perceptive account of the relationships between Parliament, Ministers and Nationalised Industry Boards in which he argues that the latter have much more independence of Ministers than is commonly supposed and that the often advanced distinction between policy making (a Ministerial responsibility) and policy implementation (the Boards) is simply not operational. Only part of the difficulty can be poorly framed statutes and unclear objectives, but in any case, the result is that the industries frequently attract criticism, by no means always justifiably, for their relatively low efficiency, over-manning, poor marketing and slow rates of technological progress (e.g. Redwood, 1984, takes an exceedingly critical view of most of the public enterprises he examines). Public attitudes towards the nationalised industries are frequently contradictory, with high profits being seen as an indication that undue advantage is being taken of a statutory monopoly position, and low profits regarded as a sign of gross inefficiency.

At the beginning of this section it was noted that nationalisation can be regarded as an instrument of industrial policy. But it can also be regarded as an objective in itself, or as an instrument for achieving other policy goals, such as redistribution. However, the suggestion sometimes that nationalisation might help to redistribute the nation's wealth is actually another fairly weak argument. On the one hand, there has been no nationalisation in Britain without compensation of the former owners, hence little or no net transfer of wealth is effected; and it seems doubtful whether even a radical Labour government would depart from that principle. On the other hand, an effective wealth tax could be introduced to meet the redistribution objective in a more general and less selective manner. It is interesting to note, however, that no government has yet had the political courage to introduce such a tax and make it work. Presumably an important reason for this caution is fears about the possible adverse effect of a wealth tax on private sector investment.

So what can we conclude about nationalisation, in relation to economic planning? Aside from dogmatic or ideologically based predispositions to favour one particular view, there are strong arguments both for and against further nationalisation. On the whole, these arguments have little bearing on the case for planning made out in this book. Although some of the existing nationalised industries could probably be better planned than at present, and their investment structure and performance could be improved by linking into a national planning system, this in no way implies that planning must be accompanied by further nationalisations. Indeed, even a limited amount of privatisation might be quite compatible with the development of planning, since the above arguments do not imply that the existing set of nationalised industries should be accorded any particularly privileged status. (On privatisation, see

Shackleton (1984), Klein (1984), Kay and Silberston, 1984, Privatisation, 1984, and for a much more critical view, Whitfield, 1983.)

Table 6.1   *The financial institutions*

Institution	Attributes
Bank of England	Nationalised in 1944; banker to the government (i.e. funds government deficit) and to the Clearing Banks; manages foreign exchange reserves and operates monetary policy.
Clearing banks (and other banks)	Deposits from individuals, firms and government departments; loans for consumption or investment, usually short or medium term. Some assets held in company or government securities.
Merchant banks	Deposits from other financial institutions, firms: loans to firms, mainly for investment purposes.
Discount houses	Deal in Treasury Bills (short-term government debt) using short-term funds from the Clearing Banks.
Building societies	Deposits from individuals; long-term loans for house purchase; some finance for other property development.
Insurance companies	Insurance premiums from individuals, firms and occasionally government agencies; funds invested in a range of financial securities of various degrees of liquidity to ensure claims can be met.
Pension funds	Income from individuals, firms and government; funds invested in property and a variety of financial securities; limited direct investment.
Stock exchange	Transactions in company and government securities; deals in new issues as well as existing securities.

6.2   The Financial Institutions

Aside from the provision of banking services to the general public, the principal economic function of the financial institutions is to act as intermediaries between savers and investors. Since there are many reasons for saving and many forms of investment, it is not surprising to find some specialisation among the financial institutions according to the type of deposit they wish to attract, and the area of investment they favour. Table 6.1 shows the main groups of institutions currently operating in Britain together with their most significant attributes from the standpoint of the present study.

Note that the Bank of England, the National Savings Bank and the Post Office Giro (included in 'other banks' in Table 6.1) are the only parts of the British financial system that are fully nationalised. Also, it is noteworthy that a high proportion of financial dealings are in secondary securities (financial intermediation) as opposed to loans made directly for physical investment, and that only a small proportion of investment funding, except in the housing and property sector, is on a long term basis. This pattern of business is very different from what prevails in such countries as Germany and Japan, where long term investment loans to firms are much more the norm, and the loan market for house purchase is not so fully developed (e.g. see Carrington and Edwards, 1979). Some authors have criticised financial institutions in Britain for their failure to invest more in so-called productive industry but such criticism is misplaced for several reasons. Aside from this problem, which manifests itself as a short time horizon on the part of most financial institutions, a further issue is the distribution of funds between physical and financial, or portfolio investment. Both these issues concern banks as well as non-banking financial institutions, and the institutions are sometimes criticised for not applying more of their funds to physical investment. However, the prevailing allocation of funds between different types of asset is neither arbitrary nor perverse, but is governed by a number of quite simple economic factors which need to be better understood.

First, it has to be remembered that the principal objective of the financial institutions, as for any other branch of the economy operating in a competitive capitalist environment is to preserve, and wherever possible to expand the value of their capital: in other words, to seek profits. Any particular financial institution will therefore tend to hold a mix of assets with various maturities and degrees of riskiness, which enables it to make as much profit as possible while meeting its current and expected future liabilities. Since different institutions face different legal and other constraints on their behaviour, they will not all choose to hold the same mix of assets. In the last few years, however, since the lifting of exchange controls, many financial institutions have chosen to raise the share of their assets held overseas: presumably they have judged that such assets would be more profitable and/or less risky than additional holdings of British assets. Thus even in this case, the institutions concerned are merely following the available market signals efficiently. Nevertheless, depending on the prevailing policy objectives, one may wish to change the environment generating the signals. Also, given the argument in Chapter 4, the set of signals may be incomplete since most futures markets do not operate; to a large extent, therefore, the financial institutions have to take their decisions on the basis of highly imperfect and uncertain information about future market conditions.

Secondly, in view of the above stress on profitability, it is to be expected that funds would be allocated between different types of asset according to their relative rates of return, the returns incorporating interest, capital gains or losses, adjustment for inflation, adjustment for expected exchange rate fluctuations and so on. An important factor affecting relative returns was emphasised by the Meade report (Meade, 1978). The report argued that the prevailing patterns of allocation of finance in Britain were strongly influenced by distortions in the relative returns to different types of asset caused by our tax system. Some assets, such as mortgages for house purchase, were found to be heavily subsidised (interest payments set against income to obtain tax relief, no capital gains tax and no tax on imputed rental income) while others were treated much less favourably, e.g equity shareholdings (dividends taxed as unearned income, capital gains tax). Moreover, in a useful study of the fiscal privilege associated with different forms of savings, Hills (1984) has shown that the net returns to many assets are quite sensitive to the rate of inflation, while others exhibit very little sensitivity. In addition, Flemming (1976) has shown that the cost of capital (that is, the cost to a company of the finance needed to pay for physical capital) has risen since the late 1960s, while the rate of return on new investment continued to decline. Hence it is not surprising some investment has been discouraged and that even some very large companies such as GEC have preferred financial to physical investment and have found that to be a highly profitable strategy. If all these distortions are really so significant, then criticism and reforms should be directed at the tax system itself, to eliminate or reduce the main distortions. The only other option, not at all easy to achieve in the short run, is to increase the rate of return on physical investment.

Thirdly, the report of the Wilson Committee on the financial institutions (Wilson, 1980) indicated that the banks already operated both competitively and efficiently, and found that the main reason for the low proportion of loans directed to industrial investment (and within this, the low proportion of longer term loans) was low demand rather than an inability or unwillingness on the part of the banks to support industry. However, it is difficult to evaluate this claim since high interest rates and poor market prospects might well depress investment for a while, whereas the absence of long term business loans has been a persistent feature of the British financial system. The only significant problem area identified in the Wilson report concerned loans for small businesses, where the banks appeared to be extremely cautious. The difficulties here are largely associated with the high riskiness of such transactions, and the high costs to the bank of assessing the credit worthiness of the firms involved. However, the Thatcher government has introduced a number of schemes to make finance for small business more readily available. These recognise the social value of supporting small businesses more actively by subsidising, or sharing the risks of loans to businesses below a specified size.

How do the financial institutions need to be changed in order to support our proposed economic planning system? Several ideas can be found in the recent literature on planning, including

(1) Channel some pension-fund money into local enterprise boards (see Murray, 1983)
(2) Nationalise some or all of the clearing banks, or otherwise extend state ownership (FISG, 1982, and Minns, 1982))
(3) Establish a National Investment Bank (FISG, 1982, and TUC–Labour Party, 1982).
(4) Issue credit guidelines to financial institutions, based on a national economic plan (FISG, 1982).

As we remarked in Chapter 3, the last of these has been a characteristic of planning both in France and Japan; moreover the second, nationalisation of the banks, was completed in France very recently under the present (Mitterand) government. Let us now consider which, if any, of the above measures might be suitable in the British case, bearing in mind the analysis of Chapters 4 and 5. As we shall see, only the fourth proposal can be supported unequivocally on the basis of earlier analysis, though consideration of the third proposal is deferred until the next chapter.

Local enterprise boards will be discussed fully in the next section, so it is possible to be quite brief here. Existing enterprise boards have so far been funded directly by the local authorities that set them up, though most of the projects supported are not solely dependent on board funds. Pension funds are understandably reluctant to invest directly in the normally small or medium-sized firms of interest to local enterprise boards, largely because of the high risks and administrative costs that would be involved. However, the board could act as an investment manager on behalf of one or more pension funds, thereby cutting out some of these costs and, with suitable guarantees about returns, substantially reducing the risks. Essentially, this is what the already existing enterprise boards are now proposing to do, though it is too early to know what success they will experience.

From the boards' standpoint, the pension funds would be providing additional financial resources unaccompanied by the political constraints or conditions that might be associated with local authority money, though of course there would always be some conditions imposed. Some boards may wish to provide a certain proportion of their funds on a non-commercial basis, to promote some non-profit objective such as employment maintenance or expansion. It is unlikely that pension fund money could or should be used in such a way, since such funds usually have a duty to make profits in order to meet future pension obligations.

As matters stand at present this use of pension fund resources would have some local significance, but in national terms it would hardly be noticeable unless many areas set up their own enterprise boards (aside from the few already established). Nevertheless it could help to remind financial institutions that in the very long term, their success depends on profitable real investment. Although someone obviously has to hold the existing stock of financial securities, and ideally on terms which create favourable conditions for new issues to finance additional investment, it is the new investment itself which generates income and employment. This activity in turn generates further income for the pension funds, provided that the real returns are sufficiently high. This use of pension fund money could be viewed as one small step towards the socialisation of investment, on which we have more to say in the next chapter.

It does, however, raise the question of whose pension funds would be employed in this way and precisely how the money would be channelled to the enterprise boards. If the boards' activities are seen to be commercially successful, then in principle there is nothing to prevent pension funds from voluntarily investing some of their resources in such ventures on just the same basis as they would invest anywhere else. On the other hand, if the commercial viability of board-financed investment was not so assured, either because of bad luck, poor investment choices, or the pursuit of non-commercial objectives, then pension funds would not normally supply any resources unless they were compelled to do so by legislation. Whether it would be proper to apply compulsion in this area is considered fully in the next chapter, in relation to discussion of a possible National Investment Bank, since the same issue arises again there.

The next proposal is much more substantial, at least superficially; it would involve either nationalisation of the clearing banks, or some other means of extending state ownership of the banking system. There are several reasons why such measures might be regarded as desirable, such as:

(1) Strengthening government control over the banks' lending priorities and criteria;
(2) To encourage the provision of long-term loans to support the government's industrial policy;
(3) To ensure that the public sector received a higher proportion of the bank profits attendant on the power to create credit;
(4) To weaken the political influence of the 'City', as against 'industry', over the management of the economy;
(5) In the case of partial nationalisation, to weaken the monopoly power of the existing major banks.

If the provision of long-term loans (point (2)) is emphasised, then it may be enough merely to nationalise some or all of the major merchant banks, while the first three points considered as a whole apparently favour a wider-ranging nationalisation, encompassing the clearing banks. However, it is worth pointing out here that the provision of long-term loans to industry would be a form of financial intermediation which could be undertaken by the government itself without nationalising any banks at all. The government simply needs to borrow by selling gilt-edged securities and re-lending the proceeds to industry, as already happens occasionally. If such transactions became more frequent or came to involve a wide range of branches of the economy, then, effectively, the Industry Department would develop a banking section to manage the transactions. In time, it might prove expendient to hive off this section to form a new National Bank, a proposal discussed fully in chapter 7. In the meantime, let us review the principal arguments pertaining to bank nationalisation and consider how all the above points ((1) – (5)) could be accommodated by measures falling short of outright nationalisation.

First, the Bank of England has some powers to issue guidelines to the banks concerning the kinds of loan they should favour, according to criteria such as sector, term of loan, and so on. With at most some modest extension of these powers, points (1) and (2) above (and hence the point about credit guidelines based on a plan, mentioned on p.197) could be met without any nationalisation. Also, even after nationalisation, the banks would still be functioning in a predominantly private sector, market-oriented economy and this would put severe constraints on how they could be managed. Indeed the recent French experience suggests that in order to retain the confidence of the business community, nationalised banks might be obliged to operate even more conservatively than previously. So it may be highly unrealistic to expect a substantial change in the banks' behaviour to result from nationalisation (see Cobham, 1983).

Secondly, the point about the public sector's share of bank profits (point (3)) could be satisfied through a new tax. Alternatively, and I think preferably, banks could be permitted to pay interest on current accounts so that competition between financial institutions took place on a more equal basis; this in itself would reduce bank profits by undermining the banks' present unduly privileged position in our financial system, and would be effective provided that it was accompanied by measures to allow other financial institutions, such as the Building Societies, to offer a much wider range of banking services.

Thirdly, it would be foolish to ignore the fact that nationalisation of any kind is not a policy which would be politically popular in Britain today. Many people regard the performance and behaviour of our existing nationalised industries as disappointing and would not therefore support further nationalisation under similar conditions. Moreover, the banking unions themselves have made a number of policy statements opposing nationalisation of the banks, and it would be hard to proceed without staff co-operation. However, if an alternative institutional framework could be devised that met the main deficiencies of the existing arrangements, further nationalisation might attract wider support.

Fourthly, nationalisation of the banks would be an enormous legal and administrative undertaking which, if pursued in a Parliament that was also seeking to develop an economic planning system, could divert considerable amounts of government attention and energy into relatively uproductive channels. In addition, since bank nationalisation is a well-defined and fairly dramatic operation, it would be all too easy to present it as a major step on whatever socialist path the government was pursuing; it could even serve as a substitute, or smokescreen, for action in other less tractable, but more important spheres.

Lastly, as emphasised in the previous section compensation would have to be paid if the banks were taken over. Although only paying for a transfer of assets, the required compensation could hardly be paid without raising the PSBR in the year of acquisition, or in some specified future year if payment was deferred. In either case, this would almost certainly raise interest rates temporarily or delay their fall. Overall, therefore, I do not accept that bank nationalisation is either necessary or even a helpful precondition for a successful planning system.

Apart from the above economic arguments, point (4) referred to a political reason for bank nationalisation. Such an argument is based on the claim that in the last couple of decades, the 'City' has been able to exercise undue influence on British economic policy as compared to that exercised by industrial interests. However, under present international monetary relationships, neither the rate of interest nor the exchange rate are completely under the control of the British government, or indeed of the 'City'. Consequently, however influential the 'City' may actually be, and this is certainly not an easy matter to evaluate objectively, it is not at all clear why bank nationalisation should change anything essential; in particular, it would not give the government greater control over the exchange rate or interest rates.

The final point referred to partial nationalisation, to weaken the clearing banks' monopoly powers. The same effect could actually be achieved more straightforwardly by merging the National Savings Bank and the National Giro-bank into a single State Bank (such a scheme could also include the Trustee Savings Bank, TSB). This would avoid extensive political and legal disputes about which private sector bank to take into the state sector ,and could be implemented very rapidly. In practice, it would only gradually affect the behaviour of the clearing banks through competitive interaction (e.g. if the State Bank paid interest on current accounts), so a convincing case for a merger would need to be based on the administrative economies and other savings that might result.

This completes our rather sceptical analysis of nationalisation proposals within the financial sphere. The third proposal concerned the formation of a National Investment Bank, and consideration of this is deferred until the next chapter since it involves a new institution. The final proposal, issuing credit guidelines to financial institutions, based on a national plan, would have to be implemented whatever view was taken of the nationalisation issue that we have just investigated. Guidelines could be provided in two main forms, namely:

(1) Quantitative controls: limits on the volume of credit which the financial institutions as a whole, or particular institutions, may devote to specified purposes within a specified period
(2) Price-type controls: interest rate subsidies or partial capital grants, at different rates according to the type of investment project concerned.

Given a plan, quantitative controls are the easiest to introduce since the appropriate guidelines follow more or less directly from the plan, However, unless operated very flexibly or in terms of very broad categories of investment they can be too rigid. If quantitative controls are operated strictly, then the outcome will only be satisfactory if the original plan is substantially correct. This is not a defect shared by price-type controls, since these essentially represent judgements about the social, as against the private, costs and benefits of various kinds of investment. In other words, they amount to the determination of what are frequently called *shadow prices* for investment. It is then up to mainly private-sector decision-makers to decide on their demands for the different types of loan on offer. If the plan was correct, then these demands will be in line with the plan's initial assessments, but in case of misjudgements or changes in circumstances, the price-type approach permits flexible accommodation. Hence, in general, it is to be preferred. As far as specific guidelines are concerned, it might be desirable to restrict (or make more expensive) lending to the personal and overseas sectors (on the latter, see Section 6.4), in order to give preference to domestic production of goods and services. This would serve to lower the equilibrium interest rates payable on loans for productive investment, and so would be helpful as part of a general policy to raise the rate of investment. Within the sphere of production, either differential interest rates (or rates of capital subsidy) or credit limits could then be used to discriminate between different types of investment, as required.

6.3 Enterprise Boards and Development Agencies

In this section we continue the discussion of enterprise boards briefly referred to in the last section, and also cover their counterparts at regional or national level, the development agencies (or planning agencies as they were called in Chapter 5). The last few years have seen the establishment by various local authorities of a number of enterprise boards; the best known of these are probably: GLEB (Greater London Enterprise Board, established by the GLC in 1982); and WMEB (West Midlands Enterprise Board, established by the West Midlands County Council in early 1982). Other councils, such as Sheffield, have formed similiar bodies, though, since the idea is quite new, it is not surprising to find that the detailed arrangements vary from place to place.

(Much of the discussion of local enterprise boards is based on GLEB amd WMEB working papers. See also Blazyca (1983, ch. 5) and for a critical review of the National Enterprise Board, see Redwood (1984, ch. 5).)

In all cases, however, the strongest motivation for establishing enterprise boards has been the alarming rate of local job loss, especially in branches of manufacturing, coupled with the realisation that the central government itself was unwilling to act to expand the economy by applying more conventional macroeconomic instruments. Thus the formation of the boards has been associated with a very specific political conjuncture. This involved a Conservative government at national level, wedded to monetarist principles of economic management which prevented it from responding to high and rising unemployment by raising government spending or cutting taxes; and Labour-controlled authorities determined to do something about the problem. Given this background one wonders whether the same local initiative would have been exercised in the presence of a Labour government.

Enterprise boards have typically been set up as limited companies, substantially independent of the relevant local councils in their day-to-day operations, though normally with some council members on their management board or board of directors. In addition, the boards report to their councils from time to time. They seek to promote job-preserving or job-creating investment in their own local authority areas, investing mainly in existing companies judged to have reasonable growth prospects in manufacturing and 'productive' services. To enable them to do this, the boards receive funding from their founding authorities in the form of annual grants. There are some legal constraints on the power of councils to use ratepayers' money for such purposes (and, indeed, government money via the rate support grant), but so far the boards have operated on such a small scale that the constraint has not been effective. Nevertheless, this problem explains why some boards have been exploring the possibilities of alternative sources of funding such as contributions from pension funds, as outlined in the last section.

The boards use their financial resources to provide loans or grants to companies in need, or to acquire a share in their equity capital. Normally, a particular investment would only be supported in conjunction with other financial institutions such as the banks. For instance, the WMEB prefers to provide less than 50 per cent of the new finance put into a company, and up to the first quarter of 1983 its participation had actually averaged under 30 per cent.

According to WMEB policy statements, its investments will normally be in existing companies with over 100 employees, operating within the West Midlands. Finance will be supplied to support growth and expansion; financial restructuring; management buy-outs and demergers; and mergers and take-overs. As far as possible the funding is set up to allow subsequent realisation as projects develop and additional sources of finance become available; this approach allows the board to support more projects in a given period, as at least a proportion of its resources assume the form of a revolving pump-priming fund.

Before supporting a company, the board requires detailed information about the company itself (finance, marketing, product-mix, technology, staff, legal position, etc.), its proposed project, and the branch within which the project will operate (ownership and market structure, competing products, strategic considerations, etc.). Whenerever it provides substantial new funding to a company, the WMEB appoints a director to the company's board and requires, at least initially, monthly accounts to enable the company's progress to be monitored closely. In addition, the company is expected to sign a so-called planning and investment agreement with the enterprise board, which imposes a number of financial, operational and accounting constraints on the company, insists on good industrial relations practice and may contain certain special provisions reflecting the position of the individual company; the latter would not usually form part of the published agreement, but would remain confidential to the board and the company. An interesting feature of these agreements is the requirement to obtain local materials and other supplies whenever possible, thus maximising the local multiplier effects of supported projects.

At this early stage in the development of enterprise boards it is not very clear what kinds of project are most likely to attract support. The companies concerned may well be regarded as poor risks by the banks, otherwise they would not need to rely on board funding. Apart from general problems arising from the recession, which, of course, enterprise boards are powerless to counteract, there are other problems facing certain companies where the boards should be able to assist. Inadequate management is the most frequent instance of this; it can lead companies into financial difficulties, even though they have a potentially sound product range and promising markets. Since, as often remarked, financial institutions in Britain tend to be reluctant to get involved directly with company management, especially with small and medium-sized companies, such ailing companies would simply be allowed to go bankrupt and in many cases this is the most natural way of shedding ineffective managers. However, if enterprise board intervention could help to revamp the management structure (including introducing new personnel and removing some of the previous management) and the organisation of these companies and inject some capital, it could give the existing financial institutions the confidence to invest more themselves. In suitable cases, this approach could be preferable to the more usual expedient of bankruptcy.

The above paragraphs have presented a picture of enterprise boards as essentially passive bodies, merely awaiting approaches from local firms for financial assistance. However, GLEB's experience in London suggests the need for a much more active role in the local economy. In the first place, since evaluating a particular project proposal can only be done properly in the context of a survey of the whole branch in which it will be located, it is advantageous for an enterprise board to collect and organise a great deal of general economic information on the local economy. This ensures that when a specific proposal comes forward, the board concerned will be able to mount the necessary branch survey and so respond to the enquiring firm much more expeditiously than otherwise. It might also enable the board to suggest possible trading partners in the local area, thus providing an element of the information system referred to in Chapter 4.

Secondly, as a result of investigating their own local economies, the enterprise boards should be able to identify some areas or branches where investments could usefully be stimulated. In other words, the boards could move into the business of identifying possible projects for themselves, rather than just wait for external proposals. Having identified some projects, it would then be necessary to find, or even create, suitable firms to serve as vehicles for their implementation. It may seem odd to propose such a rôle for local enterprise boards in what is basically a market economy. But as we have emphasised already, market-generated signals are at best imperfect guides to the most desirable pattern of new investment; and even when the 'right' signals are generated, conventional market theories presuppose that some agent or agents will be there to receive them. If there is a lack of entrepreneurs for some reason, or those available simply fail to perceive certain economic opportunities, then it is surely entirely proper for bodies such as enterprise boards to act as I have suggested they should.

Very much the same point could also be advanced in relation to regional or national level development agencies, a group of economic institutions which were set up by the last Labour government under the 1975 Industry Act. The institutions concerned are:

National Enterprise Board (NEB)
Scottish Development Agency (SDA)
Welsh Development Agency (WDA).

The first of these was merged with the National Research Development Corporation (NRDC) in 1980 to form the British Technology Group, and its functions and budget cut back sharply in relation to what was originally envisaged. So in this section I shall discuss the NEB as the 1975 legislation intended it to operate, noting, however, the political and other constraints under which it has functioned in practice.

The NEB is supervised by the Department of Industry, while the SDA answers to the Scottish Office and the WDA to the Welsh Office. All three bodies are essentially investment agencies, though they do not all have quite the same range of activity. In particular, the WDA and SDA both invest in advance factory building and finance a variety of environmental improvement schemes, as well as investing in existing or incoming companies. The NEB concentrated much more on the latter function, and was also active in establishing or promoting a number of entirely new companies, especially in certain high technology fields, as outlined in Chapter 2.

In practice, only a small fraction of the NEB budget was available to stimulate new investments of the kind expected by its early supporters. The NEB did nevertheless engage in several novel ventures in such fields as computing, electronic office equipment, biotechnology, the manufacture of silicon chips, and so on. Its financial participation was usually a mixture of loans and equity; outright grants were also provided for to a limited extent by the 1975 Industry Act but the NEB always had to bear in mind its overall rate of return requirement, imposed after consultation with the Industry Department. Despite the hopes of some people that it would undertake socially desirable but not necessarily highly profitable investment, the NEB was actually required to earn what was virtually a normal commercial return on its assets.

I have already suggested in the previous chapter, however, that the concept of social need, and hence the unambiguous identification of socially desirable investment, is not straightforward, and is indeed open to a great deal of self-interested manipulation by firms and other organisations submitting project proposals. For this reason, one has to sympathise with the Industry Department's insistence that a clear financial criterion should be imposed instead. Moreover, from the NEB's own point of view, such a criterion, even if arguably a rather stringent one, has the merit of permitting considerable decentralisation of NEB activities from those of central government, thereby helping to de-politicise the investment process. Of course, in any system some of the very largest investments are unavoidably political, and rightly so (e.g. a major airport development). However, on efficiency grounds, and in order to operate a reasonably unambiguous set of general rules and conditions to assist potential investors, the kind of decentralisation that characterised the NEB is indeed desirable.

As hinted above, the basic economic justification for establishing bodies such as the NEB, and its Scottish and Welsh counterparts, has nothing whatever to do with 'social' investment, however that may be defined. Instead, the NEB and similar agencies can act to organise and encourage investment in areas where the private sector is either not performing well for some reason, or where the present organisational structure of the private sector inhibits its perception of certain types of investment project, such as those which cut across existing organisational boundaries or which involve new combinations of markets, products and technologies. This is in line with what was said at the end of Chapter 4, but of course it completely contradicts the widely-held view that planning, public ownership and bodies like the NEB should enable the government 'to replace or control market forces' (Coates, 1980, p. 130). Also, the fact that the private sector is not currently active in some branch does not imply that the returns there need be particularly low; so the requirement to seek a high rate of return on investment need not be incompatible with the adventurous and risky investment policy envisaged above.

6.4 Regulation of International Transactions

Since Britain is a highly open economy, it is essential for any serious proposal concerning economic planning to explain how international transactions should be managed. In this sphere it is important to distinguish between capital flows (short and long term) and current account transactions (imports, exports and flows of profits, interest and dividends). As far as the former are concerned, it is virtually inevitable that any government seriously intending to plan the economy would desire some controls on movements of capital, especially capital exports. At least in the early stages of planning, the government would be seeking to induce or compel some private firms to undertake investments which they would not otherwise choose to do; if this were not the case, then planning would scarcely be more than an attempt to forecast what was going to happen anyway. Such influence over private-sector investment in the domestic economy is all the harder to achieve if firms have an easy option of investing abroad by transferring domestic funds.

An associated reason for seeking to restrict exports of capital is the need to regain some control over British interest rates. In particular, successful control over capital exports would make it somewhat easier for the government to maintain lower levels of interest rates without any adverse consequences for the sterling exchange rate.

The government would not need to be so concerned about capital inflows unless it deliberately sought to restrain investment in some areas: this is surely not very likely. However, it is possible that the government might not wish to accept substantial control by foreign firms in certain key or sensitive industries and it might not be willing to see more profits leaving Britain in the future. On the other hand, restrictions on outflows themselves amount to a restriction on the inflow of capital, since such restrictions decrease the attractiveness of financial assets denominated in the currency concerned. In the long run, of course, flows of interest, profits and dividends depend on earlier policy towards inward and outward capital investments, as well as on exchange rates and current rates of interest here and overseas; so once an effective policy about capital flows has been adopted, there is probably no need for a separate policy to deal with the income flows generated by the capital account transactions.

Unfortunately, while it is quite easy to sketch arguments as above to explain the need to regulate capital account transactions it is extremely hard to devise and introduce effective measures. Until 1979, controls were administered by the Bank of England, but the old apparatus has now been dismantled and it would no doubt take some time to rebuild an adequate control system. If it wished to act quickly, an incoming government that was enthusiastic about planning could always close the foreign exchange markets for a few days while it began to institute new controls. However, such a drastic step would almost certainly be anticipated before an election (depending, of course, on the state of the public opinion polls at the time), leading to substantial outflows of capital and a fall in sterling's exchange rate in the period up to the election. Also, a closure of the market would have to be very brief in order to avoid disrupting normal trading transactions, and to avoid alienating and losing the confidence of the firms and traders whose co-operation the planners would subsequently wish to seek. Hence a new government aiming to introduce controls would have to be well prepared even in advance of the election that brought it to power.

In designing exchange controls, it is important to decide which economic agents are to be subject to them, and which types of transaction would be affected. For both administrative and political reasons, there seems little point in applying controls to private individuals acting on their own account, especially as the net amounts of foreign exchange involved would be quite small. But for producing and trading firms, as well as for the financial institutions, controls would presumably try to discriminate between current account and capital transactions, the latter mainly comprising portfolio and direct investment in overseas assets.The simplest way of operating the controls would then be to split the foreign exchange market into two segments, one for current transactions and the other, presumably dealing at a higher, premium exchange rate in relation to the current market, for capital transactions. In practice this would be quite similar to the system that existed in Britain until the late 1970s: for much of this period, the old system required 25 per cent of investment currency proceeds (from the sale of foreign currency securities) to be surrendered to the official exchange market, and a similar rule might be introduced again.

The long term effects of exchange controls are not easy to estimate. During the earlier period of controls it proved possible for firms to finance direct investment abroad either by selling overseas securities or by foreign borrowing, and such operations might well have reduced subsequent flows of profits or dividends into Britain. However, the controls must also have had some restrictive effect on the ability of companies to transfer British profits overseas and to the extent that they were effective, improved the market for British government securities and helped to hold down domestic interest rates. Nevertheless, it is likely that the net effect was, and would be in the future, quite modest, since firms are sufficiently ingenious to devise ways of evading all but the most stringent controls. As far as an incoming government was concerned, the main function of controls would be to prevent an initial huge outflow of funds by risk-averse companies nervous about the likely effects of a new planning system. Hence as soon as the system came to be established and accepted, it should prove possible to relax the controls.

In connection with controls on capital flows, it is also worth mentioning the experience of France and Italy. Both countries operate fairly strict controls on capital outflows, but at times of financial crisis neither actually succeeds in stemming the outflow of capital. It may be that any effective control of international capital flows would have to be multinational. Finally, note that in the argument so far there has been a presumption that capital outflows attendant on the introducton of a system of national planning would probably be harmfully destabilising. However, capital flows can also be stabilising, and it would be a serious mistake to construct economic policy on the assumption that all such flows are undesirable.

This brings us to imports and exports of goods and services. Actually there is little reason to limit exports except very occasionally when supply to the domestic market would otherwise be inadequate. As far as exports were concerned, the main problem would be to ensure that they continued to rise, especially in the presence of an expansionary domestic policy. Such a policy could hardly exert much effect on output and employment if domestic firms responded by merely switching goods out of their export markets back into the domestic market. If planning, in conjunction with other policies, does bring about domestic expansion, then it is to be expected that Britain's demand for imports of goods and services would rise substantially. This is why it is important to increase the supply of exports at the same time. It also explains why there is widespread support for the view that such a rapid expansion of demand, intended to return us to something like full employment within a few years, should be accompanied by further controls over imports. I presume that the supporters of such controls are pessimistic both about our export prospects and about the likely supply response by British industry to meet the additional demand. Personally, I do not share this pessimism and would not therefore favour the use of import controls as a general instrument of planning; however, they may be justified occasionally. Let us now review the main arguments which have been advanced for and against import controls, and then consider alternative policies.

Import controls could either be general, covering the bulk of traded output, or more selective, in order to protect specific branches of the economy. Thus the Cambridge Economic Policy Group (CEPG) has argued for general import controls for several years, though its most recent publications have become less sanguine about their likely efficacy (see Godley and May (1977), Cripps and Godley (1978), Neild (1979), *Cambridge Economic Policy Review*, various issues). This is because of the severity of the crisis which they argue the British economy now faces. Proponents of the Alternative Economic Strategy (AES) also tend to favour import controls, as does the TUC (see CSE, 1980; TUC–Labour Party, 1982; Aaronovitch, 1981). However, the latter is distinctly eclectic in that it supports a depreciation of sterling to improve competitiveness, an import deposit scheme and both general and selective import controls.

None of the supporters of controls expects the volume of imports to be cut back; instead, the object is to ensure that only a modest share of any increase in domestic demand should be provided by imports, the assumption being that without some non-market form of restraint imports would rise very sharply, causing balance of payments problems well before full employment had been restored (e.g. CSE, 1980, p. 87). Moreover, the fact that imports would not actually decline suggests that our trading partners would not have an incentive to retaliate by restricting our exports to them (Cripps and Godley, 1978).

Now, controls could either be introduced as a general tariff on the relevant category of imports, presumably manufactured and semi-manufactured goods, in the main; or the foreign exchange made available for the controlled imports could be auctioned; or individual product quotas could be determined administratively. According to calculations carried out by the CEPG, the level of tariff required for the first method could be quite high, over 30 per cent in earlier computations, and exceeding 50 per cent in more recent ones; Scott *et al.* (1980), in their comprehensive critique of this policy, also showed that the required level of tariff would increase over time, reaching 100 per cent by 1990. Such high tariffs could clearly allow domestic prices to rise very sharply. To counter the resulting inflationary pressure, the CEPG recommended that other indirect taxes such as VAT should be reduced so that the overall price level would be virtually unchanged or even fall slightly. However, relative prices would obviously change and this would stimulate changes in the patterns of domestic production and demand. To the extent that relative prices were originally aligned with marginal costs, these adjustments are bound to involve losses of consumer welfare. But the advantages of this method of control are its administrative simplicity, and the fact that firms and households responding to it would be doing so in full knowledge of the prices they faced. On the other hand, given inevitable uncertainties about the elasticities of demand for various types of imports, the government would have to accept some uncertainty about the overall impact of its policies on the trade balance. The standard rate of tariff could be adjusted from time to time to keep the trade balance satisfactory.

The second approach avoids uncertainty for the government by predetermining the amount of foreign exchange to be spent on controlled imports. Any risks are now borne by the private sector, since the domestic price at which these imports can be purchased becomes uncertain, and probably variable. Apart from that difference, this method shares with the first one the virtue of administrative simplicity.

In contrast, the third approach of setting individual product quotas is administratively cumbersome, involving numerous separate decisions, each requiring expert judgements about the products and markets concerned. On the positive side, one could argue that such controls would save foreign exchange while ensuring supplies of 'essential' products. But against that, there are the practical difficulties of judging what is essential and determining priorities in a situation where, realistically, most of the civil servants operating the controls would possess hardly any detailed knowledge of the products being controlled. Consequently, they would be open to special pleading from firms and consumer organisations and, as the experience of many other countries suggests (e.g. Eastern Europe and many developing countries), the whole system of import controls could easily become both highly politicised and highly corrupt. In such circumstances it is doubtful whether any general economic principles would exert much impact on the pattern of these controls.

Hence, of these three forms of control, I think the first is to be preferred both on the grounds of its simplicity and convenience, and because it provides the private sector with unambiguous market signals about the adjustments required in the economy. Nevertheless, critics of general import controls frequently argue that a general devaluation would be more appropriate, since it provides some positive stimulus to exports and avoids the relative price distortions associated with controls; this is an alternative also considered by the CEPG. Similarly, critics of selective controls would argue that a temporary subsidy to domestic production in the branches concerned would be a superior policy, since it has the same stimulating effect on production, while avoiding the consumption distortions associated with controls.

Nevertheless, the CEPG argue that general import controls would be associated with a lower domestic inflation rate and a more rapid growth of employment than the devaluation alternative; moreover, that to be effective, the required devaluation would have to be so large as to make retaliation by other countries a virtual certainty, whereas retaliation would be much less likely with controls. This claim about retaliation is considered further below, while here we outline the general argument over controls without worrying about retaliation. Several recent studies have taken a highly critical view of the CEPG analysis, including Scott *et al.* (1980), Collyns (1982), Greenaway and Milner (1979), and Greenaway (1983).

As Collyns points out, the CEPG analysis is not based on a conventional competitive model of the economy. Instead of competitive pricing, domestic producers set their prices by applying a mark-up to lagged current costs. In addition, the labour market is characterised by real wage resistance, in the sense that workers have a 'target real wage' which they are able to achieve by demanding increases in the money wage to compensate for expected price increases. At the same time there is domestic unemployment, with the real wage exceeding its equilibrium level. Within such a model, it is clear that devaluation is ineffective since it cannot bring about a permanent change in the relative prices between domestic and foreign goods. Controls can, however, have long term effects and can, in particular, expand employment through distributing income from profits to wages, as well as through terms of trade effects. Unfortunately, the key assumptions of the CEPG model are questionable, the expected effects on employment may be quite small, and in most cases there are alternative policies which can be expected to perform better. Finally, an implicit assumption underlying the whole CEPG approach to the analysis of import controls is that the balance of payments is the principal constraint inhibiting the British government from promoting rapid expansion. This, too, is very much open to question, since in my view fears about accelerating inflation as the pressure of demand increases are the more effective constraint on expansion at present; such an effect, via some form of Phillips curve, is excluded from the Cambridge model, yet it raises an issue that simply cannot be neglected in a serious analysis of economic planning, namely incomes policy. Some possible approaches to this question are investigated in the next chapter.

Even if the CEPG assumptions could be accepted, their conclusion concerning redistribution of income from profits to wages is not. It is true that such a redistribution increases the demand for domestic output and hence employment, given the relative price changes brought about by controls, but this is only a short term effect. In the longer term, aside from inflationary problems which are not convincingly dealt with in the model, there is the difficulty that future growth depends on investment; and as argued in Chapter 4, private investment can hardly be expected to rise substantially without a concomitant increase in profits. Consequently, it is hard to take seriously a policy which entails redistribution away from profits.

What gives proposals about import controls their plausibility and appeal is the commonplace observation that import penetration in many branches of British industry has risen sharply in the last couple of decades. Thus it is tempting to believe that further expansion will merely generate further import demand and have little or no effect on domestic production: hence the need for import controls, to prevent this from happening. However, since overall trade has remained more or less in balance, it follows that exports have risen *pari passu* with imports, with the result that much higher proportions of the domestic output of many industries are now exported, than in the past. As a result increases in domestic production have been associated with both higher imports and higher exports so that at the aggregate level, it is not possible to sustain the argument that import penetration has *caused* declines in output and employment, with its corollary that import controls offer an appropriate remedy. At most, one could accept that rising import penetration has been a symptom of slow growth in the economy: so a limitation on additional imports tackles the symptom without addressing the underlying problem. For this reason, it could help to perpetuate the problem by protecting those industries experiencing the most serious difficulties from further decline, while doing little to stimulate productivity improvements or, indeed, more radical forms of adaptation such as exit from the industry (cf. the extremely interesting discussion of adaptation to competitive pressures faced by developed countries, presented in Wolf, 1979).

I assume here that the underlying and apparently persistent problem here is Britain's declining ability to compete successfully in world markets. For a few years Britain's competitiveness fell more quickly than long term trends would have suggested, largely as a result of a strong and rising pound sterling as Britain became self-sufficient in oil. Although oil has undoubtedly contributed significantly to Britain's income, the ensuing displacement of large parts of our manufacturing industry has led to rapid increases in unemployment. Over a longer period, however, the British relative decline has more to do with our failure to improve productivity as rapidly as our principal competitors have been doing, and a lack of product development, innovation and new investment in many branches. Differential productivity alone could be counterbalanced by appropriate shifts in the sterling exchange rate but what has happened in the British case is not remediable in such a simple way. For in most areas of manufacturing, trade takes place in broadly similar products; economies of scale ensure that different countries choose different specialisations within each product range and produce different qualities of output. In Britain, we seem to have slipped down towards the lower end of the quality range in many product groups, leaving us open to competition from an increasing range of countries unless a considerable amount of effort is devoted to modernisation and re-equipment. Even when we have concentrated on the high end of a product range, the British response has sometimes been astonishingly complacent. A spectacular instance of this is the demise of the British motor cycle industry, which began with Japanese competition in small machines, a market from which Britain rapidly withdrew. But when the Japanese came along with superior large machines, there was nowhere left for the British industry to retreat to, and little possibility of active competition since hardly anything had been spent on R & D and product design.

In this context it is not clear how import controls alone could contribute towards a long term improvement in Britain's position.

However, import controls combined with a substantial increase in investment directed towards the modernisation of our more traditional industries, as well as towards some completely new industries or activities offers somewhat better prospects. This is the kind of combined policy favoured by the TUC and the Labour Party before the 1979 election. It could succeed, but I think we should appreciate the substantial risks it entails.

First, it is unreasonable to expect much beneficial change to occur in less than five or ten years, so we should have to persist with the policy for a long time; it is certainly not a short-term panacea. Secondly, to support the policy one would have to be convinced that the government, or its various specialised agencies, was able to make better judgements about certain kinds of investment than the private sector. Although evidence to date on this point is somewhat mixed, and some mistakes are inevitable, much of the argument of Chapter 4, and to some extent Chapter 5, was intended to justify such a belief.

Thirdly, there is a real risk that as a result of political and economic pressures the government would be unable to restrain itself from using the planning machinery for short term employment protection, shoring up old industries that should be encouraged to die and inhibiting change rather than fostering it. In a sense, this is reversing the position analysed in Section 4.3. There the problem was one of short-term macroeconomic policy conflicting with longer term planning decisions, whereas now the problem is more the use of planning to ameliorate short term economic difficulties to the detriment of future efficiency. Finally, import controls are very much a two-edged sword: they confer protection and thereby redistribute profits in the short run towards protected branches, but their longer term effect depends on how these profits, plus any additional government assistance, are used. It also depends on how wages respond to the higher prices of protected products. In industries that are already dynamic and profitable, one can expect substantial additional investment, and rapid technological change and productivity improvement to ensue, making their products increasingly competitive on world markets; this is a picture that might apply to much of Japanese industry, for instance. In sluggish or declining industries, the short-term gains might simply be consumed, possibly by the workers themselves if high costs are tolerated and wages are allowed to rise; and this is not an unrealistic view of parts of British industry. This latter situation would soon lead to lobbying to secure the extension or even strengthening of the initial protection. If this represents an accurate appraisal of the attitudes and behaviour of British management, then the prospects for import controls to be beneficial in the long run, even when combined with the proposed new planning framework and limited direction of investment, cannot be very great. Some fundamental changes in attitudes are essential, and this might be an area where proposals for increasing workers' role in management, such as those discussed in Chapter 5, could be instrumental in bringing it about.

If Britain did nevertheless impose import controls, the question of retaliation by other countries has to be seriously considered. Probably the degree of retaliation would depend on how extensive the controls were, in terms of the products or product groups covered, and the particular trading partners most severely affected. It is clear, however, that any move towards comprehensive controls on imports violates EEC trading arrangements as well as GATT rules. By many countries, such an abrogation of Britain's past liberal trading practices would be seen as a dangerous precedent, perhaps stimulating a downward slide into a world of managed, and possibly declining international trade. Given this possibility, the CEPG argument that there would not be any retaliation because Britain's imports would not actually fall seems to me quite unconvincing. Moreover, it forgets that many of those who export to Britain have become accustomed to see their trade volumes increasing and will have invested with this expectation. So in the face of British restrictions, these companies would have to seek other markets for their goods and services. One way of facilitating this would be for the countries concerned to import more from other countries instead of from Britain, the resulting goodwill from these countries, and their improved trade balances, easing access to their markets. Unfortunately, since there are very few products in which Britain possesses a monopoly of expertise, and since Britain's main export markets are the countries whose exports to us are also the largest, we would inevitably be highly vulnerable to this kind of substitution.

In this section I have so far concentrated on outlining some of the principal arguments against import controls. Against these, it is frequently observed that in the period since the Second World War, those countries have developed most rapidly, and most successfully, which have apparently done so behind a background of controls limiting external access to their domestic markets. Also, such countries have typically experienced an active, interventionist approach to industrial policy by their governments, as discussed in Chapter 3 for the particularly interesting instances of France and Japan. Thus the combination of policies is apparently not unlike that favoured by the TUC and the Labour Party for Britain.

Some of the arguments against controls appear to assume a world of substantially free trade with little or no government intervention, in which British trade controls and industrial policy would have to be regarded as fundamental departures from the basic operating principles of the system. To the extent that this is an oversimplified and inaccurate picture, the arguments presented earlier may lose some of their force. By operating on free trade principles, Britain may risk having its industrial policy determined by default, in other words, leaving us to produce whatever other countries – new and old competitors – have positively decided not to produce for themselves. Thus Britain could be squeezed out of many traditional markets, as is already happening rapidly in steel and shipbuilding among many other branches, and could be prevented or discouraged from entering newer branches based on the most recent technological developments.

As noted above, this kind of outcome can also be explained in terms of a loss of competitiveness, rather than as a result of active government policies elsewhere. However, it is likely that the latter explains at least part of the trading difficulties experienced by Britain in recent years, and meeting these policies with an adequate response almost certainly involves government intervention in industrial policy here, too. Nevertheless, it would be absurd to place all the blame for Britain's economic problems on allegedly unfair actions on the part of more successful competitors. Hence much of our earlier case against general import controls continues to hold good, though there may sometimes be an argument for selective controls, in the light of the above discussion.

Thus as far as institutions are concerned, what this section entails can be summarised quite simply. The first requirement is the reintroduction of some mechanism for controlling capital exports, but bearing in mind the qualifications, and practical difficulties alluded to above. The second is some organisational arrangement, presumably based in the Department of Trade but with close liaison with the EPA (and the National Investment Bank if such an institution were established (see Section 7.1)), for restraining imports in the small number of instances where some control can be justified. These would be branches of industry where the planners judged that competitiveness could be assured, following a programme of modernising investment. Industries where that condition does not hold should not be protected. Finally, the question whether temporary production subsidies to the branches concerned would be preferable to import controls needs further analysis; often, it is likely that they would be, as we argued above.

7
Institutions: Proposals for Change

Continuing the discussion of institutions, this chapter makes some concrete proposals for new institutional forms intended to facilitate the successful operation of a planning system in Britain. The consideration of particular types of institution is preceded by some elucidation of the principles and problems of the planning system that call for such an institutional solution. The first section investigates national level institutions, with the emphasis on the investment process. This emphasis is justified partly by earlier arguments about the role of investment in promoting growth and restoring full employment in Britain, and partly by my view that an important aspect of planning is its role in socialising the investment process. Section 7.2 briefly reviews a variety of lower-level institutions that may be introduced, developing out of the earlier Sections 4.4 and 5.2. Finally, Section 7.3 reviews a major field of contention in British economic policy-making, namely the regulation of prices and wages. In the past, inflation has been sustained by social conflicts about distribution, especially the profit–wage distribution. These conflicts have been suppressed either by prices and incomes policies in various forms, or more recently by the creation of exceptionally high levels of unemployment. But the introduction of planning machinery alone would not be sufficient to eliminate such intense conflict, though sustained higher output might well reduce it. Hence in Section 7.3 it is important to consider what new institutional arrangements might enable the planning system to run the economy at a high level of activity without renewed inflationary pressure.

7.1   National Level Planning Institutions

The Economic Planning Agency shown in Figure 4.1 and the corresponding national level bodies referred to in Chapter 5 have a number of tasks to fulfil, given the view of planning adopted in this book. Principally, they would have responsibility in the area of investment, involving the following tasks:

(1)   Starting from targets for job creation over a number of years, and forecasts about the relationships between the pattern of demand and income levels, elaborate an outline investment plan. This would indicate the total volume of investment required over the coming years, broken down by sector (public/ private) and by a few major branches and types of investment (e.g. construction, machinery and equipment). How such an outline might be formulated is sketched below.

(2)   Negotiating with nationalised industries or their sponsoring ministries, other public sector bodies and with major private firms, to determine the investment they envisaged in the coming period. Inconsistencies between plans might be indicated and resources made available to support investment which existing firms were not currently planning to undertake.

(3)   Assessing individual investment project proposals and arranging appropriate financial packages to fund them; alternatively, supporting organisational changes such as the formation of new firms, or mergers between existing ones, to facilitate favoured investment.

(4)   Arranging appropriate financial inflows to enable the central planning institutions to support investment projects in the areas envisaged in the plan.

The first task is really about *plan formulation*. What is quite remarkable about Britain is that there exists no government agency already charged with the responsibility outlined here. Several bodies make partial forecasts, of course. For instance, the Energy Department must forecast energy demand for far enough ahead to be able to assess the most important energy investment projects, since these can easily have lead times of ten years or more. Similarly, the Transport Department needs to estimate the likely demand for various forms of transport, in order to plan investment requirements such as new motorways, bridges, railways, etc. And the various social service departments (health, education, etc.) no doubt take a view about the investments required in their respective fields, largely dependent on demographic trends and the expected growth in incomes. However, it is most unlikely that these forecasts are at present based on consistent or even broadly compatible assumptions.

More importantly, rather than starting from the overall volume of investment needed to generate a given number of jobs in the economy, they typically start from forecasts of gross national product (GNP) or the relevant individual component of output, assuming policies not greatly different from those currently in force. As a result, it can only be accidental if the levels of investment approved in these areas are those that would be appropriate to a British economy operating close to full employment.

The volume, and to a very limited extent the structure of investment are regularly predicted in the course of short and medium term macroeconomic forecasting exercises like those carried out using the Treasury model. As emphasised earlier, although these forecasts treat investment quite correctly as a component of aggregate demand, the Treasury model (like most others) fails to relate investment to the subsequent expansion of capacity. Admittedly there are sound, empirical reasons for this, in that econometric studies have failed to identify a definite relationship between investment and increases in capacity at aggregate level. It is not clear whether such a relationship could be found in a more disaggregated study. None the less, given the importance of investment for the generation of growth, both in income and employment, this feature makes such models relatively unsuitable for planning purposes.

Thus for planning, we need a new kind of model or, to put it in a way that allows for a less formal approach, growth accounting exercise. Whatever the precise details, this would entail devising new ways of arranging information about investment flows in the economy, to display relationships not currently highlighted, and to meet objectives not at present adequately incorporated into accounting or modelling of the national economy. Developing the required techniques would not be easy, but it is clearly important.

The well-known National Plan for 1964–70 was a useful instance of this general approach, though, as noted in Chapter 2, this particular planning exercise was initiated by assuming that the economy would grow by 25 per cent over the six-year plan period, rather than by making assumptions about the required employment creation. In addition, the technical basis for planning was relatively crude then in that individual branches were merely asked to work out the consequences for their own branch of overall economic growth at the postulated rate. Attempts at co-ordination between branches or the elimination of inconsistencies were limited, not least because of the haste with which the exercise was conducted.

As in the mid-1960s, it can be expected that something equivalent to the old Department of Economic Affairs (DEA) would be needed again if Britain decided to undertake planning. In keeping with the terminology adopted in Figure 4.1, we call this body the Economic Planning Agency (EPA). So the first task for the EPA is to formulate investment plans; however, for these to be effective, the EPA or associated bodies must have additional powers in order to carry out the further tasks listed above. It is these additional powers that differentiate our EPA from the old DEA. Especially in a pre-dominantly market economy like the British, the EPA needs teeth if it is to exert some positive impact on the economy that goes beyond mere exhortation, while avoiding the rapid emasculation suffered by the DEA.

Let us next consider the remaining tasks listed at the start of this section, and the institutional arrangements they appear to call for; then we must check that the proposed institutions can be inserted effectively into the existing set of national-level institutions in Britain. The section ends with some remarks on the contrast between our own proposals and recent ideas from the Labour Party and TUC.

The second task concerned investment *co-ordination*, where it needs to be emphasised that only a limited amount is likely to be necessary. In the normal course of events, market signals and firms' uneven responses to perceived investment opportunities suffice to achieve some degree of co-ordination, though in Britain this may involve an overall volume of investment that the planning authorities (the EPA) would regard as too low. However, in many branches, investment lead times are short, of the order of one to two years, and investors are likely to be responsive to the level of aggregate demand in the economy. Hence there is little to be gained from any detailed central co-ordination from the supply side in such branches; for instance, much of retailing, other small-scale consumer services

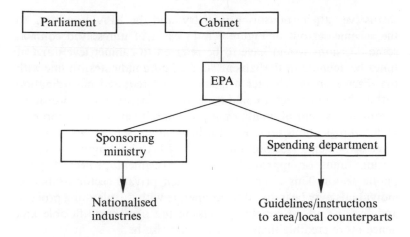

Figure 7.1   *Coordination of Nationalised Industry and other public sector investment*

and parts of light industry, as well as branches making spare parts and components, probably belong to this category.

Other branches, such as the nationalised industries, some other parts of the public sector, and the larger private sector firms whose investments often take several years to put into operation, do call for some co-ordination. As far as possible the co-ordination would seek to avoid periodic investment booms and slumps, with their accompanying harmful effects especially on the construction and engineering industries. Linkages between branches would be taken into account, while the EPA sought to persuade firms in related branches to base their investment plans on compatible assumptions. It is important that the EPA should persuade rather than compel firms to plan consistently since the EPA itself is bound to make mistakes. Hence if firms disagree with its assumptions, they must be free to act accordingly (cf. instances of Japanese firms disagreeing with MITI assumptions, referred to in Chapter 3). Naturally, such firms might not benefit from whatever grant schemes were in force to support the prevailing plan, if they chose to depart from its provisions.

With the nationalised industries, and other spending departments in the public sector, the co-ordination would involve the industries themselves, their sponsoring ministry, and the EPA, according to the scheme set out in Figure 7.1. In cases of unresolved conflict, some decisions would have to be referred to cabinet levels and at times be debated in Parliament, as the figure indicates. In line with the discussion in Chapter 4, some of the required co-ordination within the public sector could be linked to private sector decisions, through a system of conditional pre-commitments. In response to undertakings about private sector investment (see below), or about wage settlements (see Section 7.3), the EPA could agree to release certain funds or approve particular investment projects for the public sector. This is one way in which private sector firms and individuals may be induced to co-operate with the planning process, and has the added benefit of making the plan more flexible and hence more credible than it might otherwise be.

For large private sector firms, a similar scheme would hold except that the relevant ministry would usually be the Department of Industry. Planning agreements could form one way of achieving this co-ordination, although the amount of control exerted by the Department over the activities of private sector enterprises would generally be substantially less than the controls to which nationalised industries and the public sector are subject. Planning agreements are discussed more fully below.

In principle, and this is certainly the case in the centrally planned economies of Eastern Europe, co-ordination could extend beyond investment into other areas such as international trade, the structure of employment and training, and policies to do with research and development (R & D) and innovation. The last chapter suggested that relatively little co-ordination of trade was needed; however, in assessing large projects or branch development programmes which either relied on breaking into new export markets or sought to displace existing imports, it is inevitable that trading considerations would be involved in the planning process. The EPA would have to judge whether the proposed developments could be competitive in world markets, and use this as one of the main conditions for providing support. In cases where firms did not request official support of any kind, however, the problem of assessing competitiveness of the proposed products would remain with the firm concerned, just as at present. Most probably, therefore, only a small proportion of investment would have a substantial trading element of concern to the EPA. Where some co-ordination was required, I imagine it would be carried out in consultation between the EPA, the Department of Trade and the agency or other appropriate body responsible for the branch concerned. As suggested in Section 6.4, it could also involve the National Investment Bank, an institution discussed later in the present section.

In addition, the second task involved the provision of resources for that investment envisaged in the plan which existing private sector firms were not intending to undertake themselves. In the context of a market economy, this brings us to a rather delicate aspect of planning that would obviously have to be organised and managed very carefully. It concerns the resolution of significant deviations between the level and structure of investment stimulated by market signals, and that based on the planners' own calculations and judgements. An easy solution is simply to do nothing; in other words, the planners would publish their plan and then leave it entirely up to the private sector to respond as it saw fit, not taking any special action to secure implementation of the plan except as appropriate in relation to investment in the nationalised industries and public sector. At the opposite extreme, the planners or other government departments could set up new enterprises embodying the additional investment sought by the EPA. This solution *apparently* ensures that any risks resulting from activity contrary to the market signals perceived by the private sector are borne entirely by the government.

However, in view of the conflicting assessments of market demand and the corresponding requirements for new capacity, as between the EPA and existing firms, the latter are certain to feel threatened by planners' direct intervention in investment. For instance, suppose the EPA decided that the country needed more capacity in the manufacture of certain types of ball-bearing and existing firms were unwilling to install extra capacity, either because they expected it to be too costly and to be undercut by additional imports, or they saw no indication that the market was expanding. If the EPA nevertheless goes ahead and sets up a new firm to manufacture ball-bearings then the final market outcome depends on whose forecasts are correct. Should the planners' judgement turn out to be right, then everyone can achieve the sales and profitability levels they were anticipating; if they are wrong, then the original private sector firms will be facing extra competition from the new public sector enterprise, and can expect to lose sales. Consequently, despite initial appearances to the contrary, EPA-directed investment does impose risks on private sector firms especially when it raises the output of something already being produced privately and so it would be surprising if private firms did not oppose such initiatives.

When the opportunity arises, firms also oppose moves by other private companies to invest in their branch. Several instances of this have arisen when multinational companies have been considering new investments in the assisted areas of Britain. Existing firms have sometimes succeeded in persuading the Department of Industry not to support particular development proposals because the new capacity would create unwelcome competition. Just the same situation would arise in the planning context discussed above, and the EPA would therefore have to decide how to respond to this kind of lobbying. One possibility would be to adopt something akin to the French pattern referred to in Chapter 3. This effectively formalises it by setting up a number of councils and committees for various industries, and should increase the chance that the planning agency would come up with investment proposals which are compatible with each industry's views, even when they depart from the industry's own initial position; in other words, they can provide a forum within which some viable and acceptable compromises are arrived at. Needless to say, that is only a possibility if the basic procedures of the planning system are sufficiently acceptable to the private sector that firms are willing to enter into consultations and negotiations in a spirit of co-operation. Also, it is easiest to conduct such consultation with a few large firms in each branch, and it is very likely that smaller businesses would not be involved to a significant extent in these national-level discussions. On the other hand, the branch agencies discussed in Chapter 5 may be able to undertake the kind of exercise envisaged here.

However it is done, experience in many countries and regulatory bodies suggests that there would be a severe danger of regulatory 'capture', whereby the planning agencies supposedly concerned with a particular branch come to be dominated by the firms they should be regulating. Naturally, there is some advantage in having a close relationship between firms and planning agencies in that the latter might then be able to develop a good understanding of the complex issues facing the industry concerned. Nevertheless, too close a relationship can inhibit proper consideration of wider social and economic issues that should influence planning decisions within the industry. Hence regulatory capture both confers benefits and imposes costs. It has not proved easy anywhere to gain the benefits without incurring at least some of these costs.

Returning to our main theme, even with adequate consulation the EPA would sometimes wish to proceed with particular investment initiatives which the private sector was unwilling to support. The option of setting up new public enterprises for this purpose has already been canvassed. Such enterprises would presumably come under the supervision of the Department of Industry, some other appropriate ministry, or a revamped and strengthened National Enterprise Board (NEB), but with initial investment funding provided by the EPA. Another option would be to stimulate private sector co-operation by offering grants or other forms of subsidy for undertaking particular projects, to one or more of the firms already in the branches concerned. Whatever approach is adopted here it is important to emphasise that the public intervention changes both the competitive environment and the incentives of the existing firms, and hence may well induce some changes in their behaviour, including their investment decisions; this is of course one of the aims of the planning system. Hence the EPA and other agencies in the planning system cannot just assume that their decisions would have no effect on private sector behaviour.

Especially where new technology or new products are involved, there is much to be said in favour of the EPA setting up entirely new enterprises. If this induces a competitive response on the part of established firms, forcing them to develop in a similar direction, that must usually be welcome. Organisationally, these new enterprises would actually be established by the NEB acting as a holding company and a suitable management team would have to be recruited either from the private sector, or from other public sector enterprises. The NEB need not hold 100 per cent of the new firms' equity, since some private sector participation may be forthcoming, resulting in a variety of mixed public-private undertakings.

The alternative approach of paying firms grants or other subsidies to induce compliance with EPA investment plans carries the possible drawback that firms might devote too much scarce entrepreneurial effort to devising deals acceptable to the EPA to the neglect of their real market position. As observed in Chapter 3, such a concentration on vertical rather than horizontal relationships still characterises, and hinders, the post-reform Hungarian economy. Also, firms

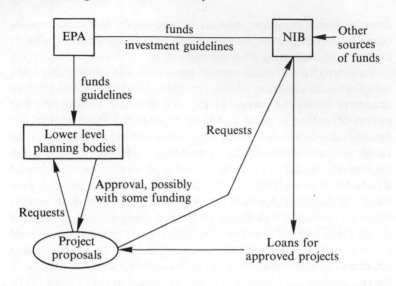

Figure 7.2 *Decentralising the implementation of investment plans*

involved with these EPA investments would naturally seek to make the EPA projects fit in as closely as possible with their existing activities, and this could easily detract from the projects' innovatory features.

Aside from these specific projects which the EPA or lower level planning agencies wish to undertake, with or without private sector co-operation, its investment plan for the economy will envisage investment in several branches over and above private sector intentions, without necessarily taking any firm decisions about precisely which additional projects would be acceptable. Hence the procedures just discussed are evidently unsuitable for implementing such investment. Instead, what is required is a National Investment Bank (NIB) which would be provided with funds and broad investment guidelines by the EPA. In addition, the next level of planning bodies (to be discussed more fully in the next section) would receive some independent funding plus the right to approve projects accounting for definite shares of the available NIB invest-ment credits. In making this proposal, I am therefore presuming that the third and fourth tasks listed earlier would not be carried out by the EPA itself, but would more properly be hived off to a combination of NIB and lower level planning bodies. The diagram opposite, Figure 7.2, indicates the structure I envisage.

The proposed NIB might begin its operations as a specialised finance department within the industry department or, given the structure outlined here, within the EPA. Initially, it would only be dealing with relatively small volumes of business, but as the planning system developed and more investment projects received long term funding from the EPA, it would be increasingly necessary to recognise the specific skills and organisational structure entailed in the finance function by forming a separate institution, the NIB. To a considerable extent, the NIB would be in a competition with the merchant banks and its appearance on the financial scene might stimulate the latter to offer more long term finance than they presently do. In such a case, the NIB could well remain a fairly small institution; correspondingly, some of the NIB functions and activities discussed below could just as well be carried out through the merchant banks, subject to suitable guidelines from the EPA or the Bank of England.

Moreover, although the ensuing discussion is conducted in terms of a flow of potential projects requiring evaluation and, where they satisfy the appropriate criteria, funding, it should not be assumed that setting up the NIB would do anything by itself to increase this flow. For one of the findings of the Wilson Committee (Wilson, 1980) was that the availability of funding was rarely the effective constraint on investment; much the most common problem was simply a lack of projects which the banks and other financial institutions regarded as acceptable risks. Now it may turn out that greater availability of long term funds might make more projects appear somewhat less risky than they are under present financial arrangements. But aside from new projects initiated by public sector bodies, which might themselves stimulate some additional private sector investment, the only effective way of generating a stronger flow of new projects is through a general improvement in confidence about the economy's longer term prospects. Initially, this could be brought about with the help of an expansionary macroeconomic policy, though the caveats of Section 4.3 should be remembered. It is important to expand in such a way that investors are confident that the expansion can be sustained.

It is apparent from Figure 7.2 that I envisage funds for investment projects flowing along two separate channels. The first is EPA, lower level planning bodies, projects; and the second is EPA, NIB, projects. In many cases, projects would only receive NIB funding, while in others they would have mixed funding or occasionally just receive resources via the first channel. At first sight my proposal for two-channel funding may appear needlessly complex, but there is a sound reason for it none the less.

This is the requirement, likely to be an important one in planning practice, to distinguish clearly between what we may term the social and economic aspects of investment. It would be difficult for the proposed NIB to operate in other than a broadly commerical manner, applying substantially the same set of investment criteria to all projects that come before it. Nevertheless, there will be projects which fit into plan guidelines but which fail to meet these given conditions. Such projects may still be accepted if they meet some recognised social need (and I have already referred to the problems involved in defining such needs, and expressed some scepticism about attempts to do so in very fine detail; see Section 5.1). For instance, it may be agreed that investment in certain regions with relatively adverse social or economic characteristics, such as Britain's present assisted areas, has greater merit than an equivalent investment elsewhere; this difference could be reflected in a subsidy to such investment, which would be paid through channel one, remaining funds coming from the NIB on a normal commercial basis. Similarly, it might be argued that investment in a given industry, or serving a particular market, should be stimulated; then again any subsidies or grants needed to support such investment preferences would be paid through channel one. These arrangements clearly allow for some conflict between the commercial criteria of the NIB and broader investment criteria operated by the planners. Projects satisfying both sets of criteria will attract funds from both channels while those satisfying neither can only go ahead on a self-financing basis or using bank credit (though this is unlikely to be available in such cases). Intermediate cases only receive funds from one or other channel.

The advantages of this procedure are twofold. First, in order to facilitate informed debate about the relative costs and benefits of different types of public expenditure, it is essential that investment subsidies should be separately identifiable, rather than being lumped together into general investment funding. The proposed organisational separation achieves this requirement quite neatly.

Secondly by separating out the social from the purely economic aspects of investment, the development of appropriate formal criteria for the social components should be stimulated. Much of the literature on cost-benefit analysis and related issues would no doubt be relevant here, but for application in a planning context I suspect that a great idea of work remains to be done.

Figure 7.2 also shows a second path for funds to reach the NIB. Once established with the basic aim of supporting the implementation of EPA investment plans, it would make sense to encourage the NIB to seek additional funding to allow it to operate in a wider sphere, while still restricting itself to providing investment finance. For example, the State Bank we referred to in the last chapter, formed by merging the Post Office Giro and the National Savings Bank, might wish to invest some proportion of its deposits in the NIB, as might a number of pension funds.

This is a convenient point to remark on Labour Party and other views about pension funds and the NIB (see FISG, 1982). The Party apparently believes that the funds should be able to purchase so-called NIB bonds bearing a guaranteed rate of return. Presumably, any failure by the NIB itself to meet this rate of return would be accommodated by exchequer funding. This contribution to the NIB, together with the smaller ones to the local enterprise boards discussed in the last chapter, mean that pension funds would be contributing a significant proportion of their resource to finance new investment. However, given the guarantees about returns, the NIB bonds would be regarded as very much the same as other government bonds by the institutions, and they would naturally be equivalent as far as the government's deficit and its financing were concerned.

Thus far, the arrangements for using pension fund money seem quite straightforward and sensible. However, others have argued that the funds should be *compelled* to invest in the NIB or some equivalent institution (e.g. TUC proposals that 10 per cent of new pension fund contributions should be channelled through the NIB, a view supported in CSE (1980, pp.75–6)). Personally, I find it hard to see any justification for taking such a position since an offer of reasonably good guaranteed returns should attract the required funds for the NIB without the need for compulsion. From an economic point of view, a serious drawback to compulsion is that it is likely to weaken the NIB's incentives to select the most profitable projects since the bank would be assured of a steady inflow of new funds each year, substantially irrespective of its financial performance.

A more radical proposal would involve the formation of so-called wage-earners' investment funds. Such funds have been debated extensively in Sweden and there was recently some legislation to support them, but in Britain they have not yet attracted much interest. However, George (1983) has argued that these funds, whereby an agreed fraction of the wages bill is invested on behalf of workers, could be a powerful instrument for equality, bringing about a gradual increase in the share of the nation's capital stock owned by the work-force. In this way, they could also act as a powerful stimulus to workers' democracy, since workers should evidently be involved in fund management. Democracy on this basis is, moreover, far less susceptible to accusations of parochialism of the kind referred to in relation to workplace democracy in Chapter 5. However, in Sweden many employers are extremely nervous about the long term implications of the measures enacted there and some firms may relocate overseas to avoid the provisions of the new legislation. At present it is not clear whether this problem is any greater than transfer pricing which can enable companies to declare most of their profits in jurisdictions with low company tax rates.

Without embarking on a full discussion of these wage-earners' investment funds, it must suffice to remark here that in the British case a proportion of the resources accumulated through the funds could be channelled through the NIB. This would not preclude the fund managers from placing the remainder of their resources in projects and firms of their own choosing. Finally, the NIB might attract some funds from other private sector institutions.

So much for our proposals regarding national level planning institutions. Whatever new organisations are established, they must somehow be fitted into the institutional structure that already exists. The result is most conveniently illustrated in a diagram, as in Figure 7.3 below. This shows the Treasury and EPA as the two 'senior' ministries, with a clear division between their responsibilities. The former's sphere of competence would be confined to the regulation of current expenditure by the public sector and, as at present, the management of the exchange rate and short-term macroeconomic policy. The EPA's principal responsibility would be to regulate the volume and composition of investment in the economy, by first formulating and then implementing plans as explained above. At

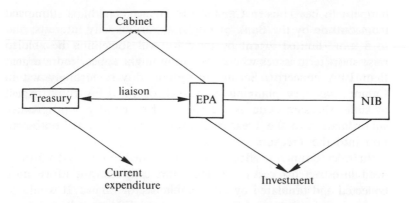

Figure 7.3 *Planning within the government structure*

present there is no single body responsible for investment in Britain; instead, responsibility is diffused throughout the economy, with only modest amounts of co-ordination even within the public sector. Hence when expenditure in general is under pressure, as public expenditure has been in the last few years, it is all too easy for investment to suffer disproportionately.

In view of the long term emphasis of planning, and its focus on investment activity, it makes sense to create an institution distinct from the Treasury, such as the proposed EPA. But it is then essential to delineate very clearly the respective powers and responsibilities of the two bodies, an operation that would not prove to be easy. The problem has nothing to do with any alleged capriciousness on the Treasury's part, as is sometimes suggested, for it is more fundamental, than that. It arises because the convenient theoretical distinction between short term economic management and regulation of the investment process is rather artificial, and frequently breaks down, as stressed in Section 4.3. Naturally, where disputes arose between the EPA and the Treasury, they could be referred to the Cabinet for resolution.

This point conveniently introduces a brief consideration of the political aspects of planning. Politics in Britain, as in many other countries, are characterised by a relatively short time perspective in relation to economic issues. Hence planning, which is essentially a long term activity, is always in danger of being superseded by short term issues, whatever the latest crisis or topical issue happens to be. Thus in Cabinet the Treasury, perhaps supported from outside by the Bank of England, various City interests, and to a more limited extent by the CBI, will sometimes be able to raise short term issues whose resolution might appear more urgent than EPA concerns. So unless supported very strongly within Cabinet any new planning body such as the EPA could expect to suffer the same fate as the 1960s DEA, namely a progressive subordination to the Treasury's priorities, culminating in absorption into the Treasury.

In order to function effectively, the proposed EPA would naturally need unrestricted access to all the economically relevant information collected and tabulated by other public sector bodies. It would be a waste of resources and time to expect the EPA to collect its own data independently. Nevertheless, since much of the data currently reported may not be in the most appropriate form for planning purposes, the EPA might have to devise its own methods of adjustment, as well as initiating, in some cases, the collection of more suitable data.

In addition, bodies such as the NEDC (National Economic Development Council) and its subordinate agencies have a potentially important rôle to play in the planning process. The agencies involved, which were first discussed in Chapter 2, are the office that services and reports to the NEDC (i.e. NEDO, the National Economic Development Office), and the various EDCs (Economic Development Councils, often referred to as Little Neddies) and SWPs (Sector Working Parties) dealing with individual branches or sectors of the economy. Apart from NEDO itself, these bodies are all characterised by a tripartite structure of government, trade union (TUC) and management (CBI) representation. They generate a great deal of interesting information about much of the economy, though they do not cover all branches and are especially weak outside manufacturing industry. These information flows should be channelled into the planning system, to assist the EPA. There is, however, one shortcoming of this source of information that needs to be borne in mind, and this has to do with its tripartite basis. In some respects this might be regarded as a strength of the NEDO system, since there are few opportunities elsewhere for these three crucial interest groups to communicate in a co-operative framework. But it can easily result in reports which refrain from criticising one or other party to the discussions for fear of giving offence or raising contentious issues, and such reports are not likely to be very useful in planning.

Strictly speaking, this completes our discussion of national level planning institutions. However, one item of unfinished business remains from earlier in the section, namely the question of planning agreements. Since these were envisaged as agreements between large firms (mainly private, but not excluding nationalised enterprises) and the EPA, it is convenient to discuss them here. In practice, it is also possible that firms might sign such agreements with branch or regional planning agencies, but this will not call for any separate comment since the issues are just the same.

As we saw in Chapter 2, planning agreements were first discussed in Britain in the 1970s, when it was envisaged that such agreements would be signed with nationalised firms and many of the larger private sector firms as a way of improving the government's control over the economy and, in particular, to encourage higher levels of investment to help protect and expand employment. Hence the agreements were expected to cover employment, output, investment and exports, among other matters. The initial intention was that public financial support (grants, loans, etc.) to firms signing such planning agreements should be strictly conditional on progress in implementing the various sections of the agreement. In other words, there was to be a clear, and in some cases quite strong financial incentive to secure co-operation between firms and government (at that time, the Department of Industry). These good intentions did not find their way into the 1975 Industry Act, which instead emphasised the voluntary nature of planning agreements and provided neither any mechanism for monitoring and securing their implementation, nor any penalties for departing from an agreement. Hence one can hardly feel any surprise at the ineffectiveness of planning agreements in the 1970s.

Estrin and Holmes (1984) investigated the rôle of planning contracts in the French system and found that, at least in their most recent form, they have forced some firms to undergo an exercise in long term planning and allowed the state to get involved with some strategically important firms without any need for day to day interference in management. At the same time, the state has been unwilling to give any funding guarantees extending beyond the first year of the current five-year period, hence undermining the whole concept of a medium term strategy. The fact that the French state cannot itself make longer term commitments suggests that the same might also be the case for individual firms, implying that planning contracts should be subject to revision under agreed circumstances, or that certain objectives should be contingent (Estrin and Holmes, 1984, pp. 20, 21).

In their paper, Estrin and Holmes also ask why private firms do not typically choose to make long term agreements among themselves. Partly it is because they prefer to keep options open and retain flexibility, and partly they are simply ignorant about what they might wish to do in the future. Hence any general case for planning contracts (or planning agreements) must rest on the view that there is some social benefit from persuading firms to accept stronger conditional pre-commitments than they choose to do voluntarily. This social benefit may take the form of better co-ordination of economic activity, especially investment, and perhaps agreement on a sufficient volume of investment to generate more rapid growth than would otherwise have occurred.

Since the legal status of a planning agreement is bound to be pretty weak (one can hardly imagine a government agency suing a firm for failing to fulfil part of an agreement, or indeed a firm suing the government for delaying, for instance, the construction of a new motorway that had been promised), the question of a suitable incentive system to stimulate compliance *on both sides* assumes considerable importance. Without some system, it matters little whether agreements are compulsory or voluntary (aside from the possible waste of managerial time and energy in drawing up an ineffective agreement): planning agreements can hardly amount to anything more than a public relations exercise in that situation. Yet the example of the recent, highly successful Chrysler rescue in the United States, in which successive tranches of the agreed financial support package were made conditional on specified performance indicators, illustrates what can be achieved within a more tightly defined framework. None the less, this kind of conditionality can increase the variance of returns expected by the firms concerned and, to the extent that it compensates for unfavourable outcomes it can weaken firms' incentives to avoid them. What we must conclude, therefore, is that although some form of conditionality is absolutely essential for a system of planning agreements to be effective, it may not be easy to devise arrangements which are completely free from the problems just mentioned. In addition, the need for conditionality means that in practice effective agreements can only be reached with firms which actually require some public funds, either to assist with restructuring, to carry out some especially risky investment, or for some other purpose. Other large firms would no doubt be willing to engage in discussions about investment and so on with government planning agencies at various levels. But without financial levers, the EPA would have to rely on its powers of persuasion to induce such firms to modify their proposed policies: as already noted, the formality of a planning agreement is worth little under these conditions.

To conclude this section, let us look at the relation between the above sketch of my own proposals, and those that emerged from discussions between the TUC and the Labour Party. In fact there is a substantial area of agreement in that, as noted above, we both support the establishment of a National Investment Bank, and recognise the need for a government department to be given formal responsibility for economic planning. In addition, we both favour some form of planning agreement. But the TUC favours the formation of a large Department of Industry and Economic Planning (DIEP) as against my preferred EPA. In my view, there are too many possible areas of dispute between industry and planning for a merger to be wise, unless arrangements could be made to ensure the predominance of the planning function. Moreover, much of the economy's investment has little or nothing to do with industry; it therefore seems more reasonable to detach planning from industry to form a body such as the EPA, capable of taking an overall view of the economy's investment activity. Such a body should also be more acceptable to other government departments, and hence elicit greater co-operation from them, since it would not be open to the accusation that it was unfairly biased in favour of investment in industry. Although industry is clearly very important, I do not think the case for planning is assisted, nor support for it widened, by an approach that emphasises industry to the extent that Labour Party and TUC proposals appear to do (see, for instance, TUC–Labour Party, 1982).

It may be that these proposals are partly modelled on Japan's MITI, whereas my own suggestion is somewhat closer to the French practice; both the Japanese and the French experience of planning were outlined in Chapter 3. I am not convinced that the Japanese approach could easily be transplanted to Britain since its apparent success must be attributed to a number of special factors that do not obtain here. These include a general acceptance by the business community in Japan of quite extensive government intervention, combined with astonishingly fierce domestic competition between the major business conglomerates; frequent movement of senior personnel between business and bureaucracy, which ensures a high degree of concordance and mutual understanding between the two sides; and a variety of other factors which Chapter 3 explains. A system not too remote from the French approach would be much less difficult to introduce here.

7.2 Lower Level Institutions

In this section we can be brief since several of the relevant institutions have already been referred to in the last three chapters and there is no need to repeat what was said there. These chapters have already covered in some detail a range of branch and regional planning agencies and their associated planning councils, as well as local enterprise boards. The British Technology Group (BTG), in its original form of the National Enterprise Board (NEB) was also mentioned earlier. At present this is subordinated to the Department of Industry; but in view of our discussion in the previous section, it might be more appropriately located under the EPA itself.

What other institutions are needed to enable a planning system to work well? In this connection, I would argue that one of the key lessons from East European planning experience is that uniformity of organisational structure is not desirable. It does, of course, have some administrative advantages, especially within a centralised system, but it is unable to meet the special requirements and circumstances of each individual branch of the economy and is generally inflexible, slow to respond to new technological (process or product) developments or market opportunities, and restricts the planners' vision.

In Britain there is little chance that we would ever develop such a uniform planning and production structure, not least because the various government agencies concerned with planning do not possess, and certainly would not be awarded by Parliament, a monopoly of the power to initiate organisational change and development. With the recent exception of Hungary, however, this is just the kind of power held by the branch ministries and central planners in Eastern Europe. By insisting that each branch should operate with a given range of technologies and produce an approved range of products the planners make it difficult for themselves to perceive economically attractive opportunities for change that cut across traditional branch boundaries. This is what I mean by the earlier remark about organisational uniformity restricting the planners' vision; it is a high price to pay for the doubtful benefits of achieving close control over current production.

To minimise such difficulties, therefore, the organisational structure of the British economy should continue to be flexible, responsive to initiatives from all levels of the system, and to include a wide variety of organisational forms. In a rapidly changing and unpredictable world it is impossible to prescribe any particular type of organisation as the ideal model for a given situation, but with a diversity of forms there is at least plenty of opportunity for learning which models appear to work and for developing new organisations or adapting old ones as economic circumstances change. In extreme cases, organisations may simply cease to be viable, and in the economic context, such a failure or inability or adapt normally entails bankruptcy or liquidation.

Thus planning institutions at local level and above would simply have to live with the prevailing complexity: it would be a serious mistake to seek to ease the planners' tasks by imposing a limited set of models on the organisation of production. In practice, much of the information used in planning would come from a relatively few large firms, and most plan negotiations and agreements would involve virtually the same group of firms. Given this, it should not matter a great deal precisely how these firms are organised, what sort of links they establish between themselves and with other, smaller firms, and how they go about adapting to changes in their environment. What is essential is that however they are organised, they should maintain reasonably good communications with the relevant part of the planning system, and should supply information in the form needed by the planners when negotiating over specific investment projects, as we discussed in the previous section. Smaller firms might maintain some links with the appropriate local enterprise board or with a local office of the NIB and might supply or receive information from the information network, but need not otherwise come into contact with the planning system. It is clear from these remarks that aside from those planning bodies listed at the start of this section, and discussed more fully earlier on, the planning system proposed in this book would not require any additional agencies to be established. Perhaps surprisingly, even the regulation of wages and prices might be managed without more bureaucracy, as we explain in the next section.

What remains for this section is to consider the detailed arrangements entailed by the information network proposed in Section 4.4 and, further, to comment on the appropriate division of labour between publicly provided and/or transmitted economic information, and its private provision. It was envisaged that the information network would be established to reduce the transactions costs incurred by firms in the process of identifying suitable trading partners. As indicated earlier, parts of the network already exist as a result of private initiatives organised by bodies like trade associations, as well as through advertisements which either offer to supply certain goods and services, or invite tenders to meet particular needs. How can the government, through the EPA and other planning bodies, assist the private sector to improve the provision of information, bearing in mind the facts that there are rather low upper limits on the volumes of economic and technical information that agents can assimilate and that too much information about potential market opportunities can make investment co-ordination more rather than less difficult?

Several approaches are possible; in the interests of conciseness I merely list them, with brief comments where appropriate.

(1)   Subsidise advertising associated with investment projects or the supply of investment goods; however, the private cost of advertising should certainly not fall to zero. A possible danger is that advertising agencies, trade journals, etc., would just charge higher fees to offset most of the subsidy, though competition between agencies, and the threat of new entry should keep this problem within tolerable limts. The advantage of this approach is that it builds on existing private sector activity and would therefore be quite straightforward administratively.

(2)   Subsidise trade associations and the publication of trade journals. To reduce fears of government intervention in the

affairs of trade associations, it may be expedient to set up a small independent committee to administer the subsidies, the necessary funds and administrative support being provided by the EPA.

(3) Set up a new information network, based on modern communications and data processing technology. This is the most interesting and in the longer term perhaps the most fruitful direction of development. It need not be undertaken as an EPA monopoly, though I imagine the EPA would determine the minimum technical standards and might well be given some licensing powers in relation to private information networks. There is no reason to expect a single comprehensive network to emerge. Instead a series of networks, possibly with some interconnections between them, and each specialising in a given region or a given range of branches of the economy seems more likely. These networks would develop data bases containing information about firms, their major product lines, and investment projects for which they sought a specified list of inputs. At least initially, it would probably be necessary to pay firms a fee for providing information to one of the systems.

Then firms using an information network would be trying to identify other firms looking for products that they could supply. Although set up with the economy's investment requirements in mind, it is clear that the networks could also facilitate trading links between firms even where investment was not involved. To deter a potential flood of casual enquiries in each network, and to earn some revenue to cover the operating and information costs, users should be charged a fee to gain access to an information network. In addition, great care would be needed to ensure that the commercial confidentiality of information suppliers was not breached. Thus even when a network identified a potentially attractive trade between two firms, it should do no more than indicate the identities of the proposed trading partners and the product(s) involved in the transactions. Other details would have to be settled directly between the firms concerned since it is unlikely, with existing technology, that the complexity of detailed contracts could be handled efficiently and securely by the network itself.

The nearest we have to an economic information network in Britain today is some commercial developments based on Prestel, the communications system linking telephone and television that was first developed by British Telecom. It may well be the case that this system could be extended to meet the needs indicated above, though the precise way of doing this would take us into technical matters well beyond the scope of this book.

To conclude this section, I should emphasise that the developments just outlined, even with existing technology, present serious technical difficulties in relation to both hardware and software (suites of computer programs to manage and control the information flows). This is why I emphasised the initial creation of smaller, interconnected networks in preference to a single huge system. Moreover, as with some other issues we have examined, this is an area where there is sufficient uncertainty about future technical developments as well as about the most effective ways of using a computer-based information network, that it would be unwise to impose a standardised specification right from the start. Lack of uniformity also involves some costs, of course, such as the need to write communications programs to enable different networks to be connected together, but the benefits – in terms of experience gained with a range of systems – are likely to be considerable. Eventually, it may well be possible and desirable for all parts of the information system to operate in accordance with an agreed standard.

7.3   Regulation of Prices and Wages

If Britain returned to a state at or close to full employment, whether as a result of the introduction of a planning system or by any other means, there is no doubt that prices and/or incomes policy would be called for to enable that situation to be sustained. In several recent publications, the TUC and Labour Party have both advocated a combination of free collective bargaining to determine wages, together with a Prices Commission to adjudicate over, and presumably restrain proposed price increases. While understandable in terms of trade union and labour movement politics, such a conjunction is not easy to defend in purely economic terms, even when supplemented by the proposed annual national economic assessment, one function of which would be to provide guidelines to assist wage negotiations.

The reports putting forward these recommendations suggested that 'the "free market" is an irrelevance in a modern and complex society' (TUC–Labour Party, 1982, para 7), a view which leads one to expect both wage and price controls to be supported. Hence, the notion that a loosely specified national economic assessment, together with free collective bargaining – whatever that means apart from its rôle as an emotive political slogan – should be the principal means of settling wage rates, is not really in harmony with most other sections of these reports. We shall have more to say about that later on.

As far as price controls are concerned, I am far from convinced that they would be desirable, at least while the great bulk of the UK's productive assets remains in private hands. Consequently, I see little need for a price commission, provided that we retain the existing legislation and institutions concerned with competition and monopoly. The only exception might arise in a few instances of natural or statutory monopoly, where it may be necessary for the EPA to regulate prices. Aside from this, there are several reasons for favouring a general laxity about price controls.

First, much empirical work suggests that a high proportion of product prices are largely formed as cost plus a mark-up, so that controlling a major element of costs such as wages should itself help to restrain inflationary pressure. Secondly, although we have this empirical finding about price formation, it is nevertheless the case that theories of price determination are in a very poor state, and it is likely that any general pricing rules applied by a price commission would contain a substantial degree of arbitrariness. For instance, the observed association between prices and costs is insufficient to indicate the direction of causality: in some cases cost changes would lead to price changes, while in others, market-constrained prices would either determine the costs at which viable manufacturers could produce or, in the short run, would simply determine profitability, with no immediate impact on costs.

Thirdly, in the most typically occurring multi-product firm, when the product mix is changing all the time as a result of shifts in market requirements and technological possibilities the assignment of depreciation and other overhead costs to individual products cannot be done according to any agreed economic principles; instead, it is done using conventional accounting rules. These inevitably impart substantial uncertainty into the measurement of production costs for each individual product, with the result that the relationship between price and cost, even though close for an aggregate of products, might provide little basis for a general price formation rule. Moreover, it is likely that the price–cost relationship will, in any case, vary over the life-cycle of any given product. Again, this impedes the effective application by an external agency of pricing rules, since it may not be easy to judge what stage of its life-cycle a particular product had reached.

Finally if it is accepted, as we argued earlier, that persistent under-investment and low profitability form at least part of the explanation for Britain's slow economic development, then a period of buoyant markets and lax or non-existent price controls might allow profits to rise again. After a lag, this improvement in profitability would help to sustain a permanently higher rate of investment; and given some restrictions on capital exports this would be investment in the domestic economy.

It may be that the pressure on the left of the British political spectrum for strict price controls and the belief in their efficacy, has been stimulated by the view that much of the economy, including the bulk of industry, is dominated by a small number of huge companies, frequently multinationals, exploiting positions of near monopoly. However, the usual implications about pricing policy that might be drawn from such an approach are not well supported. For despite the alleged prevalence of monopoly in British industry, profitability on virtually any reasonable measure has declined catastrophically in the last two decades. Present low levels of profits, though somewhat recovered from the trough of the recession, are nowhere near high enough to finance the increased investment needed to regenerate the economy. Also, profitability in the sectors supposedly more subject to monopoly is not markedly better than elsewhere. While it is true that few branches of the economy meet the classic conditions of perfect competition, most branches, and most individual firms do experience very strong competition or potential competition from a variety of sources, such as firms producing similar products, possible new entrant or imports. Unless these forms of competition are deliberately restrained through active government intervention, such as vigorous import controls or, as in the case of nationalised industries, the award of a statutory monopoly, they should normally be sufficiently strong to constrain prices to socially acceptable levels. Hence except in the occasional instances where these conditions do not obtain, I very much doubt whether a convincing economic case for price regulation by a specially constituted public agency could be made out.

There may, nevertheless, be a political argument for some limited or mild price controls. This would arise in the situation where the government was seeking to introduce a form of control over incomes. In order to secure trade union support, or at least their acquiescence, it may have to offer to control non-wage incomes as well, and possibly prices. However, such controls over prices should be as weak as possible.

Let me turn, therefore, to the question of controlling wages and other forms of personal income. The proper way of doing this depends on the theory one holds of the wage determination process in post-war Britain, and the trade-offs one is prepared to accept in relation to other economically relevant objectives in order to achieve effective control over the level and rate of change of wages.

For the economy as a whole, it is clear that if money wages rise more quickly than average productivity per employed worker then, subject to making a suitable allowance for changes in the exchange rate or in interest rates, the price level must go up. This is essentially what happens during an inflationary process. There is considerable discussion among economists about the damage done to the economy by inflation (e.g. see Bird, 1984). Many of the costs normally identified, especially distributional effects bearing on creditors, debtors and those on fixed incomes, and additional transactions costs resulting from the opportunity cost of holding money, could be remedied by indexing the tax and benefit system, and by allowing interest payments on current bank accounts.

Some other costs are more relevant to the present study and may be less easily remediable. They arise especially when inflation occurs at an unpredictable and varying rate, which is the practically important situation, as compared to the theoretically more tractable and much less troublesome situation of inflation at a uniform rate (or, slightly more generally, inflation that might be at a variable rate, but which is perfectly anticipated by all relevant economic agents). The costs I am concerned about here concern the operation of the price system as an information carrier under inflationary conditions, and the effect on investment decisions (for a critical review of the supposed 'costs' of inflation, see Hahn, 1982b, lecture III).

One such cost results from misperceptions of changing relative prices. Whether there is inflation or not, uneven rates of technical change, shifts in patterns of demand and changes in the extent of competition in various branches all combine to generate constantly changing relative prices. Observation of such changes is important for investment, since it can signal whether some branch is becoming more profitable or another less so. In the presence of erratically varying inflation, it becomes difficult for firms to discriminate between changes in the price level and these changes in relative prices; hence the forecasting required for investment decision-making becomes even more hazardous than usual. A second aspect of the same problem is that firms may find it harder than usual to assess, and forecast for investment purposes, the wage–rental ratio. Hence to the extent that substitution between capital and labour is feasible at any given time, firms would be unsure about the appropriate degree of capital intensity to adopt for new investment projects. In these conditions it is most likely that the additional uncertainty that firms face would discourage some investment, and reduce the quality of what remained. Consequently, it is worthwhile devoting some resources to controlling inflationary processes and, since I have already argued strongly against direct price controls, this inevitably refers to wage regulation.

One can readily imagine several different approaches to wage regulation, with some of which there has been some practical experience; the possible approaches include:

(1)   Reliance on market forces to regulate wages and other incomes;
(2)   Some form of incomes policy which sought to control wage settlements directly;
(3)   National level agreement between government, employers and trade unions about wages guidelines;
(4)   Tax-based incomes policy.

With the exception of reliance on market forces, (1), these all involve some degree of state intervention in the wage determination process, and hence a departure from 'free collective bargaining'.

If one believed that the labour market could be regarded, to a sufficiently good approximation, as a perfect market, then the wage should adjust flexibly to bring about equality between the supply and demand for labour. In most macroeconomic analysis it is the real wage that needs to adjust, but since only the money wage can be determined in labour markets this must serve as the instrument of adjustment. According to this approach, especially when combined with the cost-plus model of product pricing referred to above, both wage and price inflation ultimately stem from excess demand in the labour market. Hence the appropriate remedy is either to cut back the demand for labour by reducing some component of aggregate demand or somehow to expand the available labour supply. In practice, governments are more likely to restrain demand, though on occasion there has been some policy intervention on the supply side as well.

British experience does not appear to support this 'perfect market' view of the labour market. Especially in recent years, but also earlier to some degree, pressure in the labour market has had to fall drastically before wage demands, and the ensuing wage increases, are significantly moderated. This observation is more compatible with theories of labour market adjustment in which bargaining and expectations play a major rôle. The bargaining approach takes the view that workers are organised into groups based on their branch or the nature of their job, for purposes of negotiating with employers about wages. For the most part, these groups correspond to the trade unions in Britain, though it must be remembered that many workers are not unionised at all, notably those in most small businesses and industries where the labour force is widely scattered. In the latter trades, wage settlements are more likely to fit the competitive model, though their equilibrium level will be influenced by the level of settlements reached in wage bargains elsewhere.

In the context of a bargaining model, the effect of cutting aggregate demand and so reducing the demand for labour is supposedly to reduce the bargaining power of workers and hence to yield lower wage settlements. However, the bargaining power of a particular bargaining group depends on a mixture of objective and subjective factors. The objective factors include the current profitability of the firms concerned, wage bargains recently concluded elsewhere, especially by other workers in a comparable category, and the prevailing government policy, if any. The more subjective elements in the bargaining process are aspects of the general economic situation such as the prevailing unemployment rate and expectations about future price increases and the trend of real wages, as well as the profit prospects and the risk of unemployment in the particular industry over the medium and longer term.

Thus the overall unemployment rate is only one of several factors influencing wage settlements and in most instances is not likely to be the major factor. This is why, in a bargaining model, unemployment can reach the present British levels before exerting a significant effect on pay settlements. It makes nonsense of more traditional arguments based upon the now elusive Phillips curve, and suggests that to rely on unemployment to 'cure' inflation, though it will eventually succeed, involves imposing very high costs on the country, in terms of lost output and loss of income to those unemployed. Personally, I cannot believe that the harmful effects of inflation noted above are severe enough to justify such a drastic remedy.

Having suggested that reliance on market forces, method (1), could indeed control money wage increases, but only at an unacceptably high cost in terms of other economic objectives, let us next consider method (2), incomes policy. First of all, such a policy should have a clearly defined aim, namely to restrain the average rate of increase of money earnings. It should not concern itself with broad questions of distributive justice since whatever agreement exists on such issues is already embodied in the prevailing conventional differentials within certain groups of related occupations. There is unlikely to be wide agreement on the proper treatment of the low paid or on general differentials across the whole scale of incomes from work, a point argued forcefully in Layard (1982, ch.8). In addition, available evidence suggests that past incomes policies have had almost no effect on the broader distribution of income, despite attempts to pay particular attention to the low paid or other special groups. Consequently, there is little point in undermining the chances for an incomes policy to work well, by incorporating in it some of these politically sensitive distributional considerations. The only advantage of doing so would be to gain some political support for incomes policy, especially from relatively disadvantaged groups who might otherwise oppose it strongly.

The simplest form of incomes policy confines itself to specifying a norm indicating the approved rate of increase of wages. In practice, for those on salaries this also equals the rate of increase of earnings (except to the extent that various fringe benefits not included within the ambit of the official policy might also be adjusted), while for those on other payment systems the policy merely constrains the relevant basic wage rate. Hence variations in hours worked and the premia payable for work outside normal conditions allow actual earnings to increase by somewhat more or less than the norm even when the incomes policy is successful. Nevertheless, the essential feature of this kind of incomes policy is that, aside from these variations, it maintains the established pattern of relativities and ensures that all personal incomes from work rise at roughly the same rate. It is this characteristic which ensures that such a policy has a reasonable chance of attracting widespread support. Other types of incomes policy in which certain groups are treated as special cases are more problematic unless there is very general agreement as to who should be regarded as special.

In the light of British experience, it appears that wage structures only change very slowly; however, a successful incomes policy evidently prevents any significant change from happening at all in established businesses and this can lead to rapid losses of staff to new businesses in emerging industries where incomes policy cannot initially constrain the wages that can be offered. Moreover, depending on what precisely is controlled by the incomes policy, remuneration packages can shift in the direction of higher fringe benefits (bonuses, holidays, etc.) or better pension arrangements, without affecting basic pay. The efficiency losses resulting from these distortions have to be traded off against the gains from controlling inflation adequately when judging how best to control wages. A much more serious drawback of incomes policy, even when it is supported by legislation, is its reliance on at least the tacit acceptance of the major trade unions and employers' organisations concerned with wage negotiations. All that it requires is a single major bargaining group to enforce a wage claim well above the prevailing official norm and, using comparability arguments, other groups would quickly follow suit, irrespective of the formal legal position. This is the basic problem with incomes policies: they work only as long as they can command support, and embody virtually no effective sanctions to enforce compliance. Consequently, although such policies have on several occasions appeared to work for short periods of two or three years it has not proved possible to sustain the gains.

Perhaps this difficulty could best be remedied by using method (3), an agreement between government, employers and trade unions about wages guidelines. This is certainly what the TUC and Labour Party favour, for they have argued for an annual 'national economic assessment' which would seek to reach agreement on a number of national policies including both the share of national income to be devoted to investment, and wages guidelines for the coming year. The idea is an interesting one and merits much more serious consideration than it has so far received, but it is not without its own political snags. Especially at present, when real wages need to be restrained to allow investment to increase as argued earlier (Section 4.2), it may not be easy for the trade unions to reach the kind of agreement with the government that this approach assumes. Again, it is not too clear what is supposed to happen if a satisfactory agreement cannot be found, so the procedure must be regarded as incompletely specified until this question is answered. However, further study of this potentially attractive approach to wage regulation can only be welcomed.

In the meantime, rather than looking for ways of imposing unenforceable agreements, method (4), the tax-based incomes policy, relies on more conventional economic incentives. Just as with a standard incomes policy, the government would have to determine and announce a norm for pay settlements in the coming year. Firms and their workers would then be free to set whatever wage increase they could agree on, but firms would pay more tax if their wages and salaries bill per employee rose more quickly than the approved norm; conversely, firms paying less than the norm would receive a corresponding subsidy so that the net tax revenue generated by the tax-based incomes policy balanced out at around zero. Rather than relying on high unemployment to weaken the bargaining power of workers, this approach accepts a bargaining model, but sets out to strengthen the employers' side of wage bargains, by establishing a fiscal incentive to resist high wage claims. Its proponents expect that the resulting decentralisation of incomes policy, with each wage bargain reflecting its own special circumstances, should avoid the inflexibilities of conventional incomes policy and help to de-politicise the whole process of wage regulation (see Layard, 1982, and for a more critical view of tax-based incomes policies, Bosanquet, 1983).

There is room for some argument about the appropriate rate of tax to employ in a tax-based incomes policy. A tax of this kind has been applied to Hungarian enterprises with tax rates up to several hundred per cent, whereas British proposals have mentioned much lower rates, usually in the range 30–50 per cent. Since wage agreements typically apply to a large number of enterprises in

Britain (whereas Hungarian agreements are negotiated separately for each firm) and since the ability to pay the tax would vary considerably between them, we should probably have to settle for relatively low tax rates to avoid forcing many firms into unnecessary bankruptcy. At the same time, this probably means that such a tax would only have a modest beneficial effect on the level of wage settlements.

Within the public sector, of course, income determination is inseparably connected with politics. But even here it should be possible to assure the unions concerned that public sector wages would not be permitted to lag behind their private sector counterparts. With such an assurance, workers in the public sector would automatically share in the general growth of the economy and would be discouraged from striking to gain wage increases in excess of those won in the private sector. To enforce this position on relativities, something like the present cash limits systems but with a separately identified limit on wage and salaries spending for each heading of public expenditure would be needed. Then public sector wage increases above the going rate indicated by the cash limits would result in job losses and cuts in services. However, in operating this type of policy there are some practical difficulties, especially in judging the levels at which to set cash limits. The levels should have some connection, not necessarily identity, with the private sector norm forming the base for the tax-based incomes policy, and where suitable output measures are available, may also depend on expected productivity improvements.

Tax-based incomes policies are not free from drawbacks. They introduce some distortion into the labour market, for example. Thus their average wage basis is likely to encourage firms to employ relatively more unskilled and lower paid workers, in order to enable them to pay more to their skilled workers without incurring any tax liability. However, since it is the unskilled who are suffering most in the present recession, many people would find this an acceptable distortion. Similarly, it may be that firms wishing to pay high wages are also those that should be doing more investment, yet the tax-based incomes policy would impose a higher tax liability on them and so reduce their net cash flow. On the other hand, if they really have access to worthwhile investment opportunities, then external finance should be available so it is doubtful whether much efficient investment would be discouraged.

Finally, it would be incorrect to claim that a tax-based incomes policy could eliminate inflation altogether. However, to an extent depending on the tax rates built into the system it should, for any given level of unemployment and set of expectations about future rates of inflation, reduce the level of wage settlements. Hence the level of activity at which the economy can safely be operated without generating ever-increasing inflation is raised, and this is obviously an important benefit. Moreover, it is a benefit purchased at much lower cost, and with greater certainty, than would normally be possible with the other methods of income regulation discussed above. Consequently, although freely conceding that better policies might one day be devised, and that in practice one may need to apply a rather complex mixture of policies, it seems to me that an anti-inflation policy that can be positively recommended is method (4), the tax-based incomes policy.

Institutionally, this has the further advantage that it should be fairly easy to implement, especially if its operation was initially restricted to that subset of firms with, say, over 100 employees on some specified date such as the start of the fiscal year. It is true that such a provision imposes some additional administrative burden on the Inland Revenue. It also introduces an element of inequity into the tax system as between producing units of different sizes, and might even set up some incentive for demergers to take place. But such effects are unlikely to be very large and in any case the relevant tax office would already be keeping track of mergers, demergers and other organisational changes affecting firms, in order to implement the taxes that already exist. I would envisage, therefore, that a new tax on wage increases could be integrated into the existing administration of company taxation, without the need to set up an additional agency for that purpose.

The proposals recommended here merely involve a single new tax and no organisational innovations, for the EPA itself is the obvious body to set the wage norm for each period, in the light of consultations with all the interested parties. The contrast with the TUC and Labour Party proposals referred to at the beginning of this section could hardly be greater. However, the absence of an institutional solution to the problem of wage regulation is a common feature of the two sets of proposals. We are agreed that wages should continue to be substantially determined through the established bargaining machinery and procedures. The new tax leaves these procedures untouched but it does alter the terms on which bargaining can be conducted, and hence the level of wage settlements. Ideally, it might also be better to reform the wage bargaining system itself, for instance by merging unions along industry lines or some other organisational changes. At present this is not a very realistic objective for the immediate future, though the development of the sort of workplace democracy envisaged in Chapter 5 should create a more favourable environment for such change. However, I do not think it would be wise to await these developments before introducing policies – like the tax on wage increases – to improve the outcome of wage bargains. Thus the tax allows 'free collective bargaining' to continue but it does not rely on the agreement and support of all the major unions and employers' organisations to yield satisfactory outcomes. Consequently, there should be more chance of sustaining a renewed growth process in the British economy since the risks of generating a further bout of inflation would be considerably reduced.

8
Conclusions

In earlier chapters we have examined previous experience of economic planning, both in Britain (Chapter 2) and in several other countries (Chapter 3). This was followed by two theoretical chapters. The first of these, Chapter 4, concentrated on economic arguments for planning, and at times the discussion became unavoidably technical. Chapter 5 then reviewed some political aspects of planning, starting with the case for workplace democracy and moving on to the accountability of higher level planning agencies. Bearing in mind these four chapters of practical experience and formal theory, Chapters 6 and 7 surveyed some of the principal institutional implications of our proposals for a form of decentralised, market-oriented planning. At this point, therefore, it is appropriate to summarise my main conclusions about the planning system which I regard as suitable for British conditions; this is done in the first section of this chapter.

While explaining my own views, frequent reference was made to Labour Party or TUC policies on various issues, as well as to the Alternative Economic Strategy (AES), especially in the last two chapters. However, I have nowhere given anything like a full description of these policies, and this means that readers cannot readily compare my suggestions with such alternatives. Accordingly, the second section outlines the main features of the AES and discusses some of the more striking discrepancies and similarities between it and my own proposals. Labour Party and TUC policies are not discussed in detail because, at least at the time of writing, they are substantially derived from the AES, though in many respects representing a fairly cautious and moderate version of the AES.

Finally, the last section of the book broadens the discussion to include other developed countries. Although much of the detailed argument in previous chapters relates to British institutions and conditions, many of the same points would also apply more widely, and hence a case for decentralised planning can be made for certain other countries too. This case is sketched in the concluding section.

8.1 Decentralised Market-oriented Planning

My proposals for a new planning system include the following features:

(1)   A new national level Economic Planning Agency to be responsible for co-ordinating all aspects of economic policy that concern investment and growth;

(2)   Regional and branch planning agencies, especially where the pace and direction of economic change appears to be too rapid for normal market adjustment to function satisfactorily;

(3)   Local planning agencies linked to local authorities, wherever there is a clear need for them;

(4)   A National Investment Bank to support the process of raising the volume and improving the quality of investment;

(5)   Improved information flows relating to investment decisions, supported by a new information network, or series of inter-linked networks;

(6)   Workplace democracy along the lines of the Bullock Committee recommendations;

(7)   Planning councils to supervise and guide the work of the planning agencies, especially those concerned with regions and branches;

(8)   Plans to be implemented mainly through fiscal measures such as grants or subsidised loans for approved investment; with larger firms, planning agreements would be negotiated, but these should be voluntary and subject to revision under specified conditions; firms not prepared to make such agreements would not receive any state support for their investment, but would not otherwise be subject to pressure from planning bodies;

(9)   Regulation of incomes, especially the growth of wages and salaries, is essential for successful planning; one way of tackling this would be by means of a tax on wage increases, but this

may need to be supported by agreements at various levels between trade unions, planning agencies and management;

(10) Limited, and probably temporary controls over capital flows, especially while the planning system was being introduced;

(11) In occasional, special cases, temporary controls over imports of certain goods while an investment programme for the industry concerned was being undertaken to restore its competitiveness;

(12) Finally, a macroeconomic policy supportive towards planning in the sense that it should seek to maintain the level of economic activity as near as possible to full employment.

Arguments for, and detailed explanations of all the above policies were presented in earlier chapters, so there is no need to repeat myself here. However, I must emphasise that in important respects this collection of policies should be viewed as a package, and I hope one that is reasonably coherent, given the complexity of the topic (planning) and the sometimes conflicting goals of the various actors in the system. For instance, in terms of national level policy, the EPA (proposal 1) and supportive macroeconomic policy (proposal 12) are clearly strongly complementary. Likewise, while workplace democracy (proposal 6) may attract support independently of any notion of planning, it has some political significance in relation to planning in that it may render income regulation (proposal 9) more palatable to certain interest groups. Finally, without proposal 9, proposal 12 may well just be wishful thinking.

A thread that runs through virtually all these proposals is the absence of compulsion, and the explicit reliance on market forces and the market mechanism whenever these function satisfactorily. Thus I envisage a system in which plan and market elements in the economy should work together in a mutually supportive relationship, combining to yield high investment and more rapid growth in the British economy. Realistically, however, one must also note that faster growth is not something that we can expect to be achieved easily or within a short period of time. It would take some years to introduce the various elements of my proposed system and some years more for them to be firmly established and accepted to a sufficient extent to function well. For this reason, there is little chance of these, or any other planning proposals being taken seriously by the electorate (or, more especially, by the economic agents whose behaviour we are trying to change) unless planning legislation and other related measures are introduced with at last a modest amount of consensus between the principal political parties.

8.2 The Alternative Economic Strategy

There are numerous versions of the AES, all of which are essentially socialist responses to the deepening crisis experienced by the British economy. The AES seeks to bring about a sustained recovery from the crisis by restoring full employment as quickly as possible and then introducing planning and other forms of state intervention to control the subsequent course of economic development. The most important measures included in the AES are helpfully summarised in London CSE Group (1979, p.69) from which we quote as follows:

(a) A substantial extension of the public sector, including the banks and insurance companies and a number of large manufacturing companies, coupled with a strengthening of the National Enterprise Board (NEB).

(b) The development of an economic plan to provide the framework for growth and investment programmes in the public and private sectors, to be enforced by planning agreements and sanctions on uncooperative firms.

(c) An immediate improvement in living standards and the reversal of public sector cuts which, together with the expansion of investment, will cut unemployment.

(d) A sharp cut in military expenditure.

(e) Strict control over prices.

(f) The imposition of import controls to protect the balance of payments, and the sale of overseas assets to pay off foreign debts.

(g) A general democratisation of economic life through the involvement of trade unions and other popular organsations in every stage of the planning process, the development of industrial democracy, etc.

In a very useful article, Cobham (1983b) distinguishes between two forms of AES: a radical variant which he refers to as the Orthodox AES, and a more moderate variant labelled the Gradualist AES. Four tables in the paper summarise what he sees as the key differences and similarities between these two strategies (and two others which I do not need to discuss here) and Table 8.1, below is derived from these tables by selecting the items most relevant for planning.

Table 8.1 *Variants of the AES*

Policy	Orthodox AES	Gradualist AES
State intervention in industry at micro-level	substantial	some, plus creation of space for workers' initiatives.
Planning agreements	yes, imposed	yes, negotiated
Size of nationalised industry sector	large increase	little immediate change
Management of nationalised industries	primarily for social objectives	mainly commercial principles; subsidies for specific social purposes.
Import controls	general and comprehensive	limited and selective only
Controls on capital flows	general and comprehensive	limited only
Price controls	strong, anti-inflation	unclear; probably yes, pro-investment
Incomes policy	no	yes, voluntary
Industrial democracy	only in public sector	yes

It can be seen from Table 8.1 that in most respects, the Orthodox AES corresponds to points (a) to (g) listed at the beginning of this section. The only significant area of dispute relates to point (g), concerning democratisation of the economy; Table 8.1 suggests that industrial democracy would be confined to the public sector in the Orthodox AES, a much narrower interpretation than one would draw from (g) itself. However, I am not convinced that Cobham's view of the AES, as reported in Table 8.1, is correct in relation to industrial democracy, since the CSE London Working Group (1980) asserts very firmly (p.80) 'that within the AES we attach an overriding importance to the extension of workers' power – both at the point of production and within the wider democratic process of arriving at economic and social goals.' On the other hand, Sharples (1981) is more ambivalent. While recognising the possibility that planning agreements could be regarded as a development of collective bargaining to cover more aspects of company policy, including questions of strategy, he is also aware of the co-ordination problems to which such local agreements may give rise (p.82). Perhaps we should simply accept that this is an area in which various proponents of the AES have been ambiguous, a situation not altogether surprising in the light of our discussion in Chapter 5.

It should also be added here that point (c) from the earlier list may be inconsistent with point (b). For in Chapter 4 it was emphasised that more and better investment was a precondition (necessary, though not sufficient) for more rapid growth in Britain, and that if investment was to rise sharply, consumption would have to be restrained, at least for a time. To enhance its political appeal, one can see why an AES might wish to make optimistic promises about living standards, but it is surely not realistic to promise a substantial improvement right from the start, especially not in per capita terms. Even the anticipated cuts in defence expenditure (point (d)), which would certainly release some resources, could not immediately be translated into consumption. For political reasons, the cuts themselves would probably take some years to build up to their full effect, and it could take still longer either to find civilian employment for displaced military personnel or to carry out the investment required to shift production to meet civilian requirements.

My own proposals, summarised in the previous section, are rather closer to the Gradualist AES than to the Orthodox AES, the only difference being in the area of price controls which I argued against in Chapter 7. Nevertheless, one of my reasons for opposing them was related to the need to stimulate investment; so if controls themselves were used with this object in mind, my position would hardly differ from the AES.

Now it is actually a little misleading to apply the designation,

AES, to both the Gradualists and Orthodox variants' since as several commentators have observed (including Cobham (1983b), but also Lipsey (1982), Harrison (1982), Sharples (1981)), they stem from rather different economic foundations and also have very different political implications. Together they span an exceedingly broad range of opinion within the left in Britain and the label, AES, serves only to support a wholly inaccurate impression of unity.

The Orthodox AES sees economic policy largely in terms of class relationships and hence the AES itself has the principal objective of strengthening workers' positions throughout the economy and society. This is why planning agreements are to be compulsory, the public sector is to be extended considerably, and there is to be substantial state intervention in industry within the Orthodox AES. It is clear that such a high degree of intervention means, in effect, imposing decisions about production and investment on many production units, which are completely contrary to the decisions that would have resulted from unimpeded market forces. What is much less clear is how the immense political impact of such decisions might be accommodated: but let us now discuss this problem.

The authors of the AES are well aware that, at least in its more radical form, the policy would provoke vigorous resistance from capitalists who would feel directly threatened by its implementation: hence the need for stringent controls on capital flows to prevent a 'flight of capital', a great deal of publicly organised and financed investment, and state takeovers, to offset the effects of a possible 'investment strike'. But within the debates on the AES there has been surprisingly little detailed examination of the mechanics of these controls and personally, I am unconvinced about their viability. It is very hard to devise really effective controls on capital flows except in what is virtually a siege economy of the Soviet kind and I have already argued against this earlier on. I wonder how many supporters of the AES appreciate that something like a Soviet-type economy is one possible outcome of their approach to economic management.

On investment, the Orthodox AES clearly seeks to supersede the market wherever possible, regulating investment and hence the future patterns of production and consumption in accordance with criteria of social need rather than profitability. Again, I have argued against this approach on the grounds of the vagueness and subjectivity inherent in the concept of social need and therefore supported more active use of profitability and the market. Within the Orthodox AES, one has to ask who would be determining social need? Would it be workers at a particular enterprise? Or superior levels of the planning system? Or consumer groups, perhaps? It is important, indeed essential, to have detailed answers to such questions, for otherwise the AES would not even be operational. Moreover if, in the absence of definite answers, most production units went on doing virtually the same as they had been before the AES, with the same production conditions and linked to the same markets, then it would appear that little had really changed. In that case, the radical policies would merely be rhetoric.

In political terms, the Orthodox AES is not really a means of beginning the transition towards a socialist society, but it represents instead a sketch of one particular vision of the end of the transition, a sketch of the new society. Accounts of the strategy have not indicated how the transition should be effected nor what the intermediate stages might be. Consequently, it would not be surprising if the policy encountered a panicky reaction from owners and managers of large companies, and others whose interests would be prejudiced by it. I am not even very sure that the Orthodox AES would attract much support from workers themselves, in whose interests it is supposedly promoted. For while it promises much, it is both economically and politically an exceptionally risky course to follow and I suspect that many people would be unwilling to move that far from established types of policy. Though partly a result of people's natural caution in the face of change, it also seems to me that a sound case can be advanced to support such reluctance.

Ironically, I would argue that the Gradualist AES (and *a fortiori* my own recommended policies) stands a much better chance of bringing about economic and social change than the Orthodox AES. The Gradualist AES largely works within the market system, modifying its results where required to achieve particular objectives, but not otherwise seeking to supplant the market mechanism. Nevertheless, it does tackle the problem of investment that has been emphasised so strongly throughout this book and does seek to involve workers in enterprise decision-making as widely as possible. But it would achieve all this without posing an immediate threat to shareholders, managers and the like, who may indeed do rather well in the economic expansion resulting from the implementation of a gradualist AES. At the same time, while setting out in a socialist direction, it is not committed to any specific long term goal. This is an advantage in that it allows policies to be adapted to circumstances quite flexibly, and it also avoids putting forward a definite model as *the* model of a socialist society. However, it would be a weakness if it meant that there would never be any progression of development of policy beyond the Gradualist AES. Overall, I would expect the Gradualist AES to command widespread support as a result of its moderation and realism. While certainly not offering any utopia, it recognises some of the more severe problems facing the British economy and shows how existing political and institutional structures, with some significant but probably manageable changes, could be directed towards their solution.

8.3   Planning in Other Developed Countries

Apart from Chapter 3 which looked at planning in Eastern Europe, France and Japan, the remainder of this book has been devoted to planning in Britain, covering both past experience and the future prospects for a form of decentralised, market-oriented planning. However, after making suitable allowances for different institutional arrangements, much of the argument of earlier chapters is likely to be applicable to other developed countries.

One strand of the argument concerned forecasts, model building and the general question of information flows within the economic system. Chapter 4 explained why a market type economy would not normally generate information of the kinds needed to support efficient investment decision-making. Given this failure, firms themselves, as well as government departments, individuals and other agents (e.g. commercial forecasting bodies) try to compensate for the missing information by generating their own substitutes, as forecasts, expectations, sheer guesses, and so on. In this connection, the function of the proposed planning system would be to improve economic information flows in three respects:

(1)   To improve the economy-wide accounting and modelling of economic processes relevant for growth, especially investment;

(2)   As part of regular macroeconomic forecasting exercises, to provide official, medium term forecasts of key parameters, particularly prices such as the exchange rate and interest rates,

and prices of public sector outputs, relevant for public and private sector investment decisions;
(3) To foster the development of information networks linking groups of firms, to facilitate the identification of trading partners.

The theoretical analysis of information flows applies just as well to any market-type economy and nothing especially pertaining to British conditions was assumed in order to arrive at the above proposals. Accordingly, just the same conclusions could be drawn about other developed countries; improvements in economic information flows can be expected to lead to more efficient investment decisions. This may also hold for some of the developing countries, though their economic structures and institutions are often so different from the developed countries that I would hesitate to generalise that far.

A second strand of argument had to do with organisational failure. The basic notion here is that in an economy with a given organisational structure – in terms of firms and the interconnections between them, employers' and workers' organisations, government agencies and so on – that structure has important effects on the perception of investment opportunities by the agents concerned. Any particular structure will direct investors' attention to those projects which fit into the structure, which usually means those which respect the major organisational boundaries. Correspondingly, investment projects which do involve crossing these boundaries are less likely to be examined closely, or even considered at all by established firms. Of course, it would be absurd for firms to try and consider all possibilities when deciding where to invest since they could never assimilate and process all the required information. Hence a useful function of the existing organisational structure is that, by constraining perception, it makes firms' decision problems rather more tractable than they would otherwise be.

Nevertheless, some economically attractive investment opportunities are undoubtedly missed within such a framework. While some of these may be seen by new firms (which are often less committed to the given structure than older firms), planners may also play a role by facilitating investments which cut across organisational boundaries especially if these may lay the foundations for whole new industries. In addition, some projects are so large and complex, and involve so many different firms and other organisations, that some co-ordination as well as financial commitment is essential for the projects to get off the ground. Sometimes purely private consortia will be able to supply the necessary co-ordination, but in other cases one of the planning agencies may also have to be involved.

As with the informational problems discussed previously, these organisational aspects of planning are based on quite general arguments and the conclusions about the planners' role in the economy are not therefore only applicable to the British economy. However, the extent to which new entrants and private consortia are able to manage organisational change and complexity will vary a good deal from country to country. Among other factors, it will depend on the general dynamism of the economy, reflected especially in the volume and quality of investment.

This brings me to the third and final strand of the argument, on investment. In this case the analysis presented in earlier chapters on the volume and composition of investment and its connection with economic growth was not specific to Britain, but policy conclusions were, since they were based on the view that market forces left to themselves (in the presence of the kinds of government intervention experienced since the war) would not generate sufficient investment to sustain something close to full employment with steady growth. At times this particular 'market failure' has been explained in terms of deficiencies in macroeconomic policy rather than in the market mechanism *per se*: for instance, using fiscal deflation to protect the balance of payments in the 1950s and 1960s, and more recently to restrain inflationary pressure in the economy. Nevertheless, other countries have sustained much more buoyant investment even despite applying such deflationary policies on occasion, and in Britain investment has remained rather low even in the booms. Consequently, I have argued that planners in Britain, supported by an appropriate institutional framework and financial mechanism, should play a major part in improving the investment process in all its dimensions. At the same time, given the relatively superior economic performance of most other developed economies, it is doubtful whether they could employ with much advantage the approach to raising investment and directing it more productively that has been discussed at length in this book. Instead, there must still be many lessons for us to learn from them about the conduct of economic management. To learn, however, the first step is to shake off our traditional insular attitudes and mentally cross the particular organisational boundary represented by the nation state.

References

Aaronovitch, S. (1981) *The Road from Thatcherism* (London: Lawrence & Wishart).

Abell, D. F. (1980) *Defining the Business* (Englewood Cliffs, NJ : Prentice-Hall).

Alvey Committee (1982) *A Programme for Advanced Information Technology* Department of Trade and Industry (London: HMSO).

Arrow, K. J. (1959) 'Toward a Theory of Price Adjustment', in M. Abramovitz *et al.*, *The Allocation of Economic Resources* (Stanford: Stanford University Press).

Arrow, K. J. (1970) *Essays in the Theory of Risk-bearing* (Amsterdam: North-Holland).

Arrow, K. J. and Hahn, F. H. (1971) *General Competitive Analysis* (San Francisco: Holden-Day).

Arrow, K. J. and Hurwicz, L. (1977) *Studies in Resource Allocation Processes* (Cambridge: CUP).

Atkinson, T. *et al.* (1983) *Socialism in a Cold Climate* (London: Unwin Paperbacks) (edited by John Griffiths).

Azariadas, C (1981) 'Implicit Contracts and Related Topics: A Survey', in Z. Hornstein, J. Grice and A. Webb (eds), *The Economics of the Labour Market* (London: HMSO).

Azariadas, C. and Stiglitz, J. E. (1983) 'Implicit Contracts and Fixed-Price Equilibria', *Quarterly Journal of Economics*, vol. XCVIII, Supplement, pp. 1–22.

Bates, R. and Fraser, N. (1974) *Investment Decisions in the Nationalised Fuel Industries* (Cambridge: CUP).

Bauer, T. and Szamuely, L. (1978) 'The Structure of Industrial Administration in the European CMEA Countries: Change and Continuity', *Acta Oeconomica*, vol. 20(4), pp. 371–93.

Beck, P. W. (1982) 'Corporate Planning for an Uncertain Future', *Long Range Planning*, vol. 15(4), pp. 12–21.

Beckerman, W. (ed.) ((1979) *Slow Growth in Britain* (Oxford: OUP).

Berliner, J. S. (1976) *The Innovation Decision in Soviet Industry* (Cambridge, Mass.: MIT Press).

Binks, M. and Coyne, J. (1983) *The Birth of Enterprise*, Hobart Paper 98 (London: Institute of Economic Affairs).

Bird, P. (1984) 'The Political Economy of Inflation', in P. G. Hare and M. W. Kirby (eds), *An Introduction to British Economic Policy* (Brighton: Wheatsheaf).

Blackaby, F. (ed.) (1979) *De-industrialisation*, NIESR, Economic Policy Papers 2 (London: Heinemann).

Blackaby, F. T. (ed.) (1978) *British Economic Policy 1960–74*, NIESR Economic and Social Studies xxxi (Cambridge: CUP).

Blazyca, G. (1983) *Planning is Good for You: the Case for Popular Control* (London: Pluto Press).

Bornstein, M. (1976) 'Soviet Price Policy in the 1970s', in *The Soviet Economy in a New Perspective*, US Congress Joint Economic Committee (Washington, DC: USGPO).

Bosanquet, N. (1983) 'Tax-based Income Policies', in D. Robinson and K. Mayhew (eds) *Pay Policies for the Future* (Oxford: OUP).

Botham, R. and Lloyd, G. (1983) 'The Political Economy of Enterprise Zones', *National Westminster Bank Quarterly Review* May, pp. 24–32.

Bradley, K. and Gelb, A. (1980) 'Worker Cooperatives as Industrial Policy: The Case of the "Scottish Daily News" ', *Review of Economic Studies*, vol. xlvii(4), July, pp. 665–78.

Bray, J. (1982) *Production, Purpose and Structure* (London: Frances Pinter).

Brittan, S. (1978) 'How British is the British Sickness?' *Journal of Law and Economics*, vol. xxi(2), pp. 245–68.

Broadway, F. (1969) *State Intervention in British Industry 1964–68* (London: Kaye & Ward).

Brown, C. V. and Jackson, P. M. (1978) *Public Sector Economics* (Oxford: Martin Robertson).

Budd, A. (1978) *The Politics of Economic Planning* (Manchester: Manchester U.P.).

Bullock, Lord (1977) *Report of the Committee of Inquiry on Industrial Democracy* (London: HMSO).

Burton, J. (1983) *Picking Losers . . . ?* Hobart Paper 99 (London: Institute of Economic Affairs).

CSE London Working Group (1980) *The Alternative Economic Strategy* (London: CSE Books).

Carrington, J. C. and Edwards, G. T. (1979) *Financing Industrial Investment* (London: Macmillan).

Carter, C. (ed.) (1981) *Industrial Policy and Innovation*, NIESR, PSI and RIIA, Joint Studies in Public Policy 3' (London: Heinemann).

Cave, M. and Hare, P. G. (1981) *Alternative Approaches to Economic Planning* (London: Macmillan).

Cave, M. (1980) *Computers and Economic Planning – The Soviet Experience* (Cambridge: CUP).

Cave, M. (1984) 'French Planning Reforms 1981–4', Department of Economics, Brunel University, mimeo.

Coates, D. (1980) *Labour in Power? A Study of the Labour Government, 1974–1979* (London: Longman).

Cobham, D. (1983) 'The Nationalisation of the Banks in Mitterand's France: Rationalisations & Reasons', *Department of Economics Discussion Paper* No 8303 University of St Andrews.

Cobham, D. (1983b) 'Popular Political Strategies for the UK Economy', Department of Economics, University of St Andrews, July, mimeo.

Collyns, C. (1982) *Can Protection Cure Unemployment?* Thames Essay No 31 (London: Trade Policy Research Centre).

Commission Nationale de Planification (1983) *Rapport pour la Premiérè Phase de Preparation du 9eme Plan* (Paris: Documentation Française).

Commission de Reforme de la Planification (1982) *Rapport Final* (Paris: Documentation Française).

Cowling, K. (1982) *Monopoly Capitalism* (London: Macmillan).

Cripps, F. and Godley, W. (1978) 'Control of Imports as a Means to Employment and the Expansion of World Trade: the UK's Case', *Cambridge Journal of Economics*.

Crouch, C. (1983) 'Industrial Relations', in Atkinson *et al.*, *Socialism in a Cold Climate* (London: Unwin Paperbacks).

Cuthbertson, K. (1982) 'The Measurement and Behaviour of the UK Savings Ratio in the 1970s', *National Institute Economic Review*, February, pp. 75–84.

Debreu, G. (1959) *The Theory of Value* (New York: Wiley).

Dell, E. (1973) *Political Responsibility & Industry* (London: Allen & Unwin).

Denison, E. F. (1967) *Why Growth Rates Differ* (Washington, DC: The Brookings Institution).

Denison, E. F. (1979) *Accounting for Slower Economic Growth* (Washington, DC: The Brookings Institution).

Desai, M. (1983) 'Economic Alternatives for Labour, 1984–9', ch. 4 in Atkinson *et al. Socialism in a Cold Climate* (London: Unwin Paperbacks).

Devons, E. (1950) *Planning in Practice* (Cambridge: CUP).

Donovan, Lord (1968) *Report of the Royal Commission on Trade Unions and Employers' Associations* (London: HMSO).

Durbin, E. F. M. (1949) *Problems of Economic Planning* (London: Routledge & Kegan Paul).

Earl, P. E. (1984) *The Corporate Imagination: How Big Companies Make Mistakes* (Brighton: Wheatsheaf).

Estrin, S. (1984) *Self-Management: Economic Theory & Yugoslav Practice* (Cambridge: CUP).

Estrin, S. and Holmes, P. (1983a) *French Planning in Theory and Practice* (London: Allen & Unwin).

Estrin, S. and Holmes, P. (1983b) 'French Planning under the Socialists: Some Lessons for Britain', Paper presented to the *Socialist Economic Review* Conference, September. To be published in the conference volume.

Estrin, S. and Holmes, P. (1984) 'Recent Developments in French Economic Planning', *Economics of Planning*, vol. 18(1), 1982 (published in 1984), pp. 1–10.

Estrin, S. and Holmes, P. (1984) 'The Role of Planning Contracts in the Conduct of French Industrial Policy', *Discussion Papers in Economics and Econometrics* No. 8402, University of Southampton.

Fallick, J. L. and Elliott, R. F. (eds) (1981) *Incomes Policies, Inflation and Relative Pay* (London: Allen & Unwin).

Flemming, J. S. (1976) 'The Cost of Capital, Finance & Investment', *Bank of England Quarterly Bulletin*, vol 16(2), June, pp. 193–205.

Foster, C. D. (1971) *Politics, Finance and the Role of Economics* (An Essay on the Control of Public Enterprise) (London: Allen & Unwin).

Franks, Sir Oliver (1947) *Central Planning & Control in War and Peace* Lectures delivered at LSE (London: Longmans).

Friedman, M. and Friedman, R. (1980) *Free to Choose: A Personal Statement* (Harmondsworth: Penguin).

FISG (Labour Party Financial Institutions Study Group) (1982) *The City: a Socialist Approach* (London: The Labour Party).

George, D. (1983) 'Accumulation and Equality: Should we Plan a Wage-Earners' Investment Fund for Britain?' *New Socialist*.

Godley, W. and May, R. M. (1977) 'The Macroeconomic Implications of Devaluation and Import Restrictions', *Cambridge Economic Policy Review.*

Grant, R. M. and Shaw, G. K. (1980) *Current Issues in Economic Policy* (Oxford: Philip Allan).

Grant, W. (1982) *The Political Economy of Industrial Policy* (London: Butterworths).

Green, D. (1981) 'Promoting the Industries of the Future: the Search for an Industrial Strategy in Britain and France', *Journal of Public Policy*, vol. (3), pp. 333–51.

Greenaway, D. and Milner, C. (1979) *Protectionism Again . . . ?* Hobart Paper 84 (London: Institute of Economic Affairs).

Greenaway, D. (1983) *International Trade Policy: From Tariffs to the New Protectionism* (London: Macmillan).

HM Treasury (1961) *Financial and Economic Obligations of the Nationalised Industries* Cmnd 1337 (London: HMSO).

HM Treasury (1967) *Nationalised Industries: a Review of Economic and Financial Objectives*, Cmnd 3437 (London: HMSO).

IIM Treasury (1978) *The Nationalised Industries*, Cmnd 7131 (London: HMSO).

Hague, D. and Wilkinson, G. (1983) *The IRC – an Experiment in Industrial Intervention* (London: Allen & Unwin).

Hahn, F. (1982a) 'Reflections on the Invisible Hand', *Lloyds Bank Review*, April. pp. 1–21.

Hahn, F. (1982b) *Money and Inflation* (Oxford: Basil Blackwell).

Hall, P. (1980) *Great Planning Disasters* (Harmondsworth: Penguin).

Hall, Sir Robert (1962) *Planning*, The Rede Lecture 1962 (Cambridge: CUP).

Hamilton, A. (1983) 'MITI Magic at Work', *The Observer*, 14th August, p. 17.

Hare, P. G. (1976) 'Industrial Prices in Hungary', *Soviet Studies*, vol. 28 (2 and 3), pp. 189–206 and 362–90.

Hare, P. G. (1977) 'Economic Reform in Hungary: Problems and Prospects', *Cambridge Journal of Economics*, vol. 1, pp. 317–33.

Hare, P. G. (1981a) 'Aggregate Planning by Means of Input-Output and Material-Balances Systems', *Journal of Comparative Economics*, vol. 5, pp. 272–91.

Hare, P. G. (1981b) 'The Organization of Information Flows in Systems of Economic Planning', *Economics of Planning* vol. 17(1), pp. 1–19.

Hare, P. G. (1983a) 'The Beginnings of Institutional Reform in Hungary', *Soviet Studies*, vol. xxxv(3), July, pp. 313–30.

Hare, P. G. (1983b) 'The Preconditions for Effective Planning in the UK, in *Socialist Economic Review 1982* (London: Merlin Press).

Hare, P. G. (1984) 'The Nationalised Industries', in P. G. Hare and M. W. Kirby (eds), *An Introduction to British Economic Policy* (Brighton: Wheatsheaf).

Hare, P. G., Radice, H. K. and Swain, N. (eds) (1981) *Hungary: a Decade of Economic Reform* (London: Allen & Unwin).

Harrison, J. (1982) 'A "Left" Critique of the Alternative Economic Strategy', in D. Currie and M. Sawyer (eds), *Socialist Economic Review 1982* (London: Merlin Press).

Hart, O. D. (1983) 'Optimal Labour Contracts under Asymmetric Information: An Introduction', *Review of Economic Studies*, vol. l(1), January, pp. 3–35.

Hayek, F. A. *et al.* (1935) *Collectivist Economic Planning* (London: Routledge).

Hayward, J. and Narkiewicz, O. (eds) (1978) *Planning in Europe* (London: Croom Helm).

Hayward, J. and Watson, M. (1975) *Planning, Politics and Public Policy* (The British, French and Italian experience) (Cambridge: CUP).

Heal, G. M. (1973) *The Theory of Economic Planning* (Amsterdam: North-Holland).

Heald, D. (1980) 'The Economic and Financial Control of U.K. Nationalised Industries', *Economic Journal*, vol. 90, June, pp. 243–265.

Hewett, E. A. (1981) 'The Hungarian Economy: Lessons of the 1970s and Prospects for the 1980s', in Joint Economic Committee, *East European Economic Assessment* (Part 1, Country Studies 1980) (Washington, DC : USGPO).

Hills, J. (1983) 'The Industrial Policy of Japan', *Journal of Public Policy*, vol. 3(1), February, pp. 63–80.

Hills, J. (1984) *Savings and Fiscal Privilege* (London: Institute for Fiscal Studies).

Hindley, B. and Nicolaides, E. (1983) *Taking the New Protectionism Seriously* Thames Essay No 34 (London: Trade Policy Research Centre).

274   *References*

Hodgson, G. (1984) *The Democratic Economy* (Harmondsworth: Penguin).

Holland, S. (1972) *The State as Entrepreneur* (London: Weidenfeld & Nicolson).

Holland, S. (1975) *The Socialist Challenge* (London: Quartet).

Hughes Hallett, A. and Rees, H. (1983) *Quantitative Economic Policies and Interactive Planning* (Cambridge: CUP).

Hurwicz, L. (1971) 'Centralization and Decentralization in Economic Processes', in A. Eckstein (ed.), *Comparison of Economic Systems* (Berkeley: University of California Press).

Hurwicz, L. (1977) 'The Design of Resource Allocation Mechanisms', in K. J. Arrow and L. Hurwicz (eds), *Studies in Resouce Allocation Processes* (Cambridge: CUP).

Hutchison, T. W. (1968) *Economics and Economic Policy in Britain 1946–1966* (London: Allen & Unwin).

Jeffries, I. (ed.) (1981) *The Industrial Enterprise in Eastern Europe* (New York: Praeger).

Johansen, L. (1978) *Lectures on Macroeconomic Planning*, Part 2 : Centralization, decentralization, planning under uncertainty (Amsterdam: North-Holland).

Johnson, Chalmers (1982) *MITI and the Japanese Miracle* (Stanford, Calif.: Stanford U.P.).

Jones, D. T. (1981) *Industrial Adjustment and Policy: 1. Maturity and Crisis in the European Car Industry: Structural Change and Public Policy* Sussex European Papers No 8.

Kagami, N. (1983) 'Maturing of the Japanese Economy in the 1980s'. *National Westminster Bank Quarterly Review'*, November, pp. 18–28.

Kaldor, N. (1982) 'Economic Prospects of the 1980s', *Economic Notes*, pp. 67–84.

Kaldor, N. (1983) *The Economic Consequences of Mrs Thatcher* (London: Duckworth).

Kay, J. A. and Silberston, Z. A. (1984) 'The New Industrial Policy – Privatisation and Competition', *Midland Bank Review*, Spring, pp. 8–16.

Kay, N. (1982) *Strategies; the Firms, the Market and the State* typescript.

Kirzner, I. (1973) *Competition and Entrepreneurship* (Chicago: University of Chicago Press).

Klein, R. (1984) 'Privatization and the Welfare State', *Lloyds Bank Review*, January, pp. 12–29.

Knight, A. (1974) *Private Enterprise and Public Intervention: the Courtaulds Experience* (London: Allen & Unwin).

Koopmans, T. C. (1957) *Three Essays on the State of Economic Science* (New York: McGraw-Hill).

Kornai, J. (1980a) 'The Dilemmas of a Socialist Economy: the Hungarian Experience', *Cambridge Journal of Economics*, vol. 4, pp. 147–57.

Kornai, J. (1980b) *The Economics of Shortage* (Amsterdam: North-Holland).

Lange, O. (1936) 'On the Economic Theory of Socialism', in B. Lippincott (ed.), *On the Economic Theory of Socialism* (New York: McGraw-Hill).

Layard, R. (1982) *More Jobs, Less Inflation* (London: Grant McIntyre).

Leruez, J. (1975) *Economic Planning and Politics in Britain* (London: Martin Robertson).

Levacic, R. (1976) *Macroeconomics* (London: Macmillan).

Lipsey, D. (1982) 'A "Right" Critique of the Alternative Economic Strategy', in D. Currie and M. Sawyer (eds), *Socialist Economic Review 1982* (London: Merlin Press).

Loasby, B. J. (1976) *Choice, Complexity and Ignorance* (Cambridge: CUP).

Loasby, B. J. (1976) *Choice, Complexity and Ignorance* (Cambridge: CUP).

Loasby, B. J. (1981) 'The Economics of Dispersed and Incomplete Information', Paper presented at *Symposium in Honour of Ludwig von Mises*, New York University, mimeo.

London CSE Group (1979) 'Crisis, the Labour Movement and the Alternative Economic Strategy', *Capital and Class*, no. 8, summer.

Lutz, V. (1969) *Central Planning for the Market Economy* (London: Longman)

Magaziner, I. C. and Hout, T. M. (1980) *Japanese Industrial Policy* (London: Policy Studies Institute).

Marer, P. (1984) 'Hungary's Economic Reforms: From Traditional Central Planning to Market Socialism', in *Compendium of Studies on the Economies of Eastern Europe*, US Congress Joint Economic Committee (Washington, DC: USGPO).

Marglin, S. A. (1963) 'The Opportunity Costs of Public Investment', *Quarterly Journal of Economics*, vol. 77, pp. 75–111.

Meade, J. E. (1970) *The Theory of Indicative Planning* (Manchester: Manchester U.P.).

Meade, J. E. (1971) *The Controlled Economy* (London: Allen & Unwin).

Meade, J. E. (1978) *The Structure and Reform of Direct Taxation* (Report of a committee set up by the IFS) (London: Allen & Unwin).

Meadows, P. (1978) 'Planning', ch. 9 in F. T. Blackaby (ed.), *British Economic Policy 1960–74* (Cambridge: CUP).

Milward, A. S. (1977) *War, Economy and Society 1939–1945* (London: Allen Lane).

Minford, P. (1980) *Is Monetarism Enough? Essays in Refining and Reinforcing the Monetary Cure for Inflation*, IEA Readings: 24 (London: Institute of Economic Affairs).

Minns, R. (1982) *Take over the City: The Case for Public Ownership of Financial Institutions* (London: Pluto Press).

Minns, R. (1983) 'Pension Funds: an Alternative View', *Capital and Class* No. 20, pp. 104–115.

Mitchell, J. (1966) *Groundwork to Economic Planning* (London: Secker & Warburg).

Mitterand Government (1982) *Document d'Orientation pour la Preparation du IXe Plan* (Paris: Documentation Française).

Mitterand Government (1983a) *9e Plan de Developpement Economique Social et Culturel 1984–1988 Tome 1. Les Choix du 9e Plan* (Paris: Documentation Française).

Mitterand Government (1983b) *9e Plan de Developpement Economique Social et Culturel 1984–1988 Tome 2. La Strategie et les Grandes Actions* (Paris: Documentation Française).

Murray, R. (1983) 'Pension Funds and Local Authority Investments', *Capital and Class*, No. 20, pp. 89–102.

Neild, R. R. (1979) 'Managed Trade between Industrial Countries', in R. L. Major (ed.), *Britain's Trade and Exchange-rate Policy* (London: Heinemann).

Nickell, S. J. (1978) *The Investment Decisions of Firms* (Cambridge: CUP).

Nove, A. (1975) *Planning – What, How and Why?*, Fraser of Allander Institute, Speculative Papers No 1 (Edinburgh: Scottish Academic Press).

Nove, A. (1983) *The Economics of Feasible Socialism* (London: Allen & Unwin).

Oswald, A. J. (1982) 'Three Theorems on Inflation Taxes and Marginal Employment Subsidies', *Warwick Economic Research Papers*, no. 220, November.

Pinder, J. (ed.) (1982) *National Industrial Strategies and the World Economy* (London: Croom Helm).

Pollard, S. (1978) 'The Nationalisation of the Banks: the Chequered History of a Socialist Proposal', in D. Martin and D. Rubenstein (eds) *Ideology and the Labour Movement* (London: Croom Helm).

Pollard, S. (1982) *The Wasting of the British Economy* (New York: St Martin's Press).

Privatisation and After: a Symposium (1984) *Fiscal Studies*, vol. 5(1), February, pp. 36–105.

Redwood, J. and Hatch, J. (1982) *Controlling Public Industries* (Oxford: Basil Blackwell).

Redwood, J. (1984) *Going for Broke . . .* (Oxford: Basil Blackwell).

Rees, R. (1976) *Public Enterprise Economics* (London: Weidenfeld & Nicolson).

Robinson, D. and Mayhew, K. (eds) (1983) *Pay Policies for the Future* (Oxford: OUP).

Robinson, E. A. G. (1967) *Economic Planning in the United Kingdom: Some Lessons*, 1966 Marshall Lectures (Cambridge: CUP).

Sayer, S. (1982) *An Introduction to Macroeconomic Policy* (London: Butterworths).

Scott, M. FG. (1981) 'The Contribution of Investment to Growth', *Scottish Journal of Political Economy*, vol. 28(3), pp. 211–26.

Scott, M. FG., Corden, W. M. and Little, I. M. D. (1980) *The Case against General Import Restrictions*, Thames Essay, no. 24. (London: Trade Policy Research Centre).

Shackleton, J. R. (1984) 'Privatization: The Case Examined', *National Westminster Bank Quarterly Review*, May, pp. 59–73.

Shanks, M. (1977) *Planning and Politics: The British Experience 1950–76* (London: PEP/Allen & Unwin).

Sharples, A. (1981) 'Alternative Economic Strategies: Labour Movement Responses to the Crisis', in D. Currie and R. Smith (eds), *Socialist Economic Review 1981* (London: Merlin Press).

Shone, Sir Robert *et al.* (1962) *Planning* Papers read at the Business Economists' Conference at New College, Oxford, 5–8 April 1962.

Stafford, G. B. (1981) *The End of Economic Growth?* (Oxford: Martin Robertson).

Stewart, M. (1978) *Politics and Economic Policy in the UK Since 1964* (Oxford: Pergamon Press).

Stout, D. (1979) 'Capacity Adjustment in a Slowly Growing Economy', in Beckerman, W., *Slow Growth in Britain* (Oxford: OUP).

Strategy (1982) 'A Socialist GLC in Capitalist Britain?' *Capital and Class*, no. 18, Winter, pp. 117–33.

Swartz, D. (1981) 'The Eclipse of Politics: the Alternative Economic Strategy as a Socialist Strategy', *Capital and Class*, no. 13, April, pp. 102–113.

TUC (1982) *Programme for Recovery: TUC Economic Review* (London: TUC)

TUC – Labour Party (1982) *Economic Planning and Industrial Democracy: the Framework for Full Employment* (London: Labour Party).

Taylor, B. and Hussey, D. (1982) *The Realities of Planning* (Oxford: Pergamon Press).

Taylor, F. M. (1936) 'The Guidance of Production in a Socialist State', in B. Lippincott (ed.), *On the Economic Theory of Socialism* (New York: McGraw-Hill).

Thirlwall, A. P. (1982) 'Deindustrialisation in the United Kingdom', *Lloyds Bank Review*, April, pp. 22–37.

Thomas, H. and Logan, C. (1982) *Mondragon: An Economic Analysis* (London: Allen & Unwin).

Tomlinson, J. (1982) *The Unequal Struggle: British Socialism and the Capitalist Enterprise* (London: Methuen).

Trades Councils (1980) *State Intervention in Industry*. A Workers' Inquiry (Newcastle upon Tyne: Coventry, Liverpool, Newcastle, N. Tyneside Trades Councils).

Turner, R. K. and Collis, C. (1977) *The Economics of Planning* (London: Macmillan).

Ulph, A. M. and Ulph, D. T. (1975) 'Transaction Costs in General Equilibrium Theory – A Survey', *Economica*, vol. 42, pp. 355–72.

Wainwright, H. and Elliott, D. (1982) *The Lucas Plan: A New Trade Unionism in the Making?* (London: Allison & Busby).

Walker, A. (1984) *Social Planning* (Oxford: Basil Blackwell).

Ward, T. (1981) 'The Case for an Import Control Strategy in the UK', in D. Currie and R. Smith (eds), *Socialist Economic Review, 1981* (London: Merlin Press).

Weitzman, M. (1970) 'Iterative Multi-level Planning with Production Targets', *Econometrica*, vol. 38(1).

Whitfield, D. (1983) *Making it Public – Evidence and Action against Privatisation* (London: Pluto Press).

Wilczynski, J. (1983) *Comparative Industrial Relations* (London: Macmillan).

Wiles, P. J. D. (1977) *Economic Institutions Compared* (Oxford: Basil Blackwell).

William, J., Williams, K. and Thomas, D. (1983) *Why are the British Bad at Manufacturing?* (London: Routledge & Kegan Paul).

Williams, M. (1981) Review Article on 'The Alternative Economic Strategy' and 'There is an Alternative', *Capital and Class*, no. 14, Summer, pp. 112–120.

Williamson, O. E., Wachter, M. L. and Harris, J. E. (1975) 'Understanding the Employment Relation: the Analysis of Idiosyncratic Exchange', *Bell Journal of Economics*, vol. 6(1), Spring, pp. 250–278.

Wilson, H. (1980) *Report of a Committee to Review the Functioning of Financial Institutions* (chaired by H. Wilson). (London: HMSO)

Wilson, T. (1964) *Planning and Growth* (London: Macmillan).

Wolf, M. (1979) *Adjustment Policies and Problems in Developed Countries*, World Bank Staff Working Paper No 349 (Washington, DC: The World Bank).

Worswick, G. D. N. and Ady, P. H. (1962) *The British Economy in the Nineteen-Fifties* (Oxford: OUP)

Worswick, G. D. N. and Ady, P. H. (1952) *The British Economy 1945–1950* (Oxford: OUP)

Index